The World
of Angela Carter

The World
of Angela Carter

A Critical Investigation

DANI CAVALLARO

McFarland & Company, Inc., Publishers
Jefferson, North Carolina, and London

LIBRARY OF CONGRESS CATALOGUING-IN-PUBLICATION DATA

Cavallaro, Dani.
    The world of Angela Carter : a critical investigation / Dani
Cavallaro.
        p.   cm.
    Includes bibliographical references and index.

    ISBN 978-0-7864-6128-8
    softcover : 50# alkaline paper ∞

    1. Carter, Angela, 1940–1992 — Criticism and interpretation.
I. Title.
PR6053.A73Z573   2011
823.914 — dc22   2011019219

BRITISH LIBRARY CATALOGUING DATA ARE AVAILABLE

On the cover: Articulated paper doll, late 1800s
(Littauer & Boysen, Berlin); background image by J. McPhail

Manufactured in the United States of America

McFarland & Company, Inc., Publishers
  Box 611, Jefferson, North Carolina 28640
  www.mcfarlandpub.com

To Paddy,
with love and gratitude —
for everything

Table of Contents

Fantasy was an everyday, domestic business, she'd say. The ancient metaphor of yarn-spinning connected literature with the world of work. Cooking and quilt-making also had a lot in common with the craft of fiction, if you went back to pre-novel precedents.

— Lorna Sage

Rough work, iconoclasm, but the only way to get at truth.

— Oliver Wendell Holmes

Preface

*She was the opposite of parochial. Nothing, for her, was outside the
pale: she wanted to know about everything and everyone, and every
place and every word. She relished life and language hugely, and rev-
elled in the diverse.*

— Margaret Atwood

This book explores the narrative and critical writings of Angela Carter
as an author of enduring global standing, renowned for her tantalizing
interpretation — and attendant explosion — of the prolific myths which
human cultures routinely construct in order to consolidate themselves and
thus keep at bay the looming phantoms of uncertainty and fear. Time and
again, Carter shows herself willing not only to confront those minatory
presences but also, and more crucially, to engage them in rambunctious
play by recourse to a seemingly inexhaustible reservoir of creativity, adven-
turousness and dark humor. As Margaret Atwood emphasizes in the obituary published in *The Observer* on 23 February 1992, whence the above
citation derives, the driving force at the heart of this project is a vivacious
and unflagging inquisitiveness. Taking these propositions as its conceptual
launchpad, this study provides detailed discussions of a selection of novels
and short stories. These are assiduously integrated with Carter's speculative
perspectives on politics, society and aesthetics, and with her groundbreaking attempts at inventive redefinition of established popular genres through
candid hands-on appropriation of their codes and conventions.

The book does not aim to cover Carter's whole opus, seeking instead
to concentrate on a textual gallery selected on the basis of its exemplary
status vis-à-vis the author's overall output. Relatedly, even though the pri-

1

mary texts under scrutiny are chronologically situated in terms of their publication dates, this study's focus is essentially thematic. It therefore endeavors to identify salient connections among diverse stages in the writer's career, moving fluidly across the topoi and forms it encompasses. This approach is obliquely invoked by the antiteleological thrust of Carter's writings themselves, whereby metaphysical ideals of linear and upward progression are repeatedly displaced by a preference for cyclical rhythms and recurrent patterns, loops, detours, digressions and veritable flights of fancy.

The analysis is divided into seven chapters, the first of which, "Angela Carter's Vision," is devoted to a critical assessment of the author's recurrent thematics and imagery. The six chapters that follow are organized around as many ideas, overtly inspired by the author's own yarns and symbols, each of which is evaluated with close reference to one main title. Chapter 2 — Dark Play: *The Magic Toyshop*—examines Carter's alchemical fusion of fantasy and horror in the genesis of both personal and cultural identities. With Chapter 3 — Surrealist Visions: *The Infernal Desire Machines of Doctor Hoffman*—critical attention shifts to Carter's daring reconceptualization of the lessons of Surrealism as a concurrently artistic and existential world-view of unique experimental caliber. Chapter 4 — Modern Mythologies: *The Passion of New Eve*—focuses on the writer's ironic appropriation of disparate cultural stereotypes steeped in both ancient lore and the contemporary pleasure industry. Chapter 5 — Tradition Reimagined: *The Bloody Chamber and Other Stories*—investigates Carter's adventurous anatomy of the narrative formulae, rhetorical repertoire and performative implications of the traditional fairy tale to unearth the form's unabated, yet often overlooked, philosophical significance. In Chapter 6 — Beyond Gravity: *Nights at the Circus*—the discussion engages with Carter's most audacious and comprehensive expedition into experimentative territory: a venture conducive to an unprecedented blend of formal, aesthetic and ethical concepts of genuinely circensian polychromy. Chapter 7 — Mirror Identities: *Wise Children*—finally, explores the author's last novel as the apotheosis of a preoccupation so deeply ingrained in her oeuvre as a whole as to function as a latent leading thread throughout its unfolding: the conception of identity as the forever unfinished product of the specular collusion of Self and Other.

While focusing on a pivotal designated title, each chapter also addresses a suitable range of secondary titles. These are drawn from both the fiction and the nonfiction categories and include the writings listed below:

Fiction

- Novels
  Shadow Dance (a.k.a. *Honeybuzzard*)
  Several Perceptions
  Heroes and Villains
  Love
- Short Stories
  Fireworks
  Black Venus (a.k.a. *Saints and Strangers*)
  American Ghosts and Old World Wonders

Nonfiction

  The Sadeian Woman
  Nothing Sacred
  Expletives Deleted
  Shaking a Leg

CHAPTER 1

Angela Carter's Vision

Angela Carter was a thumber of noses, a defiler of sacred cows. She loved nothing so much as cussed—but also blithe—nonconformity. Her books unshackle us, toppling the statues of the pompous, demolishing the temples and commissariats of righteousness. They draw their strength, their vitality, from all that is unrighteous, illegitimate, low.
— Salman Rushdie

Fragments of high culture create not a nostalgic yearning for better, more ordered times ... but a vigorous and abrasive celebration of ambiguity. The security of our knowledge totters in the face of "the fictionality of realism." The reality of reality becomes problematic.... While for earlier highly allusive writers, for John Webster, Alexander Pope or Eliot, the ability to deploy intertextual reference marked our knowledge of and our ability to control the world, for Carter it is part of a project which combines a lively appreciation of the literature of the past with a radical demythologizing project which challenges our confidence in our social, cultural and psychic structures and the nature of reality itself.
— Rebecca Munford

In the 1980s and early 1990s, it was common for Angela Carter's name and oeuvre to be automatically bracketed together with the phrase "magical realism," and hence with an aesthetic style or fictional genre well versed in blending the real and the fantastic in such a fashion that they could be grasped as belonging to the same flow of feeling and thought. As a theoretical term, this designation has now lost much of its impactfulness, if not entirely its relevance, largely due to shallow abuse. However, it remains fundamentally appropriate as a way of describing Carter's vision, albeit cursorily, by encapsulating with aphoristic pithiness the author's unflinching attraction to both harmonious syntheses and iconoclastic collisions of ostensibly incompatible worlds. Any one of Carter's texts offers not only its individual discursive weave but also a web of specular doubles and spectral companions of itself—umbral texts either haunting or amicably complementing the phenomenal text from within the interstices of language, logic and reason. These liminal sites function as portals to an exploration of those special points where perfectly ordinary situations somehow manage to make us sense the power of fantasy as a shadowing of reality by inscrutable forces: energies that may occasionally be glimpsed but never conclusively measured. It is in such spaces that Carter stages her audacious forays into a radical interrogation of the tortuous processes through which human notions of identity, relationality, power and historical embodiment come into being. Her sustaining goal is the explosion of the doxa by which so many lives are routinely shaped and in the name of which human beings so often consent to while their days away in ponderous thoughtlessness.

Carter's writings enjoin us to engage in some courageous thinking. First and foremost, we are encouraged to reflect on the pure and simple fact of being human—which, of course, rapidly turns out to be neither pure nor simple, and hardly to qualify for definition as a "fact." As if such a task were not sufficiently onerous unto itself, Carter also dares us to address the broad epistemological implications of our humanity: that is to say, its material impact on politics and culture, the processes of artistic production and consumption, the defensibility of intellectual engagement and, ultimately, the very right to creativity. Combining the verve of the medieval jester with the curiosity and inventiveness of the archetypal *bricoleur*, Carter does not only alert us to the idea that all of the things around us are constructed rather than natural but also invites us to ponder why they are made in the way they are — and, by extension, to ask ourselves why they *are* the way they are, or indeed why they are *at all*. Carter is not satisfied with the notion that the shape which an object or concept acquires by dint of convention and convenience is an irrevocable given. Sensing that such a perspective on reality would inevitably amount to a crass cop-out, she is keen to find out what has determined the contingent forms acquired by objects and concepts in preference to the infinite range of other possible forms they could have acquired instead. Pivotal to this quest is the conviction that the truths humans live by — through compulsion, choice or apparent choice — are actually vapid opinions that can only aspire to inscription as accepted and credible facts by persistently relying on massive overdoses of mendacity.

Carter thus endeavors to free the reader's mind and senses, overthrowing the monuments erected by the self-appointed guardians of decorum to perpetuate their hegemonic ascendancy, and flinging open the fortified gates that shield the sanctuaries of propriety and pride. Relatedly Carter's thought is so resolutely inimical to dogmatism as to preclude the vaguest possibility of any one creed or philosophy ever holding sway over its capacious purview. For instance, although her works accommodate several positions one could consider feminist in the broadly philosophical sense, there is no question of Carter's mind being straitjacketed by didactic, proselytizing or messianic imperatives of the kind one encounters in more conventional feminist writers of the same generation. Similarly, it would be foolish to ignore the existence of points of contact between Carter's message and some of the major propositions advanced by structuralism and poststructuralism. Yet, it is important to recognize that those concepts are never crudely applied by the writer to an underlying fictional plan in order to flesh it out, or simply adorn it, in fashionable ways. In fact, they are subtly implied by both her fiction and her nonfiction as an underlying body of thought which she appears to have found consonant with ideas she had already intuited and tested in her own mind and writing.

Thus, although there is implicit evidence throughout her work that the author is well-acquainted with ongoing developments in the domains of critical and literary theory, an aversion so marked as to resemble an allergy to gratuitously self-inflated jargon keeps her style and register refreshingly devoid of any facile concessions to scholarly jabberwocky. By the same token, Carter unfailingly reminds us that even the most radical act of ideological debunking is always liable to reinscription by the dominant Zeitgeist, and hence to dilution, anesthetization and taming. Alternatively, we may discover that all it is ultimately capable of leaving in its wake is an unendurable atmosphere of emptiness and loss. For Carter, conversely, to question tradition and radically subvert the pre-established rules meant to bolster its functioning is more likely to yield durable and thought-provoking effects if it aims to reimagine and reconceptualize the past.

Such strategies entail a preparedness to view tradition and history through the eyes of someone who is seeing them for the very first time — as far as this is humanly possible — and, in the process, also develop novel perspectives on the present and its possible ramifications into the future. Carter's conception of textuality epitomizes this predilection for continual reassessment. No text, in her universe, is solely and unequivocally itself since all texts are forever reaching toward other texts which, in turn, always point to the existence of alternate reality levels. Any possible meaning one might hope to glean from a narrative lies in the ineffable fold engendered by each story turning into and over other plausible stories.

Carter's boundless appetite for experiment, borne out by each of her novels and collections of short stories, results in textual formations where multiple voices and meanings puckishly intermesh and where canonical forms and genres undergo incessant metamorphosis. The writer's own words corroborate this proposition with amusing directness as, averring that she is engaged "in the demythologising business," she professes her commitment to "putting new wine into old bottles, especially if the pressure of the new wine makes the old bottles explode" (Carter 1998, p. 37). The literary canon is notoriously ill-disposed toward anyone brassy or crazy enough to tamper with its bespoke cellars. As Aidan Day maintains, even as particular motifs make recurrent appearances "throughout her writing," these are constantly addressed from "new angles" and with "new emphases." Such reorientations result "partly out of Carter's immersion in the changing intellectual debates of her times" and, no less significantly, "out of the books she was reading at different stages of her life" (Day, A., p. 13).

It is indeed vital not to lose sight of Carter's identity as a reader as well as a writer. After all, her career is unthinkable independently of the kaleidoscopic range of sources from which she draws inspiration, including medieval romances and rowdy folktales, Chaucer, Rabelais, Shakespeare, Defoe, Swift, Pope, Blake, Mary Shelley, Stoke, Poe, Carroll, Melville, Baudelaire and the French Symbolists, Proust, T. S. Eliot, Dada and Surrealism, Dostoevsky, Borges, Calvino, Coover, Ballard, Hollywood cinema in virtually all its forms, Hammer Horror, Godard, Fellini, Buñuel — and this list could undoubtedly stretch further.

This quilt of influences (both overt and implicit) is quite congruous with the fluctuating cultural context in which Carter grew up and eventually matured as an artist: wartime in a Yorkshire town, the Welfare State and its educational benefits, the Sixties' rebellious anticonformism, the searching and frequently directionless disillusionment of the following decade and then Britain's Thatcher era — and hence the erosion of the social system in which Carter had developed, allied to the febrile glorification of neo–Victorian mores, rabid militarism and philistinism. "We're going to hell in a handbasket" was Carter's recurrent assessment of Thatcher's Britain (in Callil, p. 6). "She'd have hated New Labour and especially the pseudo-religiosity of Blair," Ali Smith justly opines. "She'd have known exactly what to do with terms like 'weapons of mass destruction' and exactly what to say to puncture the Age of Sincerity and its smug, lying rhetoric, the 'I believe' performance of politics and culture now" (Smith, A., 2007, p. 18). Nor would it be preposterous to opine, in an analogous vein, that Carter would have loathed the self-righteous — and abysmally boring — discourse of so-called political correctness.

Sarah Waters proffers a germane appreciation of Carter's political and broadly cultural stance in her introduction to the 2006 edition of *Nights at the Circus*, the text which many readers regard as the author's unrivaled masterpiece. "One can't help but wonder," Waters ponders "what Carter would have made of post–Communist politics, globalisation, New Labour, the invasion of Iraq, and ... it's impossible not to regret the rich and irreverent fictions she might have woven out of reality TV, the cult of celebrity, cosmetic surgery, and ASBOs" (Waters, pp. x–xi). As will be argued in detail in subsequent chapters, one of Carter's principal preoccupations lies with the pivotal role played by the dynamics of visuality and spectacle in both temporally specified historical contexts (e.g., *Nights at the Circus*) and hypothetical time zones (e.g., *The Infernal Desire Machines of Doctor Hoffman*). Hence, it is only logical, in a sense, to assume that the writer would have felt almost instinctively drawn to the performative discourses cited by Waters as alluring areas of analysis, and that her iconoclastic disposition would have fluidly led to the creation of vibrant satirical interpretations of their glamor-soaked mythologies.

The radical and relatively rapid historical shifts through which Carter developed can be said to have triggered a redefinition of the concept of reality itself. This has a lot to do with her conviction that the classic realist take on the world is not only dull and humorless (which, in the writer's purview, would be bad enough anyway) but also inadequate to capture the reality — or rather, realities — that dwell in the gaps of the visible and the empirically verifiable. "I've got nothing against realism," Carter stresses in a BBC interview. "But there is realism and realism. I mean, the questions that I ask myself, I think they are very much to do with reality. I would like, I would really like to have had the guts and the energy and so on to be able to write about, you know, people having battles with the DHSS, but I, I haven't. I've done other things. I mean, I'm an arty person, OK. I write overblown, purple, self-indulgent prose — so fucking what?" (Carter 1992a, p. 26).

This kind of remark is bolstered not only by Carter's own aesthetic agenda but also by evaluations of her fiction of the type proposed by Nicci Gerrard, who maintains that this amounts to "Undecorous, overripe and mocking tales in which nothing is sacred and nothing natural" (Gerrard, p. 20). However, Carter herself has shamelessly endorsed her own style on more than one occasion. A notable instance of this tendency is provided in the context of an interview conducted by John Haffenden in 1985, where he opines: "I think it's true that you do embrace opportunities for over-writing." To this remark, Carter zippily ripostes: "Embrace them? I would say that I half-suffocate them with the enthusiasm with which I wrap my arms and legs around them" (in Haffenden 1985, p. 91). Carter's philosophy is inextricable from her deliberate adoption of a manner that several critics and commentators would find — and indeed have found — bizarrely bloated, excessive or even downright offensive. Therefore, far from con-stituting an act of self-gratifying rhetorical overelaboration, her style con-tributes vitally to her construction of alternate, yet peculiarly credible, realities and to her power to jar the reader out of the sober conventionality from which apathy so often ensues.

The Magic Toyshop (1967) offers a felicitous point of entry to any sus-tained investigation of Carter's opus by foreshadowing many critical aspects of her mature writings. Most memorably, it articulates the idea of the ludic as an experience that is inevitably crisscrossed by sinister premonitions of sorrow, strife, and deprivation — though metaphorically and ritualistically encoded. If, to paraphrase James Joyce, it is indeed the case that kids might as well play as not given that the ogre will come regardless, Carter could be said to amplify this contention to suggest that the ogre has always already been there in the players' very midst as a key agent in the game (Joyce 1957). The murkier connotations of play are repeatedly thrown into relief by recourse to the quintessentially ambiguous figure of the doll. Sympto-matic of the human desire for self-replication, dolls do not ultimately sup-ply us with confirmation of our godlike omnipotence by simply being conceived in our own image. In fact, they insistently remind us of our inherent puniness, hinting at our status as an indifferent force's helpless playthings.

Puppets, specifically, provide Carter with an ideal means of conveying this message while also giving her opportunity to indulge in some of the most glorious expressions of the genius of the grotesque in modern literature. Especially effective, in this regard, is the author's penchant for foregrounding the intractable nebulousness of the very notion of aliveness. Carter's portrayal of the novel's inanimate characters capitalizes on the eerie insinuation that since non-human entities are capable of looking quite human, we cannot conclusively rule out the possibility of their actually being abeyantly human. (By analogy, it could be surmised that all lifeless objects might prove latently animate.) These disquieting feelings escalate to a pitch of inner turmoil as we move through the pages under the gaze of glassy-eyed puppets which, though seemingly insensate and inert, nonetheless exude an impression of vigilant awareness. Puppets, alongside clockworks and automated gadgets, also give Carter a unique opportunity to feed her fascination with "the idea of simulacra of invented people, of imitation human beings, because, you know, the big question that we have to ask ourselves is how do we know we're not imitation human beings?" (Carter 1992, p. 24). These reflections straddle ancient lore and posthuman science fiction, bringing simultaneously to mind images as diverse as Lao Tzu's butterfly dream, Hilary Putnam's brain-in-a-vat and the Wachowskis' *Matrix*. Moreover, Carter's entire oeuvre teems with simulacra-like characters and situations, from Ghislaine in *Shadow Dance* to Madame Schreck's female collectables in *Nights at the Circus* and the "empire of signs" (to borrow Roland Barthes' phrase) braided through Japanese culture as depicted in *Fireworks*.

The Infernal Desire Machines of Doctor Hoffman (1972) inaugurates a trait of Carter's writings destined to become a principal component of her unmistakable signature: a passion for Surrealist aesthetics and, relatedly, the proverbially idiosyncratic perception of beauty embedded therein. There are occasions on which the novel's imagery is so exuberantly Surrealist as to bring to mind the Comte de Lautréamont's famous celebration of Surrealism as "the chance encounter, upon a dissecting table, of a sewing machine and an umbrella" (Lautréamont). More pervasively, however, one may sense the oblique influence of André Breton's mission, encapsulated by the artist's own evaluation of his intended goal: "I hope that it stands as having tried nothing better than laying down a conductor between the far too separated worlds of waking and sleeping, of exterior and interior reality, of reason and madness, of the calm of knowledge and of love, of life for life and the revolution" (in Caws, p. 73). The novel depicts its own peculiar version of a Surrealist revolution of sorts by dramatizing with Nietzschean fervor the ever-mounting momentum of an anarchic scheme so deliriously sweeping as to promise to topple in one fell swoop the bastions of both political order and Western metaphysics. It thereby unleashes, in both its horror and its uncanny humor, a veritable pageant of chaos, irrationality, absurd pleasure and spasmodic desire. The social system envisioned by this novel is not simply a metaphor or even an allegory of psychotic derangement: it actually *is* lunacy per se. Accordingly, the reality it evokes is not so much a setting through which some barmy individual wanders in bewilderment and pain as a living entity in its own aberrant right and in the face of which the individual may or may not be able to retain a modicum of sanity depending on the extent to which he or she is equipped to negotiate its hyperbolic delusions.

The Passion of New Eve (1977) can be regarded as an alternately caustic and pugnacious catalogue of mythologies in the sense of the word immortalized by Barthes with the book of that title — i.e., a means of alluding to all of the false representations, unexamined assumptions and illusory beliefs relentlessly disseminated in contemporary societies in order to situate their members into specific signifying networks, and to perpetuate their own authority through rampant naturalization. Overtly acknowledging Barthes' influence, Carter describes these mythologies as "ideas, images, stories that we tend to take on trust without thinking what they really mean" (in Katsavos, pp. 11–12). These encompass all manner of gender-specific roles, positions and stereotypes, alternately rendered in a relatively realistic vein with reference to everyday human intercourse and its familiar power dynamics and in a flamboyantly fantastical fashion. The latter pivots on Carter's knack of literalizing some venerable myths centered on the notion of woman's life-giving powers through physical imagery so graphically tangible as to verge on the obscene. Other pervasive mythologies which *The Passion of New Eve* targets throughout pertain to the broad body of spurious role models and vapid glamor-driven aspirations out of which the contemporary cultural imaginary is fastidiously fashioned, with media-dominated practices and Hollywood cinema in axial positions.

Carter's fascination with all things liminal, ambivalent and ironical is tersely conveyed, in this novel, by the use of the term "passion" itself. This indeed combines the biblical connotations of the word rooted in its deployment as an apt descriptor for the climactic sufferings of Jesus, the secular connotations emanating from its association with earthly concepts of desire, carnal pursuit and sensory gratification and, elliptically rather than by overt reference, the symbolic connotations infused into the word by Jeanette Winterson in the novel flaunting it as its title. In one of its most iconic passages, Winterson's text provides a perfect correlative for Carter's affective universe by depicting passion as the apotheosis of ambiguity: "Somewhere between the swamp and the mountains. Somewhere between fear and sex. Somewhere between God and the Devil passion is and the way there is sudden and the way back is worse" (Winterson, p. 60).

A cornucopian bounty of voices, accents, styles, traditions and genres, *Nights at the Circus* (1984) is arguably the most joyfully unclassifiable of Carter's novels. While labels such as Picaresque, Gothic, Decadent, Satirical, Baroque, Postmodern and Metafictional (to mention but a handful) may marginally describe isolated facets of the narrative, neither these nor other terms alacritously put forward by critics and commentators since the book's first release to try and capture in their nets its untamable energy may even begin to exhaust its inebriating richness. Sublimely refined and unashamedly scatological by turns, *Nights at the Circus* brings to lusty fruition a lingering attraction to the multiaccentual image of the circus that can be felt to have abided like a hungry ghost in the wings of several of Carter's earlier narratives. The novel indeed orchestrates its tripartite plot in the guise of the closest textual equivalent one could possibly imagine to a three-ring circus — complete with sideshows.

Most appropriately, in light of this format, *Nights at the Circus* employs a particularly extensive and prismatic cast, devoting loving care to the minutest (and hence both most endearing and most infuriating) quirks and talents of each of its members irrespective of his or her dramatic prominence in the overarching storyline. Thus, its literally larger-than-life heroine, the creepy figures held to have played critical roles in her formative years, the business partners with whom she strikes deals along the way, her lovers and rivals, alongside the peripheral but unforgettable presences of countless clowns and tiger tamers, embarrassingly intelligent animals, the inmates of a panoptical penitentiary and Siberian shamans meet and merge in a swirling profusion of complications, convolutions and involutions that sway the senses without ever deteriorating into gratuitous nonsense. A sonorous testament to Carter's Rabelaisian fecundity, *Nights at the Circus* thereby defies gravity by suspending with equal glee the laws of physics and conventional morality.

Less overtly ornate than Carter's previous novel, yet no less exuberant in its cultivation of an eminently nonconformist world view most at home with the burlesque and carnival transgression, *Wise Children* (1991) revolves around a subtly diversified gallery of variations on the intercomplementary themes of replication and inversion. Duplicities, dualities and duplications work together to evoke potent symbolic analogies between the mutually reflecting members of a pair. These tropes coexist with a set of no less powerful operations ostensibly working in the opposite direction, and thus underscoring the two parties' irreducible alterity to and from each other: in this perspective, divergences, dichotomies and dissymmetries reign supreme. Employing various twin figures as her protagonists, and inter-textually beading her narrative braids with elaborate allusions to Shake-speare's megaverse, Carter hence paints a tantalizing metaphysical picture in which similarity and difference, self and non-self, presence and absence coexist at all times. In this hyperreality, identity is never anything more stable that the provisional byproduct of incessant mirroring.

From a relatively early stage in her tragically curtailed career, Carter was keen to experiment with the short story form specifically for the pur-pose of reappropriating and, by and by, drastically rethinking a number of established generic molds and corresponding audience expectations. The fairy tale played an especially important part in this venture and grad-ually rose to the status of a critical focus through which Carter was able to engage in some genuinely inspired and pioneering interventions in the domain of revisionist theory. Her speculations were fundamentally con-cerned with the prospect of redefining the literary canon in light of con-temporary realities and, by extension, impacting on anthropological research in the realm of storytelling as a vital aspect of human enculture-ment, communication and intersubjective evolution. This book makes ref-erence to several of Carter's short story collections — i.e., *Fireworks* (1973), *Black Venus* (a.k.a. *Saints and Strangers*, 1985) and *American Ghosts and Old World Wonders* (1993), as collected in the volume *Burning Your Boats* (1995). However, it devotes special attention to *The Bloody Chamber and Other Stories* (1979) as the object of study of a chapter-length discussion insofar as this is work which most resonantly declares the author's origi-nality and inventiveness in her reconceptualization of the fairy tale tradi-tion, its history and its ethics.

Sustained by a zealous desire to update and twist the yarns immor-talized by the likes of the Brothers Grimm, Charles Perrault, Giambattista

Basile and Walt Disney, Carter seeks to restore the fairy tale to its murky roots, making inspired use of archetypes in order to create autonomous tales. Even when she appears to conform to some of the more romantically idealistic formulae traditionally associated with the fairy tale parable, she never allows us to forget or ignore that any reparative resolutions we may rejoice in are only the outcome of arbitrary moves on an author's part, and that in life beyond the covers of the book, no such consolatory options are readily available. She is therefore staunchly loyal to the darker side of the fairy tale world in the communication of a grittily unsentimental lesson, honoring her instinctive attraction to that form's original ethos far more than to its edulcorated, bowdlerized and sanitized adaptations.

All of the main themes, motifs and tropes recurrently deployed by Carter in the constellation of the speculative areas discussed above are woven together into a tapestry of often mesmerizing figurative opulence and sensuous delectation by a methodical — yet by no means prescriptive — philosophical pursuit. This carries concurrently aesthetic, ethical and ideological resonance and pivots on a frank exposure of the ominous drives that lurk at the heart of any totalitarian quest for absolute control. These urges, resurfacing time after time either with measured premeditation or with convulsive instinctual compulsion, tend to acquire symbolically laden guises. Especially prominent among them is the reification of the female body. This posits woman, at times literally and at others metaphorically, as an unsettling object of both fascination and revulsion, framed as a grotesque, hybrid, composite or ghostly specimen exploitable for her entertainment value as an exhibit or her commercial worth as rare merchandise.

The psychological disturbances that can be invoked by this fertile trope are numerous but Carter adroitly suggests that she is using aberrations such as sadism, masochism, fetishistic scopophilia and necrophilia (to cite but a few) not only as convenient — and bizarrely colorful — narrative or dramatic hooks but also as allegorical correlatives for the societal evils of tyranny, intolerance, persecution and corruption. The ultimate monster, in this scenario, is not the dead-in-life curiosity encased in a perverse collector's *Wunderkammer*, appallingly macabre as this icon undeniably is. In fact, it resides with the lack of imagination gnawing at the core of the putrescent, yet stubbornly self-perpetuating, dumbing-down mentality that has tended to swamp the domains of creativity and politics alike with pandemic insistence over the past four decades. It is indeed crucial to remember that in exploring the deviousness and mendacity of innumerable belief systems, Carter does not promulgate hard-nosed rationalism but actually defends at any price the "human right to vision" (Carter 2006c, p. 73) — and therefore to envision, visualize, ideate and fantasize — as an inalienable creaturely entitlement.

The writer periodically resorts, either explicitly or allusively, to the ruse of the text-within-a-text to throw into relief the aforementioned pre-occupations. This strategy is instrumental in abetting the author's unob-trusive (and, more often than not, tongue-in-cheek) communication of a vibrantly questioning existentialist outlook. Hence, it evokes a forever pre-carious world in which words can no longer be depended upon unprob-lematically to denote the things to which they are meant to refer and become instead unfathomable things in their own right. Such a world of "nameless things" and "thingless names," to appropriate one of Samuel Beckett's most hauntingly beautiful images, cries out for rational interpre-tation only to declare it, time and again, risibly unattainable (Beckett 2009). In the process, readers are regaled with kaleidoscopic expressions of a unique ability to magnify evil through jocularity, on the one hand, and induce exhilaration through baleful visions on the other. Humor spares no flourish to intensify both the palpability and the uncanny otherworld-liness of horror by recourse to defamiliarization and irony, while a jovial down-to-earthness works to make the horror feel quite prosaic. In ideating such a reality — or reality skein — Carter reveals a mind that is not scared of confronting even the most unpalatable of taboos and in fact seeks to give them a voice in defiance of prejudice and dogma.

Carter remains bravely optimistic in the face of frightful scenarios, proving faithful to one of the key lessons of the fairy tale form so pivotal to her world picture. However, in full consonance with another message also pivotal to that same form, she does not allow her humor to divorce itself from knowledge of the darkness it so buoyantly mocks. Relatedly, her fantasies always retain an anchoring in the actual, eschewing escapism no less than classic realism. In this respect, they intimate that even though political events are not necessarily fantasies, fantasy is de facto a form of politics. As the author herself emphasizes, her take on the political is "the product of an absolute and *committed materialism*—i.e., that *this* world is all that there is, and in order to question the nature of reality one must move from a strongly grounded base in what constitutes material reality" (Carter 1998, p. 38). The fairy tale tradition again supplies a cogent reference point as the quintessential blend of reality and fantasy insofar as "fairy tales," for Carter, "are all of them the most vital connection we have with the imagination of the ordinary men and women whose labour created our world"—people whose efforts endure over the centuries even though their identities are no more enshrined in historiography than the names of those "who first invented meatballs" (Carter 1990, pp. ix–x).

By marrying fantasy to a use of language that concretizes ideas to the utmost degree, Carter deploys the fantastic in an eminently allegorical fashion, positing its bizarre characters and preposterous situations, its vertiginous plots and twists of logic as figurative correlatives for the cultural myths by which political reality is defined and corralled. Carter's mind is agilely profane but never so jokey as to become blind to the malevolence of the forces it endeavors to explode in the service of honest thinking, speculation and reflection. Ostensibly conflicting modalities collude with impish gusto, bringing forth a universe of ceaseless transmutation and flux, unrelentingly traversed by intimations of rupture, dislocation and loss — yet capable, by a glorious paradox, of dispensing no less assiduously magnanimous doses of both beauty and delight.

CHAPTER 2

Dark Play

The Magic Toyshop

Come, children, let us shut up the box and the puppets, for our play is played out.

— William Makepeace Thackeray

Play has been man's most useful preoccupation.

— Frank Caplan

Carter's passion for appropriating and reimagining traditional narrative forms declares itself from an early stage in her fictional career with *The Magic Toyshop*: a narrative shaped throughout by an unmistakable fairy tale logic. The author herself has indeed described this text as a "malign fairy tale" (in Haffenden 1984, p. 35). The fairy tale remains a virtually inexhaustible reservoir of fictional inspiration for Carter well beyond *The Magic Toyshop*—as will be demonstrated in detail in this study's fifth chapter. Furthermore, it constitutes the life and soul of her works as an editor, as attested to by the collections *Wayward Girls and Wicked Women: An Anthology of Subversive Stories* (1986), *The Virago Book of Fairy Tales* (a.k.a. *The Old Wives' Fairy Tale Book*, 1990), *The Second Virago Book of Fairy Tales* (1992, a.k.a. *Strange Things Still Sometimes Happen: Fairy Tales from Around the World*, 1993) and *Angela Carter's Book of Fairy Tales* (a compilation of the two earlier collections edited for Virago). Carter's works for children likewise deserve mention in this context. These include *The Donkey Prince* (1970), *Miss Z, the Dark Young Lady* (1970), *Comic and Curious Cats* (1979), *Moonshadow* (1982) and *Sea-Cat and Dragon King*

(2000). Finally, Carter has left us two major translations in the field: *The Fairy Tales of Charles Perrault* (1977) and *Sleeping Beauty and Other Favourite Fairy Tales* (1982), a miscellany featuring Perrault's stories alongside two tales by the novelist Jeanne-Marie Le Prince de Beaumont (1711–1780).

Carter was well aware, in translating such classics, that many of the images we automatically associate with the most famous fairy tales have been planted post hoc in the original texts in order to sanitize and edulcorate their darker components and infuse their yarns with morally edifying messages pregnant with gender-inflected prejudices. For example, Carter would have been quick to detect the bizarre disparity between popular versions of "Sleeping Beauty" culminating with the Princess' release from her long slumber as a result of the Prince's kiss and Perrault's original, where the Princess simply wakes up as the Prince enters her bedchamber for the reason that the hundred years' spell has reached its end.

In an article colorfully headed "The Better to Eat You With," whose import resonates throughout not only Carter's output as an editor and her stories for children but also the fabric of *The Magic Toyshop* itself, the author describes her perspective on the fairy tale as follows: "The notion of the fairy tale as a vehicle for moral instruction is not a fashionable one. I sweated out the heatwave browsing through Perrault's *Contes du temps passé* on the pretext of improving my French. What an unexpected treat to find that in this great Ur-collection — whence sprang the Sleeping Beauty, Puss in Boots, Little Red Riding Hood, Cinderella, Tom Thumb, all the heroes of pantomime — all these nursery tales are purposely dressed up as fables of the politics of experience. The seventeenth century regarded children, quite rightly, as apprentice adults. Charles Perrault, academician, folklorist, pedant, but clearly neither nutter nor regressive, takes a healthily abrasive attitude to his material. Cut the crap about richly nurturing the imagination. This world is all that is to the point" (Carter 1998, pp. 452–453).

The fairy tale's abiding attraction as one of Carter's pivotal frames of creative reference results primarily from its unflagging ability, as Marina Warner phrases it, "to reveal possibilities, to map out a different way and a new perception of love, marriage, women's skills, thus advocating a means of escaping imposed limits and prescribed destiny. The fairy tale looks at the ogre like Bluebeard or the Beast of 'Beauty and the Beast' in order to disenchant him; while romancing reality, it is a medium deeply concerned with undoing prejudice." While these possibilities are, in principle, available to anyone and hence unfettered by gender-specific rules, "Women of different social positions" have traditionally benefited most from the fairy tale tradition insofar as it has consistently supplied them with expressive vehicles even in cultures hell-bent on excluding their female members from the privilege of authorship. Through these channels, women "have collaborated in storytelling to achieve true recognition for their subjects: the process is still going on" (Warner 1995, p. 24).

The Magic Toyshop's entire yarn, its character cast, its recurrent imagery and, above all, its concurrently aesthetic and ethical vision could therefore be said to epitomize, in an embryonic fashion, an artistic predilection destined to resonate across its author's entire output for decades to come. As to the facets of the fairy tale capable of fueling most prolifically the specific world picture presented in *The Magic Toyshop*, the most crucial is undoubtedly its proclivity to enact unpredictable illusion-breaking strategies. The text accomplishes this feat, even as it enthrones itself as a narrative act devoted to the erection and maintenance of illusions, by foregrounding the principles of hybridity, openness, excess, impurity, irrationality, irreverence and exaggeration, veering with equal glee and with the same unshakable penchant for humor in the directions of both hyperbole and litotes. Also vital to the communication of Carter's vision throughout the novel is its flair for textual dispersion and playfulness. These, moreover, are allied to the insistent prioritization of random chance, contingency and coincidence over rational calculation and planning. By thus fostering a systematic subversion of causality, Carter's reimagined fairy tale provides an implicit critique of the concept of knowledge itself as an exercise of authority designed to yield incontrovertible certitudes.

Transcending the strictures of canonical periodization and formal classification, Carter's appropriation of the fairy tale modality in *The Magic Toyshop* points to a desire to utilize the traditional form not merely as an end in itself but also as a means of interrogating a substantially broader cultural heritage and thus challenging its mainstream representations. Accordingly, the author turns to the fairy tale as a means of staging the intricacies and ambivalences of desire, sexuality, fear and passion as the epitome of all that the censorious hand of reason and logic have addictively sought to quash or deride. Reason and logic, in the fairy tale's world picture, are neither coterminous with the actual world nor effectively accomplishable within its parameters. The unquestioned belief that they are is exposed by Carter as the ultimate lie sustaining the false reality of classic realism.

The narrator of the short story "The Lady of the House of Love" (in *The Bloody Chamber and Other Stories*) at one point wonders: "Can a bird sing only the song it knows, or can it learn a new song?" (Carter 2006e, p. 195). In the specific context of Carter's appropriation of the fairy tale tradition, the question is whether this venerable discourse can be revamped in such a fashion as to pose new issues — to function as an effective way of positing and fathoming a heterogeneous array of hypothetical realities. The answer extended by *The Magic Toyshop* is indubitably affirmative. This is not to say, however, that the fairy tale offers an easy ride for either its characters or its tellers. As *The Magic Toyshop* clearly shows, Carter briefly allows the fantasy to gesture toward rosy prospects of serenity and reconciliation. Yet, she does not allow it to exorcize what is obviously an inequitable and oppressive present by swallowing it up into the cauldron of timelessness. The fiction remains lucidly self-conscious throughout, thereby dissipating any possible promises of conclusive harmony.

Nicoletta Pireddu's observations on Carter's appropriation of the medieval romance — a fantasy mode germane to the fairy tale at large and most pertinent to *The Magic Toyshop* — deserve particular consideration in this context: "If, on the one hand, she urges us to flee from realism because it has been telling us stories," Pireddu maintains, "on the other hand the embrace of romances is no cozy shelter, either. Beyond good and evil, beyond any possible sublimation or symbolic appeasement, we plunge into the unconscious still burdened with our common sense, and we reemerge bringing back disquieting and irrational elements that deconstruct everyday, allegedly 'real,' life. The structural endlessness [of the] romance returns in Carter's postmodern fiction in the form of a conceptual openness. Precisely the deferred reconciliation of irreconcilable but paradoxically intertwined orders of reality makes Carter's romance rigorously 'inescapable'" (Pireddu, pp. 27–28).

Carter is clearly drawn to the quest element as one of the fairy tale's staple ingredients but does not typically engage with this motif for consolatory purposes. In other words, she is not interested in chronicling a quest for goals to be accomplished so as to secure a wish-fulfilling resolution and a metaphysical guarantee of plenitude but rather in rethinking the very idea of the quest to conceive of its import in terms of a forever unresolved undertaking or project. In Carter's reimagined fairy tale universe, quests are displaced by questions, and hence operate as metaphors for the urge to scrutinize reality at all levels — devoting special attention to those objectives, aspirations and hegemonic values that seem most natural and therefore to lie innocently beyond questioning. Storytelling, in this perspective, constitutes "a system of continuing inquiry" (in Katsavos, p. 14). For Carter, we are thereby reminded, a life unexamined is tantamount to a life not lived.

Insofar as the fairy tale's adventures and intrigues are virtually inextricable from the highly codified value systems that have been sedimented within the form for centuries, it constitutes an especially versatile tool for investigating the patterns through which our experience and knowledge of reality are mediated at all times by the ideological imperatives shaping human cultures and their sustaining power relations. Nevertheless, Carter's voyage toward the roots of storytelling is not a hunt for an ultimate urtext seeking to unearth some mythical creationist figure. In fact, as intimated in the previous chapter, it tirelessly foregrounds the concept of a collective narrative patrimony that belongs to no identifiable individual but is actually open to continual dissemination, manipulation and — most critically — reinvention. Hence, tales of fantasy and magic are capable of morphing relentlessly into anything our craft might choose to make of them. Like folklore, literature is not so much invented as recycled, adopted as raw material for the shaping of new possible stories and for the voicing of contingent concerns. In this regard, Carter's project calls to mind Linda Hutcheon's challenging question concerning the ultimate meaning of originality and derivativeness — "What is *not* an adaptation?" (Hutcheon, p. 170).

Given Carter's commitment to the sustained explosion of all manner of ossified codes and conventions, it does not seem unwarranted to propose that the facet of the fairy tale that attracts her most potently is the form's predilection for narrative and performative situations witnessing the coalescence of antithetical worlds and attendant values. These contexts supply the writer with ideal arenas for the staging of dramas that are able to emit at once a pervasive aura of timelessness and a burning sense of topical cogency by capturing realities which, afloat in fantasy and magic though they often are, are nonetheless in a position to comment dispassionately on lived material conditions. In bringing out the fairy tale's concomitantly eternal and contingent relevance, *The Magic Toyshop* seeks to map out the extension and magnitude of the range of baleful human tendencies that often gain people the titles of monsters or beasts. The novel's take on these concepts echoes Warner's contention that "Monsters aren't by any means always internal psychotic phantasies" and "Beasts aren't only within, they can also be without" (Warner 1994, p. 21).

Carter engages explicitly with the questions of monstrosity and bestiality in *The Sadeian Woman*, focusing on Donatien Alphonse François, Marquis de Sade (1740–1814). In order to appreciate the full import of Carter's iconoclastic critique, it is vital to bear in mind that there is no obvious consensus as to what exactly is supposed to constitute the essence of Sadeian iniquity. The jury is still out, therefore, on whether the Marquis himself or his characters should be considered degenerate or whether, in fact, the whole culture he portrays should be addressed as the repository of ubiquitous evil. Insofar as Sade's ideas have been routinely subject to severe silencing and blue-penciling over the centuries, these and many other related questions remain unanswered. What seems incontrovertibly evident, however, is that the ferocious acts of suppression of which Sade's works have been victims over time can only smack of hypocrisy when assessed against the corruption, perversity and brutality endemic in both his own social milieux and later epochs bold enough to deem themselves purer. In this perspective, the dismal situations he depicts should not be regarded as perverse distortions of his society's dominant tendencies but rather as faithful reflections, communicated in a metaphorical or even allegorical fashion, of the perversity and viciousness of an entire culture.

According to Carter, what has rendered the Marquis' oeuvre an object of unrelentingly severe censorship is the fact that it does not allow its readers to revel in alternately titillating and idyllic versions of erotic gratification, which is by and large the purpose of pornography, but rather to "comment on real relations in the real world" (Carter 1979, p. 19). Sade's portrayal of "the last years of the ancient regime in France," she avers, evokes "not an artificial paradise of gratified sexuality but a model of hell, in which the gratification of sexuality involves the infliction and tolerance of extreme pain. He describes sexual relations in the context of an unfree society as the expression of pure tyranny," thus construing "a diabolical lyricism of fuckery" which "makes of sexuality itself a permanent negation" (p. 26). Hence, Carter interprets Sade's philosophy as the product of a "moral pornographer," eager to "use pornography as a critique of current relations between the sexes" which holds the potential of inaugurating "the total demystification of the flesh" (p. 20).

This controversial contribution to cultural history finds a perfect companion in a text penned by Roland Barthes, one of the twentieth-century philosophers with whom Carter shares some her most fundamental convictions and critical aims: namely, the intriguing treatise *Sade/Fourier/Loyola*. Engaging with no less challenging a subject than the fundamental nature of philosophical creation, Barthes draws imaginative threads of connection between the libertine thinker, the utopian philosopher and the Jesuit saint as inventors of specific languages and related codes (the discourses of erotic experimentation, visionary contentment and divine address respectively) as major contributions to the genesis of modern notions of textuality per se. Like Carter, Barthes emphasizes the political relevance of the Marquis' opus by arguing that his "adventures are not fabulous: they take place in a real world, contemporary with Sade's youth, i.e., the society of Louis XV" and "the corrupt practice of despotism" (Barthes 1996, p. 130).

While echoing Warner's contention regarding the existence of monsters and beasts as real beings rather than sheer figments of the imagination or dark children of a troubled unconscious, Carter concomitantly alerts us to those figures' (mainly silent) omnipresence. In this respect, her position on the subject bears latent analogies with Poppy Z. Brite's presentation of monstrosity in *Exquisite Corpse*: "Some may think killing is easy for men like me; that it is a thing we murderers do as casually and callously as brushing our teeth" Brite's protagonist reflects. "Hedonists see us as grotesque cult heroes performing mutilations for kicks. Moralists will not even grant us a position in the human race, can only rationalize our existence as monsters. But *monster* is a medical term, describing a freak too grossly deformed to belong anywhere but the grave. Murderers, skilled as belonging everywhere, seed the world" (Brite, p. 66).

Fairy tale images and tropes pervade the entire fabric of *The Magic Toyshop*. At their most explicit, they draw on identifiable narratives of the kind most of us would have heard in childhood — or else sampled in their cartoon adaptations. *Snow White*, for instance, is alluded to in by the scene where Melanie beholds her reflection after donning her mother's nuptial wreath and wonders: "Am I as beautiful as that?" (Carter 2006a, p. 16). The same tale is hinted at in a later scene where the girl, disturbed by the unfamiliar darkness of the nighttime garden, sees the beautiful pomes on the tree outside her bedroom window as "sinister poison apples" (p. 20). *Bluebeard* is invoked as Melanie, struggling to rationalize her vision of a severed female hand in the cutlery drawer, somberly reflects: "I am going out of my mind.... Bluebeard was here" (p. 118). At the end of the novel,

Uncle Philip's entire house is equated to the archvillain's stronghold as the narrator notes: "One of the sinister doors of Bluebeard's castle sprang open" (p. 198).

Sleeping Beauty, as the quintessential coming-of-age tale, appropriately makes its own memorable appearance in Carter's seminal narrative of psychosexual development: "Melanie opened her eyes and saw thorns among roses, as if she woke from a hundred years' night" (p. 53). A darkly amusing part is reserved for *Little Red Riding Hood*, a traditional yarn for which Carter will go on exhibiting a marked passion in her subsequent output. "Uncle Philip's teeth aren't in the bathroom," Melanie points out to Finn after a night spent in bed together as the most chaste of siblings would, gaining Finn's sardonic riposte: "All the better to eat me with. They're in his mouth, of course" (p. 182). The cave image, one of the fairy tale's most frequently revisited tropes, informs the description of the magic toyshop itself as perceived by the orphans when they first arrive at their new home: namely, as a signally unwelcoming "dark cavern" (p. 39). Caves, it will be recalled, are traditionally deployed as pivotal locations in the fairy tale's representation of rites of passage entailing problematic discoveries — as famously shown by *Ali Baba and the Forty Thieves*.

The Magic Toyshop partakes of the darkness pervading the fairy tale tradition in its uncensored and unsweetened manifestations in the sequence where Melanie emerges into the nocturnal garden wearing her mother's oversized wedding dress and is suddenly overwhelmed by a reality for which she is — quite simply — not yet ready: "The loneliness seized her by the throat and suddenly she could not bear it.... Too much, too soon" (p. 18). The feeling of utter helplessness escalates as Melanie begins to fantasize about the "monsters ... whose flesh was the same substance as the night" lurking in the shadows, and "'nothing' clanged inside her head" (p. 19). The epic tone is bathetically disrupted by the statement "the blackness mewed" (p. 20), at which point it becomes obvious that the heroine's only company in the engulfing gloom is Mrs. Rundle's fat cat. Carter is clearly keen to perform a fine balancing act between real terror and parody. Yet, the humorous touches do not cheapen the overall pathos imbuing Melanie's rite of passage as the narrator is also eager to show that the tenebrous isolation suffocating the girl in the course of her foray into the unknown is the very darkness which the fairy tale tradition repeatedly revisits in order to emblematize, as Diane Purkiss puts it, the "dissolution of identity."

The principal reasons for which "we fear the dark," the critic contends, are that "we cannot see in it" and, at the same time, "cannot be seen in it, cannot be known, recognized." Darkness is a liminal territory between presence and absence, plenitude and the void. The figurative equation of darkness to the dissolution of identity reaches a spine-chilling climax with the equation of darkness to the abyss of "unlife" (Purkiss, p. 15) — with "the darkness of death" itself, where a person's existence might be "forgotten" altogether, and selfhood might be irrevocably "lost in the sense of never having been known" (p. 22). As argued in more detail later in this analysis, *The Magic Toyshop* colors its drama's perception of darkness with distinctive hues by foregrounding the troubling connotations of the phenomenon of marginality with a specific focus on its generational dimension. It does so by focusing on the vicissitudes of adolescence and early adulthood as proverbially borderline moments in human development.

A seminal component of the fairy tale which *The Magic Toyshop* discreetly foregrounds is the form's ceremonially official register. A fitting illustrative instance is supplied by an early conversation between Melanie and Finn. "It is beginning to get dark," the girl observes on the way to her new family home, to which her companion cryptically ripostes: "And will get darker." As the narrator interjects, there is "a certain ritual quality in this exchange," which imparts it with a distinctively otherworldly tenor and suggests that Melanie might have inadvertently "stumbled on the secret sequence of words that would lead her safe over the swordbridge into the Castle of Corbenic" (Carter 2006a, p. 37). The fairy tale's rhetoric of haunting plays no less conspicuous a role. In the wake of her parent's fatal accident, in particular, Melanie believes that a part of her own self has perished and assumed a spectral guise: this is "the daisy-crowned young girl who would stay behind" as the flesh-and-blood Melanie moves to London "to haunt the old house, to appear in mirrors ... to flash whitely on dark nights" (p. 31). The magic toyshop itself is later referred to as a "haunted" venue as Melanie catches sight of her parents' wedding photograph in Aunt Margaret's bedroom (p. 187). At the same time, Melanie emulates the typical fairy tale heroine in her ritualistic respect for all sorts of superstitions. This is evinced by the girl's linguistic register, where religious and magical elements coexist and blend at every turn of her ordeal. This ruse affords scope for an implicit debunking of religion of precisely the kind which the staunchly antitheist and iconoclastic Carter characteristically cherishes.

In *The Magic Toyshop*, as in the fairy tale tradition, clothes carry unique importance. Melanie is obviously invested with an alternate identity by her clandestine donning of her mother's wedding-dress and comes to see the act as so blasphemous a violation of social decorum and filial obedience as to have triggered her parents' catastrophic demise. Apparel is also accorded special significance in the scenes where Melanie endeavors to imagine sexual intercourse between her parents, and notes that even in the depths of intimacy, her mum appears "to be wearing her black, going-to-town suit" and her dad, "the hairy tweed jacket with leather elbow-patches" (p. 10). Clothes and accessories feature prominently in fairy tales as major personality markers and as talismanic agencies capable of investing their wearers with more or less temporary preternatural powers: invisibility cloaks, metamorphic ball gowns and seven-league boots clearly exemplify this proposition. The connection between apparel and magic reaches deeper still if one considers its ritualistic connotations. These are famously thrown into relief by Sir James George Frazer, who posits garments as particularly versatile tools in the practice of "Sympathetic Magic" as theorized in *The Golden Bough* (1913–1920). One of the key principles by which this type of magic abides is that "things which have once been in contact with each other continue to act on each other at a distance after the physical contact has been severed." This tenet is known as "the Law of Contact or Contagion" and from it the practitioner "infers that whatever he does to a material object will affect equally the person with whom the object was once in contact, whether it formed part of his body or not.... Charms based on the Law of Contact or Contagion may be called Contagious Magic" (Frazer).

Clothes play a crucial part in the process of personality construction by investing the bodies that wear them with distinctive stylistic and formal attributes and, by extension, symbolic identities. In its partnership with apparel, the human body functions as a fundamentally osmotic vessel since, whenever it adopts particular items of dress, it simultaneously assimilates them — makes them akin to its own flesh. This perspective intimates that garments may operate as the physical organism's substitute or deputy. The body's situation in a cultural formation, its symbolic systems of signification, its codes and conventions inevitably entails that it is inconceivable outside language and representation — in other words, cultural inscription robs the body of its concreteness. In its capacity as surrogate flesh, dress could therefore be said to operate not only as an alternative to the body's depleted materiality but also as a fairy godmother of sorts by filling the gap opened up by the symbolic suppression of the corporeal dimension.

Apparel, in this regard, concurrently polices the body's boundaries by insulating it from the outside world and imparts it with a comforting level of physical density. As in the phenomenon of contagion theorized by Frazer, so in the transfer of affects from dress to the body, what is involved is not merely the individual self but a collectivity or ensemble. As the wedding photograph on display in Melanie's parental bedroom indicates, the process of transmission takes place on a communal plane. That is to say, the individual body is not only susceptible to the influence wielded by the specific garments it wears: it is also open to figurative contamination by other people's clothed bodies — i.e., to the ideological, psychological and emotional energies pervading their structures and textures. These may be perceived *in absentia* through the rhetoric of the photographic image (as in the case of the nuptial family portrait) or as actual physical presences (as in the case of Melanie's actual donning of her mother's wedding dress).

In order to give her vision graphic incarnation, Carter ideates an intriguing heroine, carefully avoiding the trap of simplistic idealization and playing with ingenious contrasts instead. Melanie is prey to patriarchal expectations regarding femininity and therefore cannot help perceiving herself stereotypically as either a prospective bride or a muse, obsessively nourishing the myth of the ideal feminine body in strict accordance with conservative male desires. Nevertheless, she is also spunky and independent, and capable of tenaciously rejecting the submissive roles designed by Uncle Philip to keep his family in his thrall. This is most invigoratingly conveyed by the segment of the narrative in which she defies the tyrant's ban on festive solace by purchasing Christmas presents for her siblings and for Aunt Margaret. In this respect, *The Magic Toyshop*'s heroine could be said to emblematize the fairy tale's amalgamation of conflicting world views. This systematic avoidance of pedestrian stereotyping also impacts felicitously on Carter's portrayal of Finn. On the one hand, the "supple and extraordinary grace" (p. 33) which characterizes the youth's patterns of motion and imparts them with "lyrical" fluidity (p. 34) hints at a delicate and feminine sensibility. On the other hand, Finn exhibits disquieting traces of lupinity redolent of *Little Red Riding Hood*'s villain as the epitome of the predatory male. As he urges Melanie to undo her torturing plaits and display her mane in all its glory, for example, Finn acquires a dangerously seductive aura: "his squinting eyes slithered and shifted like mercury on a plate," matched by "the pointed tip of his tongue" flashing "between his teeth" (p.45).

While both Melanie and Finn are depicted as multifaceted individuals, Carter's presentation of their interaction likewise transcends the attribution of monolithic roles. This is eloquently attested to by their shared peep show. At a critical point in the story, the girl discovers a hole in the wall of her bedroom which, on close inspection, turns out to have been carefully crafted in order to spy on her. However, she does not simply succumb to the role of passive object to which this ruse might easily consign a less resourceful heroine and resolves instead to use the fissure herself in order to peer into "the terra incognita" of Finn and his brother's bedroom (p. 108). Thus, her prospective lover is not the uncontrasted possessor of the proprietorial gaze — as she spies back, he becomes something of a feminized object of the look in turn. Furthermore, when Melanie asks Finn, at a later juncture in the narrative, why he has made the hole, he disarmingly states: "Because you are so beautiful" (p. 123). There is clearly no trace of malice, cunning or possessiveness in the youth's frank explanation. Melanie and Finn's mutual peep show draws attention to the politics of visuality at large, inviting us to ponder the extent to which all social relationships are intrinsically mediated by vision and therefore by images. Visual performance, in Carter's novel, is shown to penetrate deeply the psychology and fantasy apparatuses of individuals, and to have the capacity to define whole ways of life by producing identities on the basis not solely of conscious choices but also of unconscious associations endowed with visceral affective appeal. At this level, subjectivity is ideated as a product of a person's constitution as both an agent and an object of sight: a process through which the categories of being, seeing and being seen become utterly interdependent.

The total absence of mirrors in Uncle Philip's household can be read as a denial of narcissism. This entails a drastic suppression of the self-indulgent autoeroticism in which Melanie is shown to be engrossed in the novel's early portion, as she gazes at her nude body for hours on end in the mirror of her chamber, posing in arty attitudes meant to emulate the female beauties immortalized by painters as diverse as the Pre-Raphaelites, Toulouse-Lautrec and Cranach. Overcoming her narcissistic proclivities is obviously a necessary step in the heroine's process of maturation. At the same time, the absence of mirrors figuratively alludes to the exclusion from Melanie's (and her new family's) domain of any Carrollesque portals to alternative realities. This, however, is not a strategy designed to further the interests of rationality since, in the magic toyshop's world, reality and dream tenaciously coalesce and there is therefore no real need for world-bridging portals in the first place. In this context, the novel's priority is again the explosion of binary oppositions: the goal which, as argued earlier, guides Carter's characterization of her principal personae. With its setting, *The Magic Toyshop* reinforces the same basic world view by intimating that an apparently oppressive and inimical environment does not necessarily represent an undilutedly adversarial force and may actually turn out to function as a salutary space in which conventional boundaries may be transgressed and positive transformation initiated.

It should also be borne in mind, on this point, that the specular world actually rejects Melanie prior to her relocation to London, as the looking-glass complicit with her autoerotic fantasies is shattered, thereby seeming to erase the very girl's identity, in the immediate aftermath of the announcement that Melanie's parents have died (pp. 24–25). A comparable state of affairs marks the dénouement of the short story "Reflections" (in *Fireworks*), where Carter explores the collusion of actuality and virtuality by utilizing the familiar image of the mirror as a means of initiating a drastic reality reversal, and hence defamiliarizing the ordinary in order to impel recognition of the iniquities underpinning its unexamined authority. "The "glass gathered itself together like a skilful whore and expelled me," the narrator-protagonist gravely states as he ponders his specular journey's precipitous end. "The glass rejected me; it sealed itself again into nothing but mysterious, reflective opacity" (Carter 2006e, p. 94).

As suggested earlier, *The Magic Toyshop* revels in the bizarre rhetoric of liminality. This applies in equal measures to the novel's representation of space and to its handling of the temporal dimension. At the spatial level, Carter's passion for borderline situations finds perfect expression in the orphans' transition from the country to the city, from the neatly mapped middle-class domain of Melanie's early life to the blurry hyper-reality of the magic toyshop. The nebulousness of the demarcation between consciousness and dreaming pervades this world from beginning to end. Thus, Melanie is powerless to ascertain whether the "soft-looking, plump little hand" she sees in the knife drawer is real or not — all she can do is turn to the collective imaginary enshrined in the fairy tale tradition in an attempt to keep her immobilizing hesitation at bay: "From the raggedness of the flesh at the wrist, it appeared that the hand had been hewn from its arm with a knife or axe that was very blunt" (p. 118). Likewise, she cannot establish whether the dining-table is a solid object or a specular impression:

"her eyes turned again and again to the plausible distortion of the witch-ball. She found herself wondering which was the real tea-table and which was the reflection" (p. 169). Concurrently, Melanie's hallucinatory dreams remain precariously suspended between the anguish of simple nightmares and the mystical sphere of prophetic warnings — as borne out by the dream in which she identifies so intimately with her brother as to actually become convinced that she occupies Jonathon's body.

So committed is the novel to the systematic erosion of clear distinctions between the solid and the oneiric that it takes time to throw into relief the inarrestable interplay of reality and fantasy even prior to the move to London. The spirit of liminality so pivotal to the magic toyshop can therefore be seen also to animate the text's non-magical settings. Fantasy, accordingly, already penetrates the characters' musings and sustaining dreams at an early stage in the narrative, coursing vibrantly not only through Melanie's but also through Mrs. Rundle's and Jonathon's psyches. Thus, while the heroine ideates her "phantom bridegroom" so powerfully as to be able to "feel his breath on her cheek" (p. 2), the elderly housekeeper has a similar tendency to conjure up the features and mannerisms of the spouse she has never actually had out of thin air (p. 3), and Jonathon, for his part, is so engrossed in the punctilious construction of model boats as to inhabit at all times an alternate world of "blue seas and coconut islands" and to even walk "with a faintly discernible nautical roll" (p. 4). Importantly, in the course of the journey from the familiarity of the countryside to the mystery of London, the train's liminal space itself is referred to as "purgatory" (p. 32).

On the temporal plane, *The Magic Toyshop* highlights the significance of liminality by concentrating on the borderline status of its key character's age. In this regard, it echoes Arnold van Gennep's contention that liminality characteristically denotes a stage within a maturation process in the course of which a person faces a transitional realm hovering between two discrete social roles: "whoever passes from one [zone] to the other finds himself physically and magico-religiously in a special situation for a certain length of time: he wavers between two worlds" (van Gennep, p. 18). If, as Peter Narváez suggests, the "temporal usage of liminality" is extended to "a spatial understanding of areas between known space (purity) and unknown space (danger)," it is plausible to view the magic toyshop as a topographical concretization of the heroine's state of psychological suspension (Narváez, pp. 337–338).

The fairy tale's proverbial fascination with borderline conditions is corroborated by fairy lore itself. As Purkiss observes, the fairy folk's location in interstitial portions of reality is a crucial facet of that tradition issuing from a transcultural *horror vacui* whereby "human nature seems to abhor a blank space on a map." The reason for which the lacunae in our world come to host fairies — and areas of the universe unoccupied by heavenly bodies are often held to accommodate alien beings — is that the human psyche is incapable of enduring the thought of empty "darkness" (Purkiss, p. 3). Furthermore, the fairy figure's apparently natural bond with marginality could be said to derive from her standing as "a gatekeeper," a being who "guards the entrance to a new realm" and is hence regarded, in numerous cultures, as a supervisor of "the borders of our lives" — e.g., transitional phases such as "adolescence, sexual awakening, pregnancy and childbirth" (p. 4). The temporal significance of liminality emphasized by van Gennep is again thrown into relief by this proposition, and carries considerable weight in the generational context of *The Magic Toyshop*.

Central to Carter's articulation of her vision in *The Magic Toyshop* — as indeed elsewhere — is the intimation that all identities ultimately amount to roles, masks, costumes. Throughout the entire novel, each and every character ultimately stands out, above all else, as a performer. It is primarily for this reason that the writer, as we have seen, allows her methods of characterization to make no facile concessions to the classic realist passion for so-called fully rounded personae. It is in light of this recognition that the centrality accorded by the text to the puppet figure can be fully grasped: everybody is a puppet of sorts in *The Magic Toyshop*'s logic. The shop itself is depicted as practically inseparable from the puppets it hosts from the very first moment we are allowed to catch a glimpse of its portentously dusky façade: "In the cave could be seen ... stiff-limbed puppets, dressed in rich, sombre colours, dangling from their strings" (p. 39). Puppets are presented as even more prominent actors right from the start in the film version of *The Magic Toyshop* (1988) directed by Stephen Morrison. As Laura Mulvey explains, "Unlike the book, the film opens with a short sequence in the puppet theatre in the basement of the toyshop" (Mulvey 2007, p. 245). The movie then transits smoothly to the image of Melanie playing out her fantasies in front of the mirror, thus silently proposing a direct link between the reality level symbolized by the artificial creatures and the reality level embodied by the heroine herself as virtually interdependent affective zones.

Uncle Philip is portrayed as this dark fairy tale's arch-manipulator: an unscrupulous handler not only of artificial dolls but also of his entire family, whose flesh-and-blood members he regards merely as toys molded by dread and economic dependence. In this matter, the novel echoes Mikhail Bakhtin's symbolic interpretation of the "puppet as the victim of alien inhuman forces" (Bakhtin 1984, p. 40). The culmination of the despot's mania is the section in which he throws Finn from the flies during a show to punish him for handling with unpardonable clumsiness his precious puppets. From that point onward, Finn is a different — much graver — person: "After he fell, he changed.... Worst of all, his grace was gone" (p. 134). Yet, the dire episode also paves the way to revenge and to the oppressor's undoing, standing out as a life-transforming change — the kind of crucial narrative pivot which Carter would have eagerly identified as typical of the fairy tale form at its best. However, Uncle Philip himself is just a role, not a three-dimensional human being: totally dependent on his freedom to manipulate others at will, he falls apart the very moment his power is questioned.

The crux of the matter comes into full evidence, in this respect, with the episode chronicling the Leda and the Swan puppet show, where Uncle Philip forces Melanie to play the role of the mythological maiden with a massive swan of his own making in the role of her celestial deflowerer. The pivotal significance of this portion of the story is corroborated by a sprinkling of earlier swan references. For instance, we are told at an early stage in the narrative that "Jonathon roved uncharted seas under a swan-spread of canvas" (p. 4), and that the sleeves of the wedding dress are as "wide as the wings of swans" (p. 11). When the garment becomes an unbearable burden and threatens to engulf Melanie's body as she struggles to climb the apple tree to the safety of her chamber, it acquires a far more sinister identity and comes to resemble a "giant albatross" (p. 22). At this point, the dress is far less reminiscent of a swan than of Charles Baudelaire's albatross — the erstwhile majestic "winged voyager" ("*voyageur ailé*") reduced by captivity to a "comical and ugly" ("*comique et laid*") freak (Baudelaire). This same image, incidentally, is explicitly invoked in *The Passion of New Eve*, where Tristessa is at one point compared to "a great, dead bird blown by a gale far inland from its ocean, the veritable, Baudelairean albatross" (Carter 2009b, p. 143). The iconic bird gains unrivaled prominence in Carter's revisionist portrait of Jeanne Duval in "Black Venus," where Baudelaire's famous mistress is herself compared to a "sooty albatross"

yearning "for the storm" that would provide her with her true "element" (Carter 2006e, p. 239).

Not content merely to indulge in his own symbolic rape of the girl, Uncle Philip also instructs Finn to seduce Melanie prior to the show, wishing to humiliate her even before inflicting the coup de grâce. The cruelty of this carefully staged vicarious violation lies not so much with the theatrical rape itself, disturbing as this undoubtedly is, as with Uncle Philip's determination also to besmirch other people's honesty and innocent emotions. Nevertheless, the metaphorical rape is also presented in an unequivocally ludicrous vein: "It was a grotesque parody of a swan; Edward Lear might have designed it" (p. 165). Hence, as Gina Wisker argues, while the "horror of this enacted relationship is emphasized," it is simultaneously "debunked, satirised, laughed at" (Wisker 1994, p. 111). It is though this fusion of the horrific and the comical that *The Magic Toyshop* succeeds in destabilizing the seemingly immutable ideology in which its puppet-like characters are trapped. According to Sarah Gamble "herein perhaps lies Carter's clue to the deconstruction of patriarchy — its greatest horror and its greatest weakness is that it is sustained by the force of its subjects' belief. Cease to believe, and it becomes nothing more than a masquerade or a puppet show in the simplest, most obvious sense: theatrics" (Gamble 1997, p. 72).

Carter's darkly satirical tone is further fueled by the aura of stultified mechanicity surrounding Uncle Philip's avian artifact, an aspect of the drama that brings to mind Henri Bergson's definition of laughter: "in laughter we always find an unavowed intention to humiliate and consequently to correct our neighbour." The philosopher views the comic as a product of the sense of relief we feel when we can laugh specifically at life forms degraded to the status of mechanisms and can therefore free ourselves from any apprehension of our own mechanistic and materialistic substratum. "A situation is always comic," he states, "if it participates simultaneously in two series of events which are absolutely independent of each other, and if it can be interpreted in two quite different meanings." Laughter, in this perspective, constitutes the corrective punishment meted out by conventional society upon the antisocial or unsocialized individual: "It seems that laughter needs an echo. Our laughter is always the laughter of a group" (Bergson).

It should also be borne in mind, in assessing the transgressive proclivities inherent in Carter's text, that the grotesque puppet show results in Finn's destruction of the swan and that this act, in turn, paves the way to Uncle Philip's disintegration, as though the despot were powerless to survive in the absence of his puppet-avatar. Finn's meticulous dismemberment and ensuing burial of the infamous bird, conducted with ceremonial reverence, exudes an aura of gravity worthy of the most solemn of rites — though plausibly Bacchic ones, given the extent of Finn's inebriation at the time of their enactment. The seriousness of the youth's devotion to his task results precisely from the conviction that the artificer and the artifact are inextricably intertwined: "He put himself into it" he maintains (p. 174).

As mentioned in the opening chapter, Carter capitalizes on the intense feeling of dislocation generated by the ontological ambivalence of the puppet figure as the very distillation of the uncanny at work. This concept is famously theorized by Ernst Jentsch in the 1906 essay *On the Psychology of the Uncanny*, where the uncanny is defined as a state engendered by the presence of "doubts whether an apparently animate being is really alive; or conversely, whether a lifeless object might be, in fact, animate." Jentsch further elaborates this general proposition with specific reference to the domain of fiction, maintaining that "in telling a story one of the most successful devices for easily creating uncanny effects is to leave the reader in uncertainty whether a particular figure in the story is a human being or an automaton and to do it in such a way that his attention is not focused directly upon his uncertainty, so that he may not be led to go into the matter and clear it up immediately" (cited in Freud). Jentsch singles out E. T. A. Hoffmann as an author worthy of special consideration, in this respect, due to his knack of deploying uncanny effects throughout his oeuvre. A paradigmatic case in point is the story "The Sandman" ("Der Sandmann") with its distressingly lifelike doll, Olympia. In Sigmund Freud's own evaluation of the uncanny, so pervasive is Hoffmann's evocation of uncanny effects that upon close inspection, the tale turns out to be veritably saturated with their aura: "the theme of the doll Olympia, who is to all appearances a living being," turns out to be neither "the only" nor ultimately "the most important, element that must be held responsible for the quite unparalleled atmosphere of uncanniness evoked by the story" (Freud).

Another apposite example of uncanny affects unleashed by puppet-like or doll-like creatures is supplied by the Classical legend of Pygmalion, a sculptor reputed to have fallen in love with an ivory statue of his own making and to have made offerings to Venus while wishing that his artifact could morph into a real woman. Sent by Venus in response to this silent prayer, the ever zestful Cupid kisses the sculpture on the hand, thereby triggering its translation into a gorgeous woman, and places a ring on her finger to ensure she will reciprocate her maker's feelings as his loyal spouse Galatea. Like the legend of *Leda and the Swan* so pivotal to Melanie's rite of passage in *The Magic Toyshop*, the mythological anecdote in which Zeus is said to come to Leda in the form of a swan, the story of Pygmalion and Galatea has proved hugely popular as a source of inspiration for countless works in disparate media. Both subjects undoubtedly owed much of their tremendous sixteenth-century popularity, specifically, to the fact that they allowed artists to indulge in some daring depictions of nudity without incurring their contemporaries' moral opprobrium. In the case of Leda and the Swan, moreover, the legend benefited from the warped ethical notion that portraying a woman in the act of copulation with a lecherous male in the guise of a swan was somehow acceptable even though an analogous scene featuring an actual man would have been deemed scandalous in the extreme.

While the genius of the grotesque no doubt reaches its apotheosis in *The Magic Toyshop*'s puppet rhetoric, it is also important to recognize its influential presence in the novel's interstitial imagery. A case in point is the early description of the heroine's hyperbolic feelings toward a traditional recipe which tends to feature with obsessive regularity in Mrs. Rundle's culinary repertoire, bread pudding. Melanie comes to regard the dish as a dark enemy, fearing that it will cause her to degenerate into a monstrously swollen grotesquerie. The image ideated by Melanie is intensely redolent of the pathetic character of the "Fat Lady" as portrayed in the novel *Lady Oracle* by Margaret Atwood, an author harboring great admiration for Carter's work: "The Fat Lady kicked her skates feebly; her tights and the huge moon of her rump were visible. Really it was an outrage. 'They've gone for the harpoon gun,' I heard the commentator say. They were going to shoot her down in cold blood, explode her, despite the fact that she had now burst into song" (Atwood 2004, p. 274).

Furthermore, in the toyshop's parallel world, the image of the mask is consistently deployed as an ideal complement to puppetry in the evocation of the grotesque at its most baleful. Masks, in this context, do not only function as visual props intended to bolster the novel's eerie ambience, however. They also operate, in fact, as an integral component of one of *The Magic Toyshop*'s principal thematic concerns: namely, the tension between reality and illusion. In chronicling Melanie's fairy tale Bildungsroman, the text repeatedly intimates that masks have the power to become incrementally more real than the identities supposed to underlie them. The logical — and profoundly unsettling — corollary of this proposition is that masks might ultimately serve to screen not a presence but an absence, not an authentic identity but the suffocating void left in its wake by the self's evaporation into a pageant of fictitious personae. *The Magic Toyshop's* take on the concept of the mask is concurrently suffused with echoes of shamanism, which could be seen to foreshadow a critical aspect of *Nights at the Circus*. This is tersely conveyed by Carter's economical depiction of Melanie's intercourse with the masks on display as objects of both revulsion and fascination — autonomous entities which appear capable of infusing her being with traces of felinity or vulpinity as she tentatively tries them on.

Carter's fascination with puppets and masks finds further articulation, albeit in a highly capsulated fashion, in the short story "The Loves of Lady Purple" (in *Fireworks*). As Jeff VanderMeer observes, "The story's sweeping aside of the mystique to reveal the wires and machinations behind the puppetry ... reveals Carter's life-long fascination with surface appearances and their symbolic underpinnings." Relatedly, the story as a whole "succeeds not because of the fantasy element but because it deals with the invention of masks, with the way men try to re-invent women in order to control them. Thus, the tale the puppeteer tells his audience about The Lady Purple becomes reality, and the reality devours the puppeteer" (VanderMeer). There can be little doubt that this short story is indeed a paean to Carter's seemingly irresistible attraction to those areas of experience (and speculation) where the barrier between the real and the imaginary becomes so nebulous as to fizzle out altogether. This is poetically borne out by the opening portrayal of the "puppet master," an enigmatic figure "always dusted with a little darkness." At the heart of his "skill" there lies a baffling irony since "the more lifelike his marionettes, the more godlike his manipulations and the more radical the symbiosis between inarticulate doll and articulating fingers." Hence, he inhabits a "a no-man's-limbo between the real and that which, although we know very well it is not, nevertheless seems to be real" (Carter 2006e, p. 41).

One of the most distinctive aspects of the particular style employed by Carter in *The Magic Toyshop*, and bound to be progressively consolidated over time to reach the heights of refinement in the late novels, lies with her explicitly anti-cliché use of literary and artistic allusions. Apposite examples are the scenes in which Melanie adopts theatrical poses inspired by all manner of famous artists (pp. 1–2) or visualizes her and her siblings' fate in terms of narrative tableaux of Pre-Raphaelite orientation (p. 53), the haunting proposition that Uncle Philip appears out of place in the wedding photograph taken at Melanie's parents' wedding as a result of his having encountered an "ancient mariner" en route to the ceremony (p. 13), the suggestion that Victoria might be abnormal and destined to infest Melanie's household as a latter-day "Mrs. Rochester" (p. 7), and the *Hamlet*-inspired description of the meal served by Mrs. Rundle in the immediate aftermath of the disaster as "funeral baked meats" (p. 27).

At the same time, Carter is keen on conjuring an eminently "affective" kind of space, to use Henri Lefebvre's cumulative term for all manner of locations saturated with symbolic connotations, mnemonic vestiges and oneiric residues, and hence resonating with multiple levels of imagery — a fluid, dynamic and concrete dimension inextricably intertwined with the body's lived experience. The space depicted in *The Magic Toyshop* is no less alive, ultimately, than Uncle Philip's uncanny puppets. Lefebvre seeks to demonstrate that the widespread tendency to conceive of space in terms of social practices does not de facto reduce it to an assortment of merely political or economic data, insofar as all imaginable forms of space defined by social practices (including, among them, domestic life and attendant familial interactions) also constitute at all times myriad facets of a geography of emotions, experiences and desires. In other words, they chart a mobile dimension which Lefebvre graphically describes as "representational space." This realm, "is alive: it speaks. It has an affective kernel or centre: Ego, bed, bedroom, dwelling, house; or, square, church, graveyard. It embraces the loci of passion, of action and of lived situations" (Lefebvre, p. 42).

Numerous examples of Carter's penchant for the evocation of affective space punctuate *The Magic Toyshop* but a couple of illustrations will have to suffice in the present context. When Melanie finds herself on her own in an early segment of the narrative, the atmosphere of the empty house is described as "the strange not-being of a houseful of deserted rooms" (pp. 23–24). After the move to London, the narrator points out that Melanie is bound to perceive her new family's kitchen as a space replete with "other people's unknown lives" (p. 59). These images bring to mind the atmosphere evoked by T. S. Eliot in "Burnt Norton," where the abandoned garden oozes with aliveness despite its utter vacantness: "for the leaves were full of children,/Hidden excitedly, containing laughter" (Eliot).

The novel's cumulative message could be described as a sustained dismantling of the myth of identity as a unified, stable and autonomous endowment. This is intended to expose not solely the constructedness of what is so often and so unthinkingly referred to as a person's identity but also its vulnerability and mercurial elusiveness qua construct—a goal achieved by Carter by puncturing it, fragmenting it and dispersing it until the self's boundaries shake and then topple altogether. However, the writer also deploys a self-conscious cultivation of constructedness to her own creative ends in order to pursue its potentialities as a survival strategy. Her priority, in this respect, is the bold appropriation of established formulae to promote alternate ways of constructing personhood in language and imagery. The ultimate challenge for us all — not just authors and artists — is to make do with any available tools just to stay afloat, however precariously. This is where the quintessential genius of *bricolage* shines forth in its full mocking glory. Carter assiduously reminds us that there is no point in pretending that the status quo, tradition and the canon can be erased. In fact, we have no choice but to go on working *within* them and *with* them, all the time acknowledging their oppressiveness but also pursuing the possibilities which they liberate — albeit inadvertently or even accidentally. It is from the sustained adoption of this survivalist strategy that we may ultimately derive the ability to perceive hope amid calamities (real and figurative alike), surprises and challenges amid ossified conventions, humor amid despair. Yet, Carter promises no utopian celebration of laughter as equivalent to undiluted joy: no doubt laughter can be devilishly transgressive but it can never fully divest itself of its own inherent darkness: its awareness of stemming from a lucid recognition of madness and of pain.

The Magic Toyshop bears some interesting points of contact with Carter's other early novels. With *Shadow Dance* (a.k.a. *Honeybuzzard*, 1966), it unquestionably shares Carter's fascination with the fairy tale tradition as a lens through which contemporary writers might fruitfully explore the dynamics and politics of interpersonal manipulation. The character of Honeybuzzard, specifically, could be said to anticipate Uncle Philip as an incarnation of the quintessential manipulator who appears to derive insane satisfaction from the slightest pretext for controlling, twisting and — quite literally — sculpting other humans. *Shadow Dance*'s protagonist operates exclusively in consonance with his whimsical yearnings and impulsive urges, which tend to acquire increasingly brutal and destructive under-currents as the text careens toward its disconcerting conclusion. As Anna Watz points out, Honeybuzzard is governed at every turn by the "Pleasure Principle" (Watz, p. 1) at its most unruly, Honeybuzzard is veritably addicted to the ideation and enactment of multiple power games, regarding the people he victimizes as no more substantial than "shadows" and justi-fying the tenability of his conduct by claiming that one simply cannot "be sorry for shadows" (Carter 2009a, p. 86).

The novel's very "title," interpreted in light of this sinister character trait, foregrounds Honeybuzzard's role as vicious puppeteer keen on maneu-vering his human playthings as though they were puppets in a "shadow puppet show" (Watz, pp. 2–3). (It is also worth noting, in this context, that the term "shadow" is synonymous with "actor" in Elizabethan English.) Honeybuzzard's manipulative mania is epitomized by the pleasure he derives from constructing "jumping-jack caricatures of other characters" (p. 2). Analogously, Uncle Philip is reputed to have terrified Melanie as a little girl by sending her an uncanny jack-in-the-box modeled in her image. No less ominously, Honeybuzzard dreams of an ideal game of chess in which he "would stand on a chair and call out" his "moves from a megaphone," and flesh-and-bone "men and women ... would click their heels and march for-ward" in strict accordance with his commands (Carter 2009a, p. 117).

The hero-villain's perversity is openly announced from the start, as the drama is ushered in by the portrayal of the villain's lover, Ghislaine, in the immediate aftermath of her release from hospital, where she has endured many weeks of torment after having her face slashed by him. Carter's depiction of the young woman unsentimentally throws the horror of her disfigurement into relief: "the scar went all the way down her face, from the corner of her left eyebrow, down, down, down, past nose and mouth and chin until it disappeared below the collar of her shirt." At the same time, the language chosen to invest the scar with a distinctive cor-poreal identity endeavors to communicate a troubling sense of its very aliveness: "the scar was all red and raw as if, at the slightest exertion, it might open and bleed." At the same time, Carter relishes the Franken-steinian connotations of Ghislaine's deformity, taking care to highlight that "the flesh was marked with purple imprints from the stitches she had had in it" and that the "scar had somehow puckered all the flesh around it, as if some clumsy amateur dressmaker had roughly cobbled up the seam and pushed her away.... The scar drew her whole face sideways and even in profile, when the hideous thing turned away, her face was horribly lopsided, skin, features and all dragged away from the bone" (Carter 2009a, pp. 2–3). Thus, Ghislaine's mark is construed as a concurrently physiological and technological event, which enables Carter to foreground the fundamental indivisibility of nature and art, spontaneity and artifice. According to Watz, it is important to acknowledge that "However gruesome this act seems to the other characters in the novel, as well as to the reader, Honeybuzzard's moral standpoint is clear: the violence he exacts on Ghislaine is just play" (Watz, p. 2).

In addition, as the critic also observes, Honeybuzzard's annihilation of the girl's celebrated beauty carries erotic connotations (p. 3). According to Gamble, his weapon could indeed be seen to carve a grotesque replication of the female sexual organs on her visage (Gamble 1997, p. 55). Ghislaine herself describes her lover's attack with masochistic gusto as an act of "spiritual defloration" (Carter 2009a, p. 132). Not content to bring his ferocious manipulation of Ghislaine's body to a close simply with her abduction to an abandoned house and subsequent murder, Honeybuzzard crowns his perverse game with a quasi-satanic ritual of his own conception. As Watz comments, he proceeds to place the corpse on an "altar-like table" and then maniacally revels in a flurry of nechrophiliac fantasies while he continues to play with her "dead body" in a state of utter "delirium" (Watz, p. 3). Given that Ghislaine is "a clergyman's daughter" (Carter 2009a, p. 132), Honeybuzzard's sustained violation of her being throughout the text acquires the significance of a bold celebration of "blasphemy" (Watz, p. 3). *Shadow Dance* dwells on the ubiquitous victimization of its female personae much more explicitly than *The Magic Toyshop*. Yet, both narratives persistently intimate that the creatures involved in their grisly dramas are primarily artifacts, costumes, masks, and not the bearers of authentic identities: Ghislaine, in particular, is compared explicitly to a doll and an automaton.

Moreover, there is a peculiar sense in which Honeybuzzard's actions do not domesticate Ghislaine but actually *liberate* unforeseen possibilities. This hypothesis, argues Watz, is upheld by the aura of subversive ambiguity gained by her erstwhile perfect mien as a result of the hideous injury (pp. 3–4). By erasing the distinction between innocence and experience, virginal purity and erotic provocativeness, Ghislaine's grotesque face constitutes a riotous assault on patriarchal and Classical notions of female beauty: "the whole cheek was a mass of corrugated white flesh, like a bowl of blancmange a child has played with and not eaten. Through this devastation ran a deep central trough that went right down her throat.... Grainy fragments of cosmetics were lodged in the crevices and crannies of the shattered face, whitewash slapped on a crumbling wall. But the other half of the face was fresh and young and smooth and warm as fruit in the sunlight. The two sides of the moon juxtaposed" (Carter 2009a, pp. 152–153). This irreverent desecration of canonical conceptions of beauty and grace is comparable to the deformation of the image of the divine swan seen in *The Magic Toyshop*.

On one level, as Watz suggests, Honeybuzzard is comparable to the Marquis de Sade (Watz, p. 1) as portrayed by Carter in *The Sadeian Woman*—i.e., a subversive agent whose intervention can be seen as salutary despite its apparently obnoxious exterior. This is the character's positive side, so to speak. Yet, Honeybuzzard is also depicted as a consummate and ultimately self-destructive narcissist: these characteristics can again be seen to foreshadow Uncle Philip. According to Watz, "in the instant when Honeybuzzard's surrealist play seems to have completely shattered the boundary between the dimensions of play and reality, and when it seems to have fully achieved its subversive and blasphemous goals, it simultaneously undermines itself" (p. 5). At this juncture, the character is sucked into a whirlpool of utterly wild and uncompromising disreality, his lunacy economically conveyed by his portrayal as a fiend with "hair" streaming behind him "like mad Ophelia's" and "eyes ... too large for his head"—until everything which has been hitherto "familiar about him" appears to be "pared away," and "the daytime flesh" to have been "carved off his bones" to expose the "skeleton" in all its intractable vulnerability (Carter 2009a, p. 179).

While at one level Honeybuzzard's deed amounts to nothing more heroic or adventurous than a ghastly "murder" (Watz, p. 5), it is nonetheless important to acknowledge that the transgressive implications of his unrestrainable appetite for the ludic in its most scandalous manifestations echoes the politics of "surrealism" (p. 6). The same ethos is succinctly captured by Ghislaine's warped beauty after her mutilation—a work of art (of sorts) redolent of many famous representations of women by Surrealist artists as diverse as "Alberto Giacometti, Max Ernst and Hans Bellmer" (p. 4), as well as Leonora Carrington, Remedios Varo, Hanna Höch, Frida Kahlo and Pablo Picasso in his Surrealist phase. In this respect, *Shadow Dance* can be assessed not simply as *The Magic Toyshop*'s immediate predecessor but also as a worthy anticipation of Carter's paean to Surrealism: *The Infernal Desire Machines of Doctor Hoffman*.

The other two novels deserving of consideration in the present context are *Several Perceptions* (1968) and *Love* (1971): the two texts which, in conjunction with *Shadow Dance*, are commonly held to constitute the so-called "Bristol trilogy." Just as *The Magic* Toyshop reimagines the fairy tale modality to comment on a particular nexus of power that throws into relief familial and intergenerational tensions of considerable magnitude, so *Several Perceptions* endeavors to focus on its setting's material conditions. To this extent, the novel captures one of Carter's most enduring and pressing preoccupations, as outlined in the previous chapter. Focusing on Joseph, a permanently mystified and directionless rebel without a cause whose shapeless existence has been drastically disrupted by the desertion of his cherished girlfriend, Charlotte, the novel provides a humanely irreverent allegory of the shattered dreams and vicissitudes endured by a notoriously problematic generation.

As Hannah Stoneham puts it, the novel's "characters wander around in a mad hatter world where they can do anything and yet seem to do nothing.... Carter presents her characters as the flotsam and jetsam of the sixties revolution — people who have been slightly lost in a cultural idea" (Stoneham). There can be little doubt that the cast of *Several Perceptions* abides in memory principally as a mutedly carnivalesque procession of oddballs to whom the word "eccentric" might just about apply as a euphemistic compliment but not, even by the wildest stretch of compassionate imagination, in the philosophical sense of the term as connotative of defiance. What is here meant by defiance is nothing less than a brave questioning of the fixed centers on which conventionality and conformism depend for their self-consolidation, endurance and hegemonic hold. In spite of all the grandiose dreams and heroic visions which Joseph's generation might have harbored, there are intimations, once his brief and intense tale is over, that the only consolation left is that of small, prosaic and unadventurous occurrences — such as the image of the cat that sits "at the foot of the bed" in the "violet dawn" ushering in yet another ordinary day, "smiling and purring like an aeroplane about to take off giving suck to five kittens all as white as snow and beautiful as stars" (Carter 2005, p. 148).

Love echoes most sonorously the cultural atmosphere and aesthetic vision communicated by *The Magic Toyshop* by recourse to the imaginative reconceptualization of old forms as a means of commenting metaphorically on the aspirations and foibles of contemporary strata of society. In the case of *Love*, specifically, Carter deals with the false hopes nourished by the 1960s in the name of boundless freedom and a radical emancipation from stultifying mores so as to reveal their ephemeral standing as inevitable harbingers of disillusionment, nihilism and, ultimately, unnamable anguish. In her afterword to the revised 1987 edition of *Love*, Carter explicitly reveals the little known source of inspiration underlying her narrative as follows: "I first got the idea for *Love*, from Benjamin Constant's early-nineteenth-century novel of sensibility, *Adolphe*; I was seized with the desire to write a kind of modern-day, demotic version of *Adolphe*, although I doubt anybody could spot the resemblance after I'd macerated the whole thing in triple-distilled essence of English provincial life" (Carter 2006b, p. 111). Carter's reinvention of the popular eighteenth-century genre subjects the concept of sensibility to a dispassionate anatomy, seeking to throw into relief its ethical ambiguities and the unsavory motives underpinning the outward show of emotionalism, affective receptiveness and sympathetic identification with the afflicted. This cherished spectacle is thus exposed as a hypocritical travesty of sensitivity, moral refinement and compassion. At the same time, as Patricia Juliana Smith puts it, Carter "mercilessly illustrates the similarities between the excesses of the period that gave rise to Romanticism and those of the period that gave us the sexual revolution. Through the medium of the ménage à trois comprised of Lee, Annabel, and Buzz, she takes stock of our cherished and reviled conventional gender roles and to what extent they have, while changing drastically, nonetheless stubbornly remained the same" (Smith, P. J.).

The novel of sensibility, as Janet Todd explains, was initially a didactic genre intended to show "people how to behave, how to express themselves in friendship and how to respond decently to life's experiences" but rapidly morphed into a popular mode that "prided itself more on making its readers weep and in teaching them when and how much to weep. In addition, it delivered the great archetypal victims: the chaste suffering woman, happily rewarded in marriage or elevated into redemptive death, and the sensitive, benevolent man whose feelings are too exquisite for the acquisitiveness, vulgarity and selfishness of his world" (Todd, p. 4). Moreover, Carter inflates the already proverbially florid melodramatic prose of her source material (and its generic affiliates generally) in order to throw into relief through ironic parody the emotional excesses to which her own characters are prey in their vain search for goals, destinations or simply glimmers of hope. The eighteenth-century literary antecedent and its postmodernist embodiment come together in the character of Annabel: the "mad girl plastered in fear and trembling against a thorn bush," all the time trapped in a phantom world of delusions resulting from her pathological tendency to treat "All she apprehended through her senses ... only as objects for interpretation in the expressionist style," and hence prone to see, "in everyday things, a world of mythic, fearful shapes of whose existence she was convinced although she never spoke of it to anyone" (Carter 2006b, p. 3).

As Carter sardonically observes in her Afterword, "even the women's movement would have been no help to her and alternative psychiatry would only have made things, if possible, worse" (p. 111). Carter's inveterate attraction to the fairy tale tradition also makes itself felt throughout the text (amid imagery laced with varyingly overt allusions to Emily Brontë, Edgar Allan Poe and Gothic terror at its most feverishly unbridled). This is patently evinced by Annabel's pictures of Lee as a mythological creature redolent of heraldic unicorns and lions, as well as references to *Bluebeard*. These images and allusions can be regarded as symptomatic of a yearning for a parallel life peopled by fairy tale types congruous with not only Annabel's but all three protagonists' submerged fantasies.

Like *The Magic Toyshop*, *Love* resolutely eschews strict binary oppositions — an especially arduous task in the context of a creative borrowing inspired by a genre that would seem to favor, in fact, the adoption of ultra-conventional ethical parameters. Accordingly, much as Annabel outwardly typifies the feminine attributes of physical and psychological vulnerability characteristic of the novel of sensibility's conventional heroine, her relationships with Lee and Buzz disclose alarmingly sadistic tendencies. At their most extreme, these manifest themselves in the guise of a temporary assumption of roles which one would normally associate with the aggressive male type, as indicated by the sequence in which Annabel forces Lee to bear a permanent mark of her own conception. This is described as a "baroque humiliation" consisting of his body's inscription with "her name indelibly in Gothic script" within a "rosy red heart" which becomes the "visible" replacement "laid bare for all to see," as Lee himself views it, for his inner and private heart (p. 67).

As far as Lee himself is concerned, this character undoubtedly offers a feminine façade and may therefore seem to conform to the stock figure of the sensitive male portrayed by Todd: an individual who typically eschews "manly power" and exhibits instead "the womanly qualities of tenderness and susceptibility," even though he could not "be raped and abandoned" himself (Todd, p. 89). It gradually transpires that Lee is motivated entirely by narcissistic and solipsistic urges akin to Annabel's own self-imprisoning obsessions. Carter ironically debunks Lee's potential heroism by emphasizing the character's stereotype-dominated self-dramatizing proclivities. This is paradigmatically demonstrated by the following passage: "Lee sank more deeply into a melancholy so alien to his nature it never occurred to him he might be unhappy for he associated unhappiness with a positive state, with scarcely tolerable grief or furious sorrow authenticated by a death or a disaster, not with this unmotivated absence of pleasure that dulled the colours of the approaching spring" (Carter 2006b, p. 71). Carter's characterization of Buzz also serves to challenge the tenability of stark binaries. His ludicrously fierce deportment, inarticulateness and utter lack of any hint at sophistication or urbanity impart him a superficial shell of hypermasculinity. However, he turns out to be driven not only by homosexual but also by incestuous longings.

By hanging her motley adaptive cloak on the hook of the classic erotic triangle, Carter ideates a penetrating and sad satire of the shortcomings of her own generation by candidly exposing its inherent emotional brittleness. She thus presents *Love*'s protagonists, as Smith maintains, as "self-deluded relics of a bygone age dressed in a newer fashion." By integrating the novel of sensibility into an experimental adaptation, Carter turns the popular formula on its head, to the point that love itself is posited as a state "more likely to invoke fear and revulsion than tears and sympathy." The novel as a whole, in this regard, stands out as "a study in how not to deport oneself" (Smith, P. J.). Resolutely severing itself from this paltry ancestry, Carter's vision of love soars to exhilarating heights in her next major novel, *The Infernal Desire Machines of Doctor Hoffman*, where "Love is the synthesis of dream and actuality; love is the only matrix of the unprecedented; love is the tree which buds lovers like roses" (Carter 2010, p. 241).

CHAPTER 3

Surrealist Visions

The Infernal Desire Machines of Doctor Hoffman

How prone poor Humanity is to dam up the minutest remnants of its freedom, and build an artificial roof to prevent it looking up to the clear blue sky. ... Think of the wonderful circles in which our whole being moves and from which we cannot escape no matter how we try. The circler circles in these circles.

— E. T. A. Hoffmann

What is a television apparatus to man, who has only to shut his eyes to see the most inaccessible regions of the seen and the never seen, who has only to imagine in order to pierce through walls and cause all the planetary Baghdads of his dreams to rise from the dust.

— Salvador Dalí

Carter wrote *The Infernal Desire Machines of Doctor Hoffman* in Japan, where she had traveled with the funds provided by her Somerset Maugham Award, received in 1969 for *Several Perceptions*. Commenting on her exposure to Japanese culture and society, the author implicitly sheds light on the experiential circumstances likely to have influenced the novel's genesis. "Since I kept on trying to learn Japanese, and kept on failing to do so," Carter frankly admits, "I started trying to understand things by simply looking at them very, very carefully, an involuntary apprenticeship in the interpretation of signs" (in Smith, A. 2010, p. ix). Given the nature of the Japanese language — and its underlying cultural heritage at large — the "signs" referred to by Carter are not to be understood merely as conceptual

47

abstractions but also, perhaps primarily, as tactile objects. In *The Infernal Desire Machines of Doctor Hoffman* itself, signs transcend the status of graphic conventions to become the (seemingly) solid avatars of intricate alternate realities.

These realms' artificer is the titular Doctor Hoffman, a godlike scientist and professor of metaphysics who has the power to bring into being any reality he fancies. Exploiting futuristic technologies of his own conception, the Doctor has inundated the city — the capital of an unnamed South American country — with all manner of hypnotically enthralling delusions, woven from a baroque pandemonium of enfleshed metaphors, sophisms and blazons. As his ambassador puts it, Doctor Hoffman operates on the assumption that "time and space have their own properties.... Time and space are the very guts of nature and so, naturally, they undulate in the manner of intestines" (Carter 2010, p. 32). "For us," the same character later avers, "the world exists only as a medium in which we execute our desires." Accordingly, just as "the real world ... is formed of malleable clay," so for the visionary scientist and his acolytes, "its metaphysical structure is just as malleable" (p. 34). As a result of the Doctor's rampant defilement of logic, reason and order, the city has precipitated into chaos: trade with the outside world has ceased, crime rates have soared exponentially and there have even been sporadic reports of outbreaks of cholera and the plague. Sadly, "only a few of the transmutations" triggered by Doctor Hoffman's incursions into reality are "lyrical." More often than not, "imaginary massacres" glut the streets "with blood." As a corollary, a "deep-seated anxiety and a sense of profound melancholy" are endemic throughout all social strata of the capital's population and these deleterious affects, in turn, are frequently conducive to "suicide" (p. 15).

The city upon which the diabolical scientist wreaks havoc by giving palpable, and even sanguinary, incarnation to his wildest desires may initially come across as the totally fabulous product of myriad, subtly interlocked cultural allusions — as a site of intertextual invagination, to resort to the evocative term used by Jacques Derrida to designate the situation in which one term secretly resides inside another (Derrida and Ronell). However, it rapidly transpires that Doctor Hoffman's idiosyncratic semiosis is in fact grounded in a material reality endowed with powerful, albeit elliptical, ties to actual history. The dense tangle of hieroglyphs relentlessly dished out by the city itself at every twist and turn of its protean map can be interpreted in strictly materialist terms. According to Scott Dimovitz, the city as a whole stands out as "a personification of contemporary postmodern patriarchy." Admittedly, its historical and geographical identity is shrouded in mystery, insofar as Carter avoids the insertion of cultural indices which would indicate unequivocally the action's temporal or spatial situation. The "Catholic cathedral and the immigration patterns Desiderio describes" are evocative of Brazil but these elements are intermingled with allusions to diverse Western milieux and to Japanese society. At times, the text makes use of "culturally specific verbal tags." The "country's currency," we are informed, "consists of quarters and dollars, implying that it is the United States," while the employment of the term "'torch' rather than flashlight" suggests that the story "takes place in England." Through these carefully distributed hints, the narrative combines "multiple cultural forms to create a kind of Ur-patriarchy" (Dimovitz, p. 85).

Paradoxically, although Doctor Hoffman is the figure responsible for investing the urban fabric with its most painfully memorable attributes, the text itself ironically associates the city with the social camp championed by the figure of the Minister of Determination. In so doing, it entwines its history and reputation with bourgeois patriarchy and, behind that construct, with a morally questionable legacy of piracy, crime, arm trade, colonial expansion and prostitution. Doctor Hoffman's infernal delusions, in this perspective, can be read as "projections of the patriarchal city's unconscious desires" (Carter 2010, p. 86)—an idea corroborated by Albertina's revelation that the images conveyed to the city by her father can be repelled by the Minister's mental barriers: a clear metaphor for the psychic mechanisms of disavowal and repression. Following Nicoletta Vallorani's suggestion, it could be suggested that Carter's city—here as in *The Passion of New Eve*—operates as "the secular celebration of chaos" (Vallorani, p. 368). Yet, it is vital to realize that such a celebration is by no means conducive to facile utopianism since, as Dimovitz reminds us, much as "Carter's vision of contemporary urban culture ... serves as a metaphor for a postmodern topos of nonhierarchical, fragmented identity, culture, and ontology," *The Infernal Desire Machines of Doctor Hoffman* evidently regards its hypothetical setting as a "negatively oppressive place, not at all the liberating potentiality of postmodern urban space theorists" (Dimovitz, p. 87).

Carter's opulently poetic prose evokes a ubiquitous atmosphere of both sensory and intellectual intoxication—an apt stylistic correlative for Doctor Hoffman's cunning disruptions of time and space. Most fittingly, the recurrent imagery adopted throughout the text in order to fuel this concurrently seductive and disruptive scenario is veritably saturated with words such as such as mirage, hallucination, vertigo, delirium, magic, labyrinth and — perhaps above all else —*desire*. In addition, Carter's fabulatory pyrotechnics abound with allusions and references to Classical mythology, the Bible, Chaucer, Shakespeare, Chuang Tzu, Marvell, Descartes, Pope, Defoe, Swift, Emily Brontë, Hoffmann, Kafka, Poe, Mallarmé, Proust, the Marquis de Sade, Hegel, Bach, Mozart, Chopin, Berlioz, Schubert, Wagner, Van Gogh, Freud, Barthes, Foucault, Calvino, Fritz Lang, de Mille, Fassbinder — and this list is by no means exhaustive. At this level of the narrative, *The Infernal Desire Machines of Doctor Hoffman* eloquently attests to Carter's exhaustive knowledge of the canon but also demonstrates that this is a knowledge that never deteriorates into self-complacent name dropping because it is underpinned at all times by an even more profound understanding of that canon's evolution and glorification as an eminently ideological fabrication.

This, in turn, is allied to an inexhaustible appetite for experiment: a creative option which Carter cultivates no less enthusiastically than she treasures traditional stories. *The Infernal Desire Machines of Doctor Hoffman*, accordingly, is continually engaged with the ideation of novel possibilities — and with the formulation of fresh storytelling codes and conventions — even as it harks back to the old methodologies of legend and folklore, fireside yarn-spinning and marketplace gossip. It is as a logical corollary of this passion for experimentation that throughout the textual orchestration of Doctor Hoffman and Desiderio's ordeals, Carter is drawn to both the Surrealists' iconoclasm and the Romantics' visionary *afflatus*. Yet, in accordance with that same drive, the writer knows that she could not remain loyal to her self-appointed task if she were to embrace unequivocally either the Surrealist agenda or the Romantic credo, and chooses instead to put to the test the kind of aerial act destined to come to superb fruition two decades later in *Night at the Circus*. (Carter's relationship with both Surrealism and Romanticism will be revisited in greater depth later in this chapter.)

According to Ali Smith, the novel's experimental verve entails that *The Infernal Desire Machines of Doctor Hoffman* still stands out, "in literary terms," as "a matrix of the unprecedented" (Smith, A. 2010, p. vii). Its "cornucopic and virtuoso performance," the critic later remarks, "is a visionary book for a virtual age" (p. viii). As a corollary, it can be argued that "right now, in the emergence of the virtual age, the age [Carter] foresaw nearly forty years ago.... *The Infernal Desire Machines of Doctor Hoff-man* never looked more relevant" (p. xii). As Cornel Bonca remarks, it is also vital to bear in mind that even though the "mythic conflict" addressed in this text "is as old as the hills — Dionysus vs. Apollo, Orc vs. Urizen, Eros vs. Civilization," Carter "pulls it off with that insolent brilliance that characterizes many of the writers who came of age in the 1960s, mixing genres high and low, brazenly appropriating literary images cherished by British culture, and fearlessly tapping into a countercultural rage at a world lorded over at the time, remember, by arch–Determinators Leonid Brezh-nev and Richard M. Nixon" (Bonca).

The narrator is Desiderio (the Italian word, quite simply, for "Desire"): a half-breed junior civil servant at the time of the adventure chronicled in the main body of the novel, and now an old man hailed as a national hero as a consequence of his having been responsible, in his youth, for vanquishing Doctor Hoffman at the behest of the Minister of Determination. A lucid and solid individual who has deliberately divested himself of any possible "Faustian desires" (Carter 2010, p. 25), the Minister acts as the chief emissary of a hyperrationalist government that abhors Doctor Hoffman's schemes and is therefore determined to return their world to its pristine state: that of a functional, highly efficient and pro-ductive — albeit also obtusely unimaginative — modern metropolis. Deside-rio has been selected for a number of fundamentally disconnected reasons: "I was chosen for the mission," he explains, "because: (a) I was in my right mind; (b) I was dispensable and (c) the Minister's computers decided my skill at crossword puzzles suggested a facility in the processes of analogical thought which might lead me to the Doctor where everyone else had failed" (p. 39).

Above all, Desiderio is a perfect candidate for the task because the phantasmagoric "complexity" of the parauniverse concocted by the Doctor simply "bored" him (p. 3) — a result, he reckons, of his being "too sardonic" and "too disaffected" (p. 4). He also admits, however, to having been an "exceedingly romantic young man" in spite of all his "indifferences" (p. 41), and this apparently inconsistent facet of his personality indeed turns out to have played a vital part in the Doctor's undoing. As argued later, the character is not only romantic in the affective understanding of the term but also Romantic in a philosophical sense, especially in his assessment of the Doctor's ultimate agenda.

Through the character of Desiderio, Carter performs an acrobatic feat of narrative subversion, drastically exploding the myth of the omniscient and dependable author. Desiderio's unreliability as a narratorial authority is conveyed from the start by his attitude to memory. In the novel's introduction, he boldly states: "I remember everything perfectly" (p. 3). Yet, only a few pages later, in the context of the actual first chapter, he concedes that he "cannot remember exactly how it began" (p. 9). The narrator's rational control over the text is further eroded by his undying infatuation with Doctor Hoffman's elusive, ambiguous and shimmeringly beautiful daughter, Albertina. In fact, Desiderio falls desperately in love with Albertina at an early stage in the story, and remains motivated throughout his adventures by the yearning to be united with her — an achievement which the narrative itself insistently defers and from whose postponement, accordingly, it derives much of its impetus. If this aspect of the novel's structure bears witness to the aesthetic proclivities harbored by Carter the experimental writer, it simultaneously recalls a form dear to Carter the medievalist: namely, the romance.

David Lodge has highlighted the erotic implications of the romance mode by contrasting it with the epic. "Epic," like "tragedy," is held by the critic to "move inexorably to ... an essentially *male* climax — a single, explosive discharge of accumulated tension. Romance, in contrast, is not structured this way. It has not one climax, but many, the pleasure of this text comes and comes and comes again. No sooner is one crisis in the fortunes of the hero averted than a new one presents itself; no sooner has one mystery been solved than another is raised; no sooner has one adventure been concluded than another begins. The narrative questions open and close, open and close.... Romance is a multiple orgasm" (Lodge, pp. 322–323). This reading is paralleled by W. P. Ker's seminal definition of the romance form as the province of the fantastic, and hence as the antithesis of the substantial world immortalized by the epic. "Whatever Epic might mean," Ker argues, "it implies some weight and solidity; Romance means nothing, if it does not convey some notion of mystery or fantasy.... Beowulf might stand for the one side, Lancelot or Gawain for the other" (Ker, p. 14). Relatedly while in a properly heroic narrative, characters "always have good reasons of their own for fighting," the "wandering champions of romance" often appear to be driven by purely irrational "readiness" (pp. 15–16).

Thus, epic is typically sustained by the principles of martial prowess, fortitude and virility, allied to the imperative to uphold feudal loyalty, and to harmonize the aspirations of freshly formed or gestating nation states with the transnational edifice of Christianity. Romance mischievously punctures these lofty ideals to give free rein to magical phenomena, erotic exploits and a childlike curiosity, in the service of open-ended narrative tapestries of kaleidoscopic unpredictability. The sequential accumulation of frequently discontinuous and even incongruous incidents treasured by the romance rebels against the idea of textual construction as a quest for a privileged center of meaning, gesturing instead toward a potentially limitless horizon.

The adventures dramatized by most medieval romances of the chivalric ilk do not normally tend to gather momentum in the service of a grandiose climax, an explosive expression of accumulated energy. In fact, they meander episodically from one provisional resolution to the next to reveal, on numerous occasions, that any ostensible resolution is only a springboard to yet another narrative complication. Structural rhythms of repetition, recapitulation, anticipation, mirroring and duplication are critical — as indeed they increasingly are in Carter's oeuvre — to the orchestration of an enthusiastically multilayered textual mesh. Carter maximizes the attributes of ephemerality and illusionism attributed to the romance form in the modern age (most often with derogatory intent) as crucial components of her tirelessly iconoclastic game. It must also be stressed, in pursuing this kind of comparative evaluation, that the brave and stalwart world of epic is inhabited principally by either literal males or women admitted to the ranks of honorary males. The domain of romance, by contrast, places female characters and the vagaries of Eros in a pivotal position: an aspect of the form immediately relevant to Carter's gender-inflected priorities.

Desiderio does not realize until his odyssey has reached its climactic stages that "the reciprocal motion" of his and Albertina's "hearts ... was a natural and eternal power" (p. 166) and that this power is pivotal to the Doctor's machinations. Albertina eventually clarifies the issue for both the narrator and the reader's sake as follows: "My father has discovered that the magnetic field formed by our reciprocal desire ... may be quite unique in its intensity. Such desire might be the strongest force in the world" (p. 242). The entire web of Doctor Hoffman's "reality modifying machines" (p. 250) is revealed to depend on the generation and diffusion of "eroto-energy," which is described as "the simplest yet most powerful form of radiant energy in the entire universe" (p. 256). However, the quintessential lovers' "conjunction" is supposed to hold inimitable potentialities within the broader eroto-energy network insofar as it could, if accomplished, "spurt such a charge of energy" that their "infinity would fill the world and, in this experiential void, the Doctor would descend on the city and his liberation would begin" (p. 257)—i.e., he would be in a position to replace reality with his delusions for good. At the same time as it echoes the textual operations of the romance mode, Carter's enthroning of sexual desire as the driving force of a chronicle of endless postponement brings to mind Roland Barthes' "reasonable" and "amorous" feelings: "*reasonable* sentiment: everything works out but nothing lasts. *Amorous* sentiment: nothing works out, but it keeps going on" (Barthes 1990, p. 140). Furthermore, the whimsical character of erotic comportment is inherently discursive: i.e., governed by the logic of "*Dis-cursus*—originally the action of running here and there, comings and goings, measures taken, 'plots and plans'" (p. 3).

Doctor Hoffman himself has reimagined the Cartesian *Cogito* in the form of the statement "I DESIRE THEREFORE I EXIST" (Carter 2010, p. 252). So has the character of the Count, incidentally: "I ride the whirlwind of my desires," the latter proudly declares (p. 198). The inextricability of desire from the Doctor's diabolical apparatuses brings to mind the concept of "desiring-machines" theorized by Gilles Deleuze and Félix Guattari in *Anti-Oedipus: Capitalism and Schizophrenia*—a text originally published in the very same year in which Carter's novel entered the public domain, 1972. The phrase desiring-machine is used by Deleuze and Guattari to capture the mechanistic character of desire: a force operating as a kind of circuit breaker in the wider circuit of disparate machines to which it is bound.

Concurrently, the desiring-machine is also capable of releasing a stream of desire from its own structure. On this basis, Deleuze and Guattari conjecture a multi-functional reality consisting of inextricably interconnected machines: no desiring-machines exist without the social machines which they form and no social machines, conversely, exist without the desiring machines that inhabit them. Deleuze and Guattari's machines — largely conceived as a brassy joke at the expense of classic psychoanalytical theory — are as densely and sexually corporeal as Carter's, as born out by this inceptive statement: "It is at work everywhere, functioning smoothly at times, at other times in fits and starts. It breathes, it heats, it eats. It shits and fucks. What a mistake to have ever said the *id*. Everywhere *it* is machines — real ones, not figurative ones: machines driving other machines, machines being driven by other machines, with all the necessary couplings and connections. An organ-machine is plugged into an energy-source machine: the one produces a flow that the other interrupts" (Deleuze and Guattari, p. 1).

Conflations of machines and desires of the kind theorized by Deleuze and Guattari are endemic in Carter's oeuvre even though it is specifically in Desiderio's saga that they are so blatantly central as to deserve titular ascendancy. Indeed, they can be seen to run as a powerful thread from Honeybuzzard's perverse reconstruction of his lover's body in *Shadow Dance*, through Uncle Philip's puppet-maneuvering equipment in *The Magic Toyshop* and Hollywood's cinematic apparatus in *The Passion of New Eve*, to the baroque acrobatic machinery of *Nights at the Circus* and the stage technology of *Wise Children*. As one turns to Carter's prolific brood of short stories of diverse amplitude and genre, yet a greater variety of desiring machines reveals itself in the guise of alternately literal and figurative diabolical contraptions intended to articulate the symbiotic interplay of diverse human-made constructs and networks of desire which connect and separate people by turns. In this context, the most effective device turns out to be the medium of the short story itself as a studiously constructed form — more so, arguably, than the novel due to its highly compressed discursive economy. This form lends itself ideally to the uncompromising exposure of the dominance of desire in human existence thanks to its ability to enact its expressions in a tight-knit capsulated fashion.

Desiderio has ultimately no choice but to destroy Doctor Hoffman because he knows that the scientist's creation of an alternate reality unfettered by the strictures of rationality and authority is not conducive to freedom but only to yet another form of despotism. "I might not want the Minister's world," he declares, "but I did not want the Doctor's either.... He might know the nature of the inexhaustible plus but, all the same, he was a totalitarian" (p. 247). The character's decision is fueled by his realization that Doctor Hoffman's world is not even endowed with the glamour one might be inclined to accord it on the basis of its superficial effects: "I was not in the domain of the marvellous at all. I had gone far beyond that," Desiderio reminisces, and "reached the power-house of the marvellous, where all its clanking, dull, stage machinery was kept" (p. 239).

Just as even the most ethereal theatrical and cinematic effects ultimately turn out to have been generated by ugly cogs and wheels (or, at best, by blandly impersonal computers), so the fantasy woven by Carter's mad scientist loses its aura of otherworldly refinement once its intimate workings are penetrated. Albertina herself is eventually a victim of her patriarchal lord's despotism: much as he may claim to abhor rules and restraints, the Doctor cannot contemplate the idea of according the right to total freedom to anyone, and his own precious daughter is no exception. As Dimovitz observes, even at end, after she has discarded "her outward idealist manifestations and become the guerrilla commando, Generalissimo Hoffman," Albertina remains bound to the Doctor's tyrannical will and agrees to fight on his behalf (Dimovitz, p. 100).

Resorting to the narrative form most avidly cherished by Carter throughout her career, the fairy tale, it could be suggested that while on the surface Doctor Hoffman evinces the debonair seductiveness of *Little Red Riding Hood*'s lupine arch-predator, at heart he is as mechanistically repetitive, and hence ultimately monotonous, as the figure of the compulsive serial killer notoriously epitomized by *Bluebeard*'s eponymous villain. We are hence obliquely invited to ponder Simone Weil's famous distinction between hypothetical and realized versions of evil: "Imaginary evil is romantic and varied; real evil is gloomy, monotonous, barren, boring. Imaginary good is boring; real good is always new, marvelous, intoxicating. Therefore 'imaginative literature' is either boring or immoral (or a mixture of both). It only escapes from this alternative if in some way it passes over to the side of reality through the power of art" (Weil, p. 120). Doctor Hoffman's evil, in terms of this philosophical pronouncement, is exciting as long as it is contemplated from the outside, and hence evaluated entirely in terms of its sensational manifestations — of the sheer spectacle it unfurls. It becomes tedious, dreary and uninspiring, however, the moment the façade of its histrionics is pierced and the actuality of the ponderously pumping machinery at its core is exposed.

In his capacity as the so-called hero responsible for defeating the evil scientist, Desiderio himself is neither truly boring nor truly marvelous, insofar as he is simply not portrayed as a personification of goodness but simply as an instrumental agency with scarce control over his own fate. As for Carter's mediating presence, many readers would agree that her imagination succeeds in bypassing the strictures of both tedium and immorality, and in deploying its artistry to transition to reality through a trenchant allegorical commentary on the horrors of totalitarianism and its consciousness-numbing myths.

Doctor Hoffman's flamboyantly Surrealist forays into plural states of intoxication, hallucination and delirium cannot ultimately be prevented, in spite of their revolutionary potentialities, from deteriorating into either vapid mysticism — at the publicity-oriented end of the spectrum — or robotic repetition — at the brutally pragmatic end. The Doctor's acolytes might choose to romanticize his exploits by recourse to affected behavior, inflated rhetoric and fanatical religiosity but these uncritically assumed attitudes are powerless to dissipate the sheer drabness and emptiness of what is ultimately just one single madman's polluted vision. As Bonca argues, what Desiderio ultimately finds out is that "Dr. Hoffman' plan is just as fascistic as the Minister's.... The liberation of imagination and desire, in other words, creates its own power vacuum, which authoritative impulses rush to fill. So it's not just Reason that suppresses, as the liberal tradition insists; the images of Dr. Hoffman's desire machines, when totally unrestrained, create their own inexorable logic of domination that, at their extremes, lead to bondage, cruelty, even murder." On his way to this epiphanic revelation, Carter's narrator is wedged between the two sets of incompatible objectives pursued by the "Reason-freak Minister," on the one hand, and the deranged "Dionysian genius," on the other. This conflict is vividly reflected by Desiderio's narrative voice, which comes across as a disorienting admixture of "English empirical exactitude" and "Gothic decadence whirling with emotional tumult" (Bonca).

According to Andrzej Gasiorek, Desiderio's dispassionate recognition of Doctor Hoffman's despotic drives can be read as symptomatic of the narrator's maturation. His ordeal has taught him to recognize "the debilitating dichotomy of lawlessness and moralism" for what it truly is and hence the need to go on striving toward a resolutely non-binary ethos. Thus implying that the novel harbors a positive message despite its ostensible pessimism, Gasiorek puts forward an imaginative allegorical interpretation of Carter's text which, like the novel itself, revels in intertextual allusion. The critic's pivotal frame of reference is provided by Plato's corpus, and specifically the dialogues directly concerned with the nature and function of the poetic imagination. The battle engaging the Minister and the scientist, argues Gasiorek, "replays the Platonic conflict between the appetitive and the rational parts of the soul" central to the *Republic*. As Desiderio's mindset, initially "caught between two equally intransigent opponents," gradually evolves in a more speculative and less starkly Manichean direction, the character learns to transcend "the dichotomous choice they propose." His stance therefore comes to resemble the position advocated by the Greek philosopher in a later dialogue, the *Phaedrus*, where poetry's power to "express truths inaccessible to dialectic" is acknowledged, and the necessity to reconsider "the latter's claims to knowledge" is accordingly accepted.

Moreover, just as Plato's earlier works (e.g., the *Ion*) insist that "poets are in the grip of an irrational possession that should be derided," whereas later dialogues such as the *Phaedrus* posit "the frenzy that creates poetry as springing from a divine source," so "Desiderio's conception of the respective claims made by reason and desire, soul and body, philosophy and poetry" grows "more discriminating" as he grows older (Gasiorek, cited in van de Wiel, Chapter 1). Most vitally, Carter's narrator comes to recognize that for the imagination to bring forth a genuinely inspiring and stimulating vision of the word, it must be allied to reflection and should not, therefore, be allowed to run amok in sole consonance with an individual's will. At the same time, as Raymond van de Wiel suggests, the novel could be read as a warning against the inflamed idealism of its era, and hence as "a disillusioned response to the counter-culture which emanated graffities [*sic*] like 'Be realistic: demand the impossible'" (van de Wiel). David Punter embraces a cognate perspective by contending that "we can read the text as a series of figures for the defeat of the political aspirations of the 1960s, and in particular of the father-figures of liberation, Reich and Marcuse" (Punter 1984, p. 212).

In this regard, Desiderio's perspective echoes the aesthetic and ethical lesson promulgated by E. T. A. Hoffmann, the author behind the designation of Carter's titular hero, and specifically the tale of "The Nutcracker and the Mouse King." This narrative indeed proposes that while humanity's ability to fantasize, dream and contemplate the impossible is an endowment to be defended at any price, it is nonetheless vital to recognize that such a power, if left entirely to its own devices, is destined to degenerate into perversity. In Hoffmann's tale, this idea comes to the fore with the oneiric sequences, set in exuberantly visionary realms, in which the unbridled satisfaction of desire is seen to be ultimately conducive not to the triumph of the pleasure principle and its imaginative drives but rather to stultifying repetitiveness and spiritual corruption. These scenes are most poignantly replicated by Carter through the representation of Doctor Hoffmann's castle. According to Peter Christensen, this key location, "like the enchanted land in 'Nutcracker and Mouse-King,' appears at first to be beautiful, but we soon realize that it is corrupted by the surfeit of desire.

Winter never touches Hoffman's castle, and it is filled with fruit, flowers, deer, birds, and rabbits. However, on inspection, its sinister aspect becomes obvious"— it indeed turns out to be the park foreshadowed by a pornographic peep show intent on the obscene reification of the female genitalia (Christensen).

It is with his appeal to imaginative discipline in the reconfiguration of reality through the lenses of the fairy tale — rather than in some unrestrained idealization of fantasy of the kind one could easily encounter in a less astute Romantic — that Hoffmann proclaims his work's groundbreaking caliber. This, as Jack Zipes observes, lies with his fairy tales' ability to perpetuate the progressive ambitions promulgated by the French Revolutionary period, and thus advocate "the freedom of the creative individual" while resisting "the growing mechanization of life and the alienation caused by capitalism," in order to promote the idea that "human beings must master both their talents and time to create a new world where humanism reigns, not harmony." Among the fairy tale authors of his time, Hoffmann is arguably the most effective in "demonstrating how revolutionary and utopian the fairy tale could become" (Zipes 1979, pp. 35–37). Hoffmann indubitably endeavors to usher in an alternate and more commodious reality but this is not a realm predicated on the uncontrolled expression and fulfillment of individual desires. In fact, it consists of "an imaginative projection of real possibilities for changing human and productive relations" (p. 39).

Carter's novel also alludes to "The Nutcracker and the Mouse King," incidentally, through the scientist at the head of the team of "physicists" employed by the Minister of Determination in his endless battle against the diabolical Doctor. This character is obviously named "Dr Drosselmeier" after the clockmaker, toymaker and inventor from Hoffmann's story, Drosselmeyer. Carter's persona, as it happens, loses his mind as a result of having "unwittingly exposed himself to an overdose of reality" (Carter 2010, p. 19). This incident offers an ironically twisted adaptation of the idea — famously advocated by T. S. Eliot and Carl Jung in quite distinct contexts — that human beings simply cannot tolerate too much reality. It is through Doctor Hoffman himself, however, that Carter creates her closest adaptation of Hoffmann's Drosselmeyer. Most crucially, both Hoffmann and Carter' respective dramatizations of the vicissitudes of creativity and desire bring to mind the teachings of Jacques Lacan in their profound awareness of the chasm separating what we regard as reality from the Real as such. The latter, in this context, designates the realm of absolute undifferentiation situated beyond language and therefore, by definition, a level of being which the adult encultured mind, firmly inscribed within the Symbolic order as it is, can only experience as unnamable, unrepresentable and ultimately impossible even to contemplate (Lacan).

Carter has explicitly professed her attraction to Hoffmann's work. "I'd always been fond of Poe, and Hoffmann," she states in the afterword to *Fireworks*. "Gothic tales, cruel tales, tales of wonder, tales of terror, fabulous narratives that deal directly with the imagery of the unconscious — mirrors; the externalized self; forsaken castles; haunted forests; forbidden sexual objects." However, she is not interested in upholding these narratives in a stereotypically mystical Romantic fashion as portals to dominions of superior knowledge. In fact, what she commends is their disarming honesty — the fact that they "cannot betray" their "readers into a false knowledge of everyday experience." Here as elsewhere, Carter's priority is a radical unhinging of everyday existence that does not seek refuge in some submerged fantasy but is rather prepared to confront reality with unruffled dispassionateness. "Let us keep the unconscious in a suitcase, as Père Ubu did with his conscience," she advise "and flush it down the lavatory when it gets too troublesome" (Carter 2006e, p. 459).

In addition, the climactic discoveries which Desiderio makes at the heart of Doctor Hoffman's intricate machinery suggest that even the most radical iconoclastic gesture claiming to function solely in the name of the imagination, creativeness and desire should not finally amount to a vapid veneration of irrationality per se. After all, societies based on principles of normality, conventionality and propriety hide behind the authority of so-called reason to behave most irrationally. Carter and Hoffmann alike emphasize that in order to expose this unpalatable state of affairs, it is useless — indeed even deleterious — simply to replace hegemonic pseudo-rationality with blatant irrationality. Indeed, this is ultimately a despotic move conducive to no less repressive a society than the one from which it claims to release us. Hence, Carter's — and Hoffmann's — message could be interpreted as an encouragement to work bravely with the here-and-now, and to abet this task by assiduous recourse to the imagination without, however, indulging in utopian glorifications of this faculty, and understanding instead the importance of harmonizing it at all times with the powers of rational examination and questioning.

Carter's own vision can thus be regarded as a perpetuation of Hoffmann's mission in her own times, and especially of the German writer's adventurous explosion of consolatory fictions. At the same time at it faithfully reflects Hoffmann's specific perspective, however, *The Infernal Desire Machines of Doctor Hoffman* also reflects a broader tendency within Romantic aesthetics to differentiate between productive and self-indulgent types of imagination. A paradigmatic instance of this propensity is supplied by Samuel Taylor Coleridge's contrastive definitions of "imagination" and "fancy" in Chapter XIII of his *Biographia Literaria*. The former "dissolves, diffuses, dissipates, in order to recreate: or where this process is rendered impossible, yet still at all events it struggles to idealize and to unify. It is essentially vital, even as all objects (as objects) are essentially fixed and dead." The latter, conversely, "has no other counters to play with, but fixities and definites. The fancy is indeed no other than a mode of memory emancipated from the order of time and space.... But equally with the ordinary memory the Fancy must receive all its materials ready made from the law of association" (Coleridge). Doctor Hoffman might at first appear to hold the power to generate a fluid universe uninhibited by ordinary ontological categories and boundaries and irreverently transgressive of the law of causality. Nevertheless, he finally turns out to have no power other than a prestidigitatorial knack of reshuffling the given and the ordained according to his whims. There is every chance, therefore, that he is not really creating anything especially new — and that even if this could be shown to be the case, the novelty itself would be no guarantee of spiritual, mental or bodily emancipation.

At the end of his odyssey, Desiderio does not only learn that Doctor Hoffman is a despot: he also realizes that his own real goal, in hunting down the monomaniacal scientist, has been all along the discovery of a person he could admire unreservedly and to whose will he could readily bow. According to Helen Butcher, this facet of Carter's narrative lends itself to Hegelian interpretation as a dramatization of the "theory of lordship and bondage" (a.k.a. "Master/Slave dialectic") put forward in *Phenomenology of Spirit*: an allegory for the genesis of self-consciousness and for the conflict between self and other undermining the establishment, preservation and consolidation of identity. In the reactive phase, the self perceives the other and, in becoming aware of the other as a separate entity, it simultaneously becomes aware of its own separateness: its own existence as an independent being. Yet, the self also regards the other's presence as a threat to its own influence and ascendancy, and determines that the sole means of restoring its shattered confidence — and of concurrently advancing toward self-consciousness — is to embark on a deadly struggle for pre-eminence.

Ironically, should either party actually die and vanish, the achievement of self-consciousness would be curtailed, insofar as the self and the other are mutually interdependent, complementary polarities. Thus, the two parties have no choice but to enter the dialectical master/slave relationship and, through this bond, maintain reciprocal recognition. This is no guarantee of definitive happiness, however, for the master must negotiate the slave's acquisition of skills and capacities to which he has no direct access: powers which the slave accomplishes by working intimately with nature and learning to shape its raw materials into artifacts for the master. As the slave creates an incrementally wide variety of products with greater and greater refinement by recourse to his own creativity, he comes to see himself reflected in his creations, while the master becomes more and more reliant on the slave's creative talent and his artifacts: in other words, he is at once alienated from the natural realm and enslaved by his slave's own creativity.

The master's sense of inadequacy is complicated by the fact that the moment the self extends its awareness of both itself and the other as distinct entities into a desire to assert its existence through domination of the other, problems ensue. The other indeed comes to be perceived as an inferior, second-rate or even inessential subject, and this inevitably undermines the self's authority: power wielded over a lesser being cannot be perceived — let alone paraded — as a momentous endowment. This situation entails that on the one hand, the other can be seen to bolster the self by helping it achieve self-consciousness, while on the other, it dwarfs its status by throwing into relief the paltriness of its authority. Strictly speaking, the only possible other capable of *both* supporting the self's consciousness of its own existence as a separate entity *and* of satisfying the self's desire for a truly significant expression of power must be an other that somehow replicates the self. According to Butcher, this is precisely the state of affairs depicted by Carter in *The Infernal Desire Machines of Doctor Hoffman*. The critic proposes that in light of Hegel's parable, it is possible to view the aim of Desiderio's pursuit not merely as a "leader" in the general sense of the term but specifically as "a Hegelian lord capable of providing recognition."

It is in the person of Albertina that Carter locates not simply the hub of Desiderio's erotic yearnings but also "the object of his quest for recognition." However, it is vital to acknowledge that Doctor Hoffman's shape-shifting daughter is not only "positioned as the ideal potential master." In fact, the text's insistent emphasis on her physical and cultural affinities with Desiderio — reinforced by the narrator's own tendency to regard Albertina as an ideal female version of himself— makes it feasible to read the novel as a variation on the Hegelian trajectory. Whereas in *Phenomenology of Spirit*, the "experience of being recognized" by the other can be perceived as "a subtle form of subjugation which destabilizes identity" insofar as it entails the self's marginalization, in *The Infernal Doctor Machines of Doctor Hoffman*, Desiderio would seem able "to circumvent this issue" by ideating an other that is really just another expression of his own self.

This bizarre resolution of the conflict presumed to underpin the birth and nurturing of self-identity for all humans does not, ultimately, deliver any lasting consolation within the compass of Carter's text. In fact, it simply inaugurates a vicious circle in which the self never genuinely confronts itself— and never accepts, therefore, its limitations and foibles alongside its capacities — but only ever sees replicas of its own being. In other words, its only viable outcome is an impasse of paralyzing solipsism. This contention is validated, as Butcher maintains, by the novel's repeated use of the trope of the "reflecting eye." A paradigmatic illustration is supplied by the scene in which Desiderio, in looking at a peep show exhibit, reckons that all he can see in looking at the image of the two eyes placed before him is a magnified reflection of his own eyes, and that his own eyes and the fake eyes of the exhibit mirror each other — backward and forward — in a forever bounding and rebounding scopic game. Thus, the value of recognizing the autonomous individuality of the other is effaced by the urge forcibly to imprint one's identity onto the other, and "the ethical act" of recognizing that self and other alike have a right to "possess viewpoints that are similarly contingent" is accordingly negated (Butcher).

The same existential drama is staged by Carter in the short story "A Souvenir of Japan," a gem of lyrical compression included in the intensely atmospheric (and often melancholy) collection *Fireworks*. This narrative is here worthy of privileged attention on two counts. Firstly, it offers a poignant dramatization of the problematical desiring machines activating — and yet simultaneously disabling — many human relationships. Secondly, it stands out as an intrepid attempt to tackle the issue of identity formation in a manner analogous to the one adopted by Carter in *The Infernal Desire Machines of Doctor Hoffman*. Both of these aspects of "A Souvenir of Japan" are instantly thrown into relief by the tortuous nature of the sentimental affair around which its entire yarn revolves: a British woman's liaison with a Japanese man named Taro after the character of Mamotaro, the Peach Boy so prominent in indigenous lore. According to his European lover, who also operates as the story's narrator, the present-day Taro shares with his legendary namesake "the inhuman sweetness of a child born from something other than a mother, a passive, cruel sweetness I did not immediately understand, for it was that of the repressed maso-chism which, in my country, is usually confined to women" (Carter 2006e, p. 30).

As these reflections indicate, the central relationship explored in "A Souvenir of Japan" is tainted by an ostensibly insoluble culture clash. The affective machine at its core would be able to animate it in a healthy fashion if the desires emanating from its two parties could be allowed to flow and intersect freely over a shared terrain. As it happens, the movement of desire is disastrously forestalled by the narrator's irresistible temptation to objec-tify her foreign lover lest he should attempt to objectify her in the style she recognizes as typical of her original culture — a measure intended to help her retain her own sense of self-identity in the face of the other. As a result, she soon arrives at this discomforting realization: "I knew him only in relation to myself.... At times I thought I was inventing him as I went along" (p. 32). Thus, Carter points to the critical and debilitating flaw thwarting the desire machinery at the heart of legion relationships: the acceptance of objectification — as a fate which we inflict upon others or to which we submit ourselves depending on the contingent balance of power — in return for a modicum of pleasure. It is by bravely confronting this somber truth that the narrator, putatively speaking on behalf of all the victims of dysfunctional desiring machines, brings the piece to a close in mesmerizingly poetic language: "we were surrounded by the most mov-ing images of evanescence, fireworks, morning glories, the old, children. But the most moving of these images were the intangible reflections of ourselves we saw in one another's eyes, reflections of nothing but appear-ances ... and, try as we might to possess the essence of each other's other-ness, we would inevitably fail" (p. 34).

It is also interesting to note that although the gaze is here posited as an instrument for self-assertion and self-consolidation, it is nonetheless conceptualized with reference to the image of *two* eyes: hence, the text deliberately refrains from regimenting vision on the basis of the authority of monocularity, which has traditionally been the case in the West since at least the Renaissance and its codification of perspective. Although in purely technical terms, perspective commonly designates the employment of devices meant to convey the illusion of three-dimensionality on a two-dimensional surface, its ideological implications are far-reaching. Indeed, the logic of perspectivalism aims at disciplining vision in accordance with rigid mathematical principles by ratifying a single, putatively correct, way of seeing the world and thereby enthroning the myth of the observer as an uncontrasted master of vision. Monocular vision is concurrently upheld as a means of severing vision from the material reality of the body — and the related vagaries of binocular rivalry and polyopia — in order to promote the concept of a highly civilized, rational, stable, incorporeal and desensualized eye/I.

As Martin Jay emphasizes, the most effective measures implemented to geometricalize space and vision, as germane emanations of a cultivated being, have indeed posited the eye "as singular, rather than the two eyes of normal binocular vision. It was considered in the manner of a lone eye looking through a peephole at the scene in front of it. Such an eye was, moreover, understood to be static, unblinking and fixated, rather than dynamic ... thus producing a visual take that was eternalized, reduced to 'one point of view'" (Jay, pp. 7–8). Unitary perception is clearly a fantastical construct — in much the same way as the notion of a unified subjectivity belongs to the domain of myth, naturalized though this might have become — and yet has retained almost uncontrasted authority within the politics of visuality fostered by Western and Westernized societies for several centuries. Carter undoubtedly uses Desiderio's peep show experiences to throw into relief the adaptability of vision to the erection of sensory and sexual fantasies intended both to bolster the budding subject and, sadly, to acquiesce to its self-absorption. However, in foregrounding the binocularity attendant upon her hero's perceptions, she subtly refuses to pander to the myth of unitary vision which Western ocular centrism has so often and so uncritically espoused, and therefore questions the related ideals of disembodiment, de-eroticization, eternity and stability nestled in its viperous core.

Despite this implicitly uplifting message, the novel's emphasis on the ubiquity of self-engrossment and misrecognition can feel overwhelmingly dispiriting. Nevertheless, it is scarcely deniable that such a strategy is also the most honest way of encapsulating the political tragedy at the heart of *The Infernal Desire Machines of Doctor Hoffman*: namely, its frank portrayal of a world of rampant egocentrism — a massive prison in which the self relies routinely on acts of misrecognition intended to fashion the other in accordance with its own rapacious fantasies, and hence reduce it to a passive projection or appendage of itself. The reflective imagery deployed by Carter throughout the saga is the perfect trope for a novel about the seeming inescapability of absolutist oppression and about mythology's inveterate tendency to reinvent itself whenever its bastions are challenged. Desiderio himself emphasizes that he does not wish to be thought of as a national hero because he does not authentically deserve this privileged status, claiming that his victory does not represent a genuine triumph of good over evil insofar as the new order he himself as helped to erect is just another system, another potential cage. The character's discontent is further augmented by the unhealable fracture between Desiderio the narrator and Desiderio the questor, the past and present Desiderios as it were. Paradoxically, the ideal of unity so madly pursued through the rampant acts of misrecognition performed by various characters throughout the fiction is shattered by the intrinsic nature of the textual weave itself.

Furthermore, the spuriousness of Desiderio's so-called heroism replicates the questionable nature of the very premise underpinning the narrative task he has been enjoined to undertake — i.e., the chronicling of the adventures that befell him as a young man. This assignment indeed consists of isolating from the tangled skein of events surrounding the war between the Minister of Determination and Doctor Hoffman "the single, original thread of [his] self" (Carter 2010, p. 3) — that is to say, a fictitious entity that never actually existed for the simple reason that Desiderio never possessed a unitary self which could reliably function as a leading thread throughout the saga's convolutions and involutions. In fact, his supposed self only ever amounted to a bundle of projective fantasies, specular doublings and artificially concocted infernal desires. The logical corollary of this misconception is that the foundation of Desiderio's entire narrative is ultimately no less of a lie than Doctor Hoffman's promise of a free world is. Seen from Carter's indomitably questioning standpoint, the notion of Desiderio as a unified and self-contained protagonist is just a risible liberal humanist fantasy. Yet, Desiderio the narrator is haunted by that mercurial figment as a reality which he must somehow call into being on the page — however spectrally — and whose authenticity he must defend at any price even though he knows full well it never obtained in the first place.

Combining sociological inquiry, satirical acumen and calm ratiocination with overwhelming romanticism and an appetite for the fantastic at its darkest and boldest, *The Infernal Desire Machines of Doctor Hoffman* eloquently attests to Carter's fascination with the Surrealist movement. In an essay on Georges Bataille's pornographic novella "Histoire de l'oeil" (1928) titled "Georges Bataille: Story of the Eye" (1979), Carter overtly admits to her admiration for the Surrealist author, whom she describes as her "grand old surrealist fellow-traveller and sexual philosophe" (Carter 1998, p. 68). Carter's interest in Surrealism is documented most explicitly in her 1978 essay "The Alchemy of the Word." "Surrealist beauty," the author declares in this context, "is convulsive. That is, you *feel* it, you don't see it — it exists as an excitation of the nerves. The experience of the beautiful is, like the experience of desire, an abandonment to vertigo, yet the beautiful does not exist *as such*. What do exist are images or objects that are enigmatic, marvelously erotic — or juxtapositions of objects, or people, or ideas, that arbitrarily extend our notion of the connections it is possible to make. In a way, the beautiful is put at the service of liberty." Carter is also acutely aware of the potently visual dimension of Surrealism's world picture, which she indeed describes as an "aesthetic of the eye at the tips of the fingers; of the preternaturally heightened senses of the dreamer" (Carter 2006c, p. 73).

This detail is of vital significance to the novel's imbrication with the dynamics and politics of visuality, an aspect of *The Infernal Desire Machines of Doctor Hoffman* to which the discussion will shortly return. It is also a clue to a stylistic priority pervading the fiction's entire texture which repeatedly announces Carter's strongest affinity with Surrealist aesthetics: her visual sensibility. In Carter's writing, as in Surrealist painting and sculpture, images are so punctiliously rendered, detailed and mesmerizingly accurate as to fool the eye into taking them as quite naturalistic reflections of the real — only to pull the perceptual rug from under our sensorium by abruptly reminding us that those images have no real-life referent except in the most elliptical and metaphorical sense one could ever consider.

Carter's carnivalesque spirit would no doubt have felt most potently galvanized by the Surrealists' use of play as a method of inquiry meant to free the pleasure principle and to displace conventional patterns of thought.

Carter's carnivalesque spirit, as Anna Watz has suggested, would no doubt have felt most potently galvanized by the Surrealists' use of play as a method of inquiry meant to free the pleasure principle and to displace conventional patterns of thought. Watz, drawing to a large extent on Susan Laxton, provides a succinct summation of such Surrealist play. "The ludic practices of the group of surrealists gathered around André Breton," she writes,*

> were centred on the potential of chance to critique and subvert rationality. They developed play strategies such as the surrealist *errance*, which Susan Laxton describes as "an aimless wandering in the city's streets meant to encourage the eruption of unconscious images into the perceptual field," or linguistic/visual games such as the well-known *cadavre exquis*. The Bataillean surrealists, on their part, focused on games of violence and transgression, largely inspired by Nietzsche's aesthetic theories. Despite their different strategies, however, both the Bretonian and the Bataillean factions saw in the nonrational status of play a potential for provocation and destruction of the propriety of the bourgeoisie as well as of "repressive conventions and the institutions of power that keep them in place" (Laxton [unpaged]). In short, they saw in play a potential for transforming reality [Watz, pp. 1–2].

Watz continues:

> As Laxton points out, play as a signifier is of course inherently flexible, even contradictory. Johan Huizinga's classic definition of play in *Homo Ludens: A Study of the Play Elements in Culture* (1955), which has its roots in the aesthetic theories of Kant and Schiller, emphasises play's opposition to reality: it is "a voluntary activity or occupation executed within certain fixed limits of time and place, according to rules freely accepted but absolutely binding, having its aim in itself and accompanied by a feeling of tension, joy and the consciousness that it is 'different' from 'ordinary' life" (p. 28). This conception of play as a bounded and regulated activity, existing purely in an autonomous dimension with no stake in material reality, is, as Laxton maintains, clearly not applicable to the "surrealist ludic." The surrealists insisted on play's *lack* of limits and its potential for liberating unconscious desires, and its purpose, ultimately, was to subvert the "real" world (Laxton) [Watz, p. 2].

As Watz observes regarding the character Honeybuzzard in *Shadow Dance*,

> in accordance with Peter Bürger's classic definition of surrealism as an attempted sublation of art in the praxis of life (Burger, 94), Honeybuzzard transforms art into life and life into art as he plays. In opposition to Huizinga's account of play as a bounded activity which exists at a remove from reality, Honeybuzzard's surrealist play is excessive and bent on transgression [Watz, p. 3].

*This portion of the discussion relies greatly on Anna Watz's seminal article "Violence as Surrealist Play in Angela Carter's *Shadow Dance*," pp. 1–2. Please note that this same article is also cited in the discussion of Shadow Dance here presented in Chapter 2.

Clearly, this observation can be applied to Doctor Hoffman's project, which similarly relies on absolute excess and absolute anarchy.

The novel's form and texture are pointedly picaresque. Yet, its rhythm is not dictated exclusively by linear and paratactical priorities since Carter resorts repeatedly to narrative stratagems such as foreshadowing, reiteration and recapitulation. In the articulation of these structural principles, a critical role is played throughout by the titular desire machines, each of which partakes more or less directly of the disturbing ethics of the peep show. Thus, it could be argued that Carter's desire machines are essentially machines of the eye and that *The Infernal Desire Machines of Doctor Hoffman* as a whole, by extension, is primarily a text about the machinery of vision. It therefore enables Carter to revisit an issue already addressed in her earlier novels in greater depth and by recourse to a more widely diversified frame of aesthetic and political reference: the relationship between power and visuality. Most importantly, the text obliquely charts the transition from the concept of power as the supreme form of spectacle, pivoting on the imperative to place its wielders, icons and paraphernalia on prominent display so as to awe the subject into submission, to the notion of power as surveillance, which is reliant instead on the subject's internalization of the dominant ideology's repressive gaze.

We are thereby reminded that in exercising the right to vision within a society, we do not operate as spectators but rather as observers: while the root of "spectator," *spectare*, translates simply as "to see" or "to look at," the root of "observer," *observare,* means "to comply with" and therefore designates the activity of seeing within prescribed sets of norms, expectations and limitations. In articulating these topoi, *The Infernal Desire Machines of Doctor Hoffman* proposes that what human beings see within the parameters of a particular culture (actual or speculative as the case might be) is always a function of what and how they are made or allowed to see, and of the extent to which they are able to sense the invisible therein. Norman Bryson pithily conveys this idea in his thought-provoking discussion of "The gaze in the expanded field," where it is proposed that whenever we use our eyes, we do not simply perceive "light" but also "intelligible form." The extrapolation of form from the raw materials of visual perception, argues Bryson, is a direct corollary of the socialization of vision: "For human beings collectively to orchestrate their visual experience together it is required that each submit his or her retinal experience to the socially agreed description(s) of an intelligible world. Vision is socialized, and visual reality can be measured and named, as hallucination, misrecognition, or 'visual disturbance.' Between the subject and the world is inserted the entire sum of discourses which make up visuality" (Bryson, p. 91).

In his peregrinations, Desiderio comes across not only as a picaro but also as a *flâneur*: a narrative identity most congruous with the novel's over-arching philosophy given its emphasis on the importance of visuality in an urban or quasi-urban context. This obtains regardless of the nature of the people contingently enthroned by the text as pivotal points of reference — who might equally well be sadistic pimps or suicidal damsels in distress, cannibalistic not-so-Noble Savages or self-dismembering acrobats. Desiderio mimics the figure of the Surrealist wanderer mentioned earlier, yet also presages, in keeping with the novel's prophetic anticipation of the virtual age, the portrayal of the *flâneur* proffered by Christine Boyer in the specific context of the cybercity. In this ambiguous reality marked by the incessant coalescence of the actual and the hypothetical, the tangible and the imagined, the wanderer's motion can be seen to generate not only ongoing dynamic flows but also ever-mutating visual arrangements — mobile imagistic tableaux akin to the text's diabolical peep shows. "At each step the *flâneur* takes," Boyer maintains "new constellations of images appear that resemble the turns of a kaleidoscope. But as these spectacles of the city are formed, the *flâneur*'s internal thoughts feel devalued and disordered, the result of figures that flow and blend into each other as if they were in a dream" (Boyer, p. 51). In principle, Desiderio's perambulations could stretch on ad infinitum — or indeed might, just as feasibly, never have commenced.

As he journeys from place to place — and from peep show to peep show — Carter's narrator captures myriad impressions in the compass of his sensorium. These are held together by a cumulative textual constellation that resembles a symphony in virtue of the elegantly patterned architectonics of reciprocally resonating images conjured by the author herself. Time and again, however, they also clash in a cacophony of emotions insofar as Doctor Hoffman's perceptual mirages tenaciously elude containment within a unified mold. In the process, Desiderio evokes several of the traits commonly ascribed to the *flâneur* in the context of modernity. Most significant, within the overall structure of Carter's novel, is that figure's equivocal status vis-à-vis his culture's power structures. As Steve Pile argues, "on the one hand," the *flâneur* is "captivated by the movement and excitement of the urban modern; on the other hand, terrified of being swallowed up by the masses" (Pile, p. 230). The capacity to register countless visual stimuli and retain no less copious an array of pictorial traces within his memory bank equates the *flâneur* to an uncontrasted manipulator of the visual field. Nevertheless, it also implicitly points to his vulnerability as an ephemeral being whose very identity would feasibly dissolve in the absence of those stimuli. Keith Tester corroborates this hypothesis, maintaining that "*flâneurie* can, after Baudelaire, be understood as the activity of the sovereign spectator going about the city in order to find the things which will occupy his gaze and thus complete his otherwise incomplete identity; satisfy his otherwise dissatisfied existence; replace the sense of bereavement with a sense of life" (Tester, p. 7).

Like the *flâneur*, Carter's narrator is a fundamentally ambiguous figure. While the mission he has been enjoined to undertake by the Minister of Determination invests him with special authority, he is also portrayed as powerless at various levels. His influence as a civil servant is paltry to begin with, and is further eroded by his subjection to the caprices of each person he meets along the way, which effectively makes him quite powerless in the face of each machine's infernal propagation of desires. At the same time, his sexual prowess as Albertina's knight-like suitor is insistently enfeebled by the endless deferral of satisfaction. These inadequacies are economically reflected, as intimated, in the character's limited narratorial authority. On all planes, Desiderio's ambivalences mirror Doctor Hoffman's metamorphic spaces as settings that simultaneously enthrone him as a seemingly powerful master of vision, able to see everything and yet remain unseen, and yet deprive him of the prospect of any rewarding connections with other creatures.

In this respect, he recalls the portrait of the *flâneur* proposed by Elizabeth Wilson, who suggests that while the character might be able to achieve "visual possession" of his environment (Wilson, p. 65), he is concurrently at the mercy of a disjointed pageant of forever partial and fragmentary narratives. Desiderio's experiences as a decoder of visual impressions and as a narrator expected to bind their jumbled threads together resemble the ordeal of the *flâneur* himself as a tentative decoder of urban life — a state of affairs tersely captured by Wilson as follows: "we constantly brush against strangers; we observe bits of the 'stories' men and women carry with them, but never learn their conclusions; life ceases to form itself into an epic or narrative, becoming instead a short story, dreamlike, insubstantial or ambiguous" (p. 73). Even though Desiderio's ego could, in principle, feel flattered by the psychedelic parade of machines and tableaux he encounters at each step of his voyage, he is nonetheless repeatedly left with an acute and inconsolable feeling of dispossession, incompleteness and lack.

It is vital to acknowledge, in assessing Desiderio's status as a *flâneur*-like wanderer, that the voyages characteristically undertaken by his modernist precursor lack any obvious point of inception and any definite destination. This proposition is famously advocated by Walter Benjamin in "Central Park," where the absence of any identifiable sense of direction in the *flâneur*'s movements is posited as an upshot of the baffling character of the labyrinth of which modern urban space ultimately consists: that is to say, "the home of the hesitant" (Benjamin 1985, p. 40). Benjamin's writings are of particular significance in the present context, insofar as they bring most inspiringly together the three interdependent aspects of *The Infernal Desire Machines of Doctor Hoffman* which could be reasonably described as its philosophical lynchpins: *flâneurie*, the peep show and Surrealist aesthetics. At face value, Carter's novel might seem awash in so wide and wild an array of temporal and generic references — the medieval romance, the quest narrative, the fairy tale, *fin-de-siècle* decadence, Golden Age detective fiction, hardboiled and noir fiction, steampunk, the heavy metal comic book, the aesthetic treatise — as to transcend history altogether. In fact, the peep show worlds visited by Desiderio in the course of his picaresque *flâneurie* are situated within well-defined socioeconomic parameters insofar as they constitute, above all else, specific sites of consumption. To this extent, they closely resemble Benjamin's arcades: that is to say, the prototypical setting of the *flâneur*'s errantry as receptacles of myriad commodities and consumers. Neither the classic *flâneur* nor Desiderio operate simply as members of the swarming crowds: more importantly, they act as spectators, who remain relatively detached from the spectacle unfolding around them even as they partake of it. The characteristic feeling induced by this experience, argues Benjamin is one of "intoxication" — specifically, "the intoxication of the commodity around which surges the stream of customers." (Benjamin 1983, p. 55).

In the face of commodities inveterately alienated from both their real and their hypothetical consumers, the classic *flâneur* and Desiderio alike are liable to feel comparably alienated and lonely. The sole weapon at their disposal to counteract this potentially disabling condition is the capacity to gaze, and hence create an imaginary space of action from the visual field at their disposal. However, even this space of dynamic interiority wherein the isolated spectator might process his empirical responses — and ensuing existential reflections — in peace is vulnerable to ideological interference and regimentation in the form of technologies of vision: strategies meant to control, direct and quantify the consumer's gaze within particular structures of material desire. This is borne out, in the specific context of Carter's novel, by Desiderio's implication, by and large against his own wishes, in nefarious power games revolving around the peep show world and its commodified subjects. At their freest, both the modernist *flâneur* and Desiderio are in a position to treat the people and objects they perceive as texts: i.e., potential narratives which it is up to them to actualize by decoding their cultures' hieroglyphs and judiciously recognizing the signs which might easily go unheeded by others as clues to a hidden yarn or else as hints at a submerged drama. In this respect, the wanderer's task echoes Carter's own favorite pursuit as a voracious hunter of even the vaguest traces of a storytelling opportunity.

Benjamin and Carter are concurrently brought together by a shared fascination with Surrealist poetics as a cultural force dedicated to the reconfiguration of reality in accordance with the polychromatic, dislocating and fundamentally palimpsestic logic of the oneiric. This illuminating strategy comes superbly into evidence when the Surrealists strive, as Benjamin's "Dream Kitsch" puts it, "to blaze a way into the heart of things abolished or superseded, to decipher the contours of the banal as rebus.... Picture puzzles, as schemata of the dreamwork, were long ago discovered by psychoanalysis. The Surrealists, with a similar conviction, are less on the trail of the psyche than on the track of things" (Benjamin 1999a, p. 4). Benjamin further declares his attraction to this particular facet of Surrealism in a letter to the poet Rainer Maria Rilke: "In particular what struck me about Surrealism ... was the captivating, authoritative, and definitive way in which language passes over into the world of dreams" (Benjamin 1982, p. 126).

This profession echoes some achingly beautiful lines, likewise devoted to the mystery of dreaming, which feature in the context of Benjamin's juvenile writings: "Daily we use unmeasured energies as if in our sleep. What we do and think is filled with the being of our fathers and ancestors. An uncomprehended symbolism enslaves us without ceremony. Sometimes, on awakening we recall a dream. In this way rare shafts of insight illuminate the ruins of our energies that time has passed by" (Benjamin 1996, p. 6). As intimated at various junctures in this study, Carter's own writings untiringly seek to alert us to the omnipresence of the past in our daily lives. This is most pointedly accomplished through the author's dauntless appropriation and reconceptualization of traditional narrative forms: an aesthetic and ethical predilection which the intricately multi-layered texture of *The Infernal Desire Machines of Doctor Hoffman* declares most emphatically with its cocktail of genres, styles, historical reverberations and cultural allusions. For Carter, as for Benjamin, conscious awareness of the past's momentous influence in the everyday tends to occur, paradoxical as this may sound, in situations in which lucid thinking and dreaming uncannily collude.

In exploring Surrealism's attitude to the oneiric, Benjamin finds an especially fertile source of inspiration in Louis Aragon's work *Le Paysan de Paris* (*Paris Peasant*), which he posits as a formative influence in the evolution of *The Arcades Project* (Benjamin 1999b). This constitutes a pioneering investigation of modern consumerism and its simultaneously ideological and psychological implications catalyzed by the iconic image of the nineteenth century glass-covered shopping mall as the meeting-place of architecture, advertising, fashion, prostitution, literature and photography (among several other cultural categories). Aragon's own depiction of the arcades as a domain in which quotidian reality is imbued with the fabulous is worthy of notice, in this context, not only as an image of inspirational value for Benjamin's seminal project but also as an apt correlative for the spaces of sensory inebriation meticulously painted by Carter to chronicle Desiderio's peregrinations through spectacles of commodification and vicarious consumption. For Aragon, the arcades are indeed "places where men go calmly about their mysterious lives and in which a profound religion is gradually taking shape. These sites are not yet inhabited by a divinity. It is forming there, a new godhead precipitating in these re-creations of Ephesus" (Aragon, p. 28).

While Benjamin is deeply drawn to the progressive potentialities of Surrealism (particularly as exemplified by Aragon's writings), he is aware of the danger, also implicitly present in the movement's philosophy, that a visionary striving toward novel possibilities may lead to a failure to understand and come to terms critically with the past, its lessons and its errors. Writing specifically about the status of the Surrealist imagination vis-à-vis *The Infernal Desire Machines of Doctor Hoffman*, Susan Rubin Suleiman communicates a terse warning against the perils of Surrealism which obliquely echoes Benjamin's own apprehensions on the subject. Carter's text, Suleiman maintains, is "a novel *of* as well as *about* Surrealist imagination." At the same time, even though it is undoubtedly plausible to conceive of the "Doctor-poet" as a "Surrealist image-maker," it is crucial to appreciate that he does not function exclusively as an allegory of Surrealism. "If he is an allegory of anything," she states, "it is of the technological appropriation of Surrealism *and* liberal philosophy" (Suleiman, p. 134).

Suleiman then invokes Guy Debord's *La Société du spectacle*, and specifically its proposition that "all the life of societies in which modern conditions of production dominate presents itself as an immense accumulation of *spectacles*," as a result of which "everything that was directly lived has distanced itself in a representation." Suleiman develops this argument by suggesting that if Doctor Hoffman's infernal desire machines "for projecting representations on the world" are interpreted in light of Debord's theories, it is possible to "see in Carter's mad scientist the nightmarish synthesis of repressive desublimation and the society of the spectacle" (p. 135). The destiny awaiting the Surrealist imagination in the society of the spectacle does not appear to be rosy: "At best," Suleiman broods, "'la révolution surréaliste' becomes a private passion, not a means to change the world" (p. 136). This outcome is clearly a far cry from the enthusiastic affirmation of Surrealism's innovatory potentialities proffered by Salvador Dalí, here invoked as a representative voice for the broader cultural movement with which the artist is conventionally associated: "progressive art can assist people to learn not only about the objective forces at work in the society in which they live," Dalí declares, "but also about the intensely social character of their interior lives. Ultimately, it can propel people toward social emancipation" (Dalí).

In this matter, both Benjamin and Suleiman's perspectives bear intriguing affinities with the pivotal message advocated by Carter in *The Infernal Desire Machines of Doctor Hoffman* as outlined earlier in this discussion: namely, the idea that a radically demythologizing act can easily be conducive to yet another — ultimately no less oppressive — myth unless its imaginative thrust is tempered by a modicum of rationality, and its revolutionary aspirations are not allowed to degenerate into a shambolic cavalcade of solipsistic compulsions. The repercussions of this perverse reinscription of mythology into an apparently demythologized reality are so deeply disappointing that even the most imperturbable soul is likely to feel their sting. This is borne out by the fact that Desiderio's eventual victory is not sufficient to fill his being with a conclusive feeling of achievement or sense of personal worth. In fact, at the end of his saga, Carter's narrator is left, though victorious, in possession of an onerous legacy of yearning and inconsolable regret. It will be for the protagonist of Carter's next novel, *The Passion of New Eve*, to find ways of owning her experiences courageously enough to walk away, if not exactly unburdened, at least positively invigorated.

CHAPTER 4

Modern Mythologies
The Passion of New Eve

Originally, ... the human race was different. Each individual was like two people with their backs pressed together. They had four arms and legs and a head with two faces, one looking forward, the other looking backward. And there were three sexes: individuals with two male organs, those with two female organs, and hermaphrodites possessing one female and one male organ. These beings could walk forward or backward with equal facility. And when they wished to move quickly they performed cartwheels, whirling along faster than any human can run today. Since they were twice as strong as men today, and much faster, they united to overthrow the gods.

— Plato

Culture itself is the limit of our knowledge; there is no available truth outside culture with which we can challenge injustice. But culture is also contradictory, the location of resistances as well as oppressions, and it is ultimately unstable. It too is in consequence a site of political struggle.

— Catherine Belsey and Jane Moore

As anticipated in this study's opening chapter, Carter's commitment to a project of uncompromising demythologization reaches unprecedented peaks in *The Passion of New Eve*, where the sheer spectrum of cultural mythologies which the writer brings to trial — and finds, by an large, not merely wanting but downright iniquitous — is so broad as to encompass at once popular images spawned by mainstream Western cinema and venerable icons enshrined in classic anthropology, the language of advertising at its tackiest and the high-brow eye-candy worshipped by museological idolatry. Of Carter's early novels, the one which most trenchantly fore-shadows the debunking mission undertaken in *The Passion of New Eve* is arguably *Heroes and Villains* (1969). Despite its Cinderella-ish status within the compass of Carter's output, this is actually, as Eva C. Karpinsky per-suasively argues, "an important novel, dealing with myth making in the Barthesian sense of culturally constructed collective fictions or clichés." In this text, the critic continues, Carter declares her impatience with cultural mythologies by showing that the latent "utopian elements of myth and the mythic element of utopian thought" (Karpinsky) are no less specious than the explicitly oppressive aspects of those ubiquitous cultural con-structs. As Carter emphasizes in "Notes from the Front Line," they, too, serve to bolster the "social fictions that regulate our lives" and hypocritically furnish us with a modicum of pampering coziness only for the purpose of concealing their true status as "extraordinary lies designed to make people unfree" (Carter 1998, p. 38).

In *Heroes and Villains*, the demythologizing quest seeks primarily to provide a rigorous, albeit occasionally facetious, critique of patriarchy inte-grated within a wider venture which aims at "decolonialising our language and our habits of thought" (p. 42). Carter, argues Karpinsky, "interrogates the binaries of self/other, body/mind, male/female, nature/culture, pas-sion/reason, or civilized/barbarian" which sustain patriarchy's "institutions and representations" in order to condone "exploitation and domination of one group by another." It is through this sustained ideological enterprise, couched in a deliberately stereotypical and tongue-in-cheek adaptation of a familiar post-apocalyptic formula, that the fiction delivers an inspired "dystopian romance" (Karpinsky). In so doing, it deploys its yarn's micro-cosmic dimension — a private liaison — to encourage us to judge the sound-ness of the macrocosmic context in which it is inscribed: i.e., the power structures and related intersubjective dynamics of a whole culture. Carter thus engages in a fervent and unremittingly self-reflexive investigation of the multifarious processes through which our bodies and minds are rou-tinely fashioned by the societies we inhabit through both explicit discipli-nary strategies and covert instruments of psychological regimentation. This preoccupation, destined to become central to *The Passion of New Eve*, is articulated throughout *Heroes and Villains* by recourse to a wide range of utopian and dystopian motifs derived from a stunning variety of literary, mythical, artistic and theoretical sources — including Jonathan Swift, Claude Lévi-Strauss, Sigmund Freud, Matthew Arnold, the Bible and the chivalric romance. This intertextual tapestry performs an important part in Carter's mapping of the liminal domain, situated between philosophical speculation and storytelling, where *Heroes and Villains* actually belongs.

Carter's ideologically subversive heroine, Marianne, declares her independence of spirit in the most radical fashion imaginable within the novel's parameters. She forsakes the rational and orderly culture of the Professors, in which she has been born and raised, in order to elope with a member of the rival culture, the magic-oriented Barbarians, and eventually ends becoming the Barbarian's leader — a role she embraces with almost alarming fortitude. "I'll be the tiger lady," she asserts, "and rule them with a rod of iron" (Carter 1969, p. 175). Carter does not aim, however, to glorify one society at the expense of the other. In fact, she cultivates a resolutely anti–Manichean world view by throwing into relief both societies' injustices and thus exposing their underlying similarities. One might expect the Barbarians to offer a more exciting lifestyle and a more adventurous attitude to knowledge and history than the Professors, who are obsessed with stability, productivity, and the cultural legacy of the past. Marianne's experience of the two adversarial cultures as both an insider and an outsider by turns starkly demonstrates that this is not the case. She rapidly discovers that life can be as tedious among the Barbarians as she knows it to be among the Professors, that blinding bigotry and an unquestioning faith in hierarchy poison the power structures of both societies — and, most importantly, that the Professors and the Barbarians alike are fundamentally patriarchal, driven by misogynistic prejudices and unthinkingly reliant on gender politics which absolve discrimination and inequity as not merely pardonable but quite natural tendencies. Most crucially, in the light of Carter's passionate exposure of all persecutory molds meant to keep the mind and body subjugated, each of the two cultures promotes a rampant psychology of fear as its governing mechanism, persistently constructing its antagonist as the dark other in which that fear may locate a stable focus.

Carter's portrayal of Marianne plays a key role in abetting the novel's anti-binary perspective. She is courageous, resolute, self-reliant and playfully androgynous, and is shown to be instinctively drawn to practically anything outlandish, bizarre or taboo. Yet, she is also resistant to clear-cut compartmentalization insofar as her experience of conflicting societal organizations serves to unleash a tantalizing mix of discordant energies. Richard Boston's assessment of the novel's cumulative import eloquently confirms its explosion of conventional oppositions at the levels of both plot and characterization. *Heroes and Villains*, the critic maintains, is above all "a fable that discusses the roles of reason and imagination in a civilized society. Marianne rejects the sterile rationality of the Laputan Professors, but she is also aware of the monsters that are brought forth by the sleep of reason. (The title of Goya's print is quoted.) Likewise, though the magician is often evil, to reject him is to reject art, culture, wit and humor; indeed, when the Barbarians throw him out, the consequences are fatal. The point that the story seems to make is that if man is not to be a Yahoo, then he needs both reason and imagination, the measured prose of Jane Austen as well as the mystery and poetry of the Douanier Rousseau" (Boston).

The chief mythology interrogated in *The Passion of New Eve* concerns the pervasive power of the eye, which enables Carter to problematize a bundle of issues already addressed in earlier novels: that is to say, the ideological and psychological complications inherent in the politics of visuality. This recurring preoccupation gains fresh resonance through Carter's keen focus on the intersubjective dynamics of the gaze. The novel insistently alerts us to the semantic significance of the gaze as opposed to other visual activities. Using the concept of the gaze to designate the power relations embedded in the interrelated regions of vision and visuality, Carter reminds us that the act of gazing differs radically from the mere practice of looking insofar as it entails acts of probing, penetration and mastery that typically coalesce into strategies of objectification of the human body — and, most crucially, its affective and sexual dimensions. Seeing, as the general term commonly employed to cover a broad variety of ocular engagements, implies the ability to register a range of sensations connected with color, light and form which is not normally bound up with any ulterior intentions. Glancing constitutes the most casual form of seeing imaginable, its tendency to caress the surfaces of objects like a casual breeze ranking it in the category of carefree and non-judgmental pursuits. With the act of observing we enter a more problematic wing of the palace of vision, since this activity involves more attentive and discriminate inspection of both our environment and our place within it. It is with the gaze, however, that the alliance of vision and control asserts itself most forcefully, and the eye's capacity to contribute vitally to the fabrication of social identities comes into unrivaled prominence.

In alerting us to the basic traits differentiating the most ubiquitous scopic phenomena, Carter alerts us to the fact that they are ideologically momentous even though many of us might be inclined to dismiss them as pedestrian and obvious — that they are often neglected, in fact, precisely *because* they carry enormous political weight, and it is therefore in the interests of the system they buttress to naturalize them to the point that they can be taken for granted and left unscrutinized. Given her fascination with traditional narratives of all sorts, Carter would also have been well aware, in investigating the dynamics of the gaze, of its inscription in ancient mythology and lore. Hence, it is possible to envisage, just beneath the textual surface of *The Passion of New Eve*, a web of allusions to images as disparate as the Gorgons' petrifying stare and Perseus' ability to vanquish their leader, Medusa, through specular play; Eurydice's eternal condemnation to the darkness of Hades as a result of her husband Orpheus' fatal look of longing; Lot's metamorphosis into a pillar of salt upon turning to look at Sodom and Gomorrah. Since popular traditions are no less dear to Carter's heart than the realm of legend, it is also possible to sense vestiges of the customs and rituals surrounding the evil eye. The character of Leilah is, after all, repeated associated with sorcery.

The dynamics of the gaze has offered particularly fertile ground for psychoanalytic theory — a discipline with which Carter is clearly well-acquainted, even though her attitude to its teachings is often facetious or even downright skeptical. A characteristic illustration of this proclivity is offered, incidentally, by the following assertion: "I don't on the whole remember my own dreams, but I quite often use the formal structures of dreams — formal structures which I tend to get from Freud rather than from my own experience" (in Haffenden 1985, p. 82). Psychoanalysis associates the gaze with four principal concepts: scopophilia, pleasure gleaned from looking; voyeurism, excitation produced from the sight of erotically charged bodies; fetishism, the obsessive attraction to an object or to part of an object associated with a sexually desirable entity; and sadism, gratification emanating from the sight of another's suffering. On the basis of these basic definitions, it is not hard to understand why so many critics with psychoanalytic leanings should have turned to the discourse of the gaze specifically in order to examine the cultural construction of sexuality and gender.

Laura Mulvey has made a seminal intervention in the debate with "Visual Pleasure and Narrative Cinema," originally published in 1975, where she embarks on a thorough investigation of the politics of visuality characterizing classic Hollywood cinema — namely, a cultural formation of production, consumption and desire which, as will shortly be shown, is of critical importance to Carter's own perspective on film. Focusing on Hollywood's articulation and choreographing of scopophilia, Mulvey posits the type of narrative cinema issuing from that prestigious system as instrumental in constructing and textualizing a specific image of woman: i.e., woman qua "signifier for the male other, bound by a symbolic order in which man can live out his fantasies and obsessions through linguistic command by imposing them on the silent image of woman still tied to her place as bearer of meaning, not maker of meaning" (Mulvey 1975). According to Mulvey, therefore, Hollywood cinema of the narrative ilk hinges on an asymmetrical distribution of power that routinely emplaces woman as the object and man as the bearer of the gaze. This power structure operates simultaneously at two levels since, at the same time as a film's male protagonist is accorded the authority to objectify the heroine by recourse to his gaze, the male spectator is likewise enabled to frame the female character as a passive icon for his own visual consumption. Triggered, in psychoanalytical parlance, by a castration anxiety, the objectifying urge tends to acquire either of two forms. On the one hand, the master of the gaze may choose to denigrate and demonize the female subject as the epitome of sexual corruption and vampiric predacity, and hence regard her as a deserving recipient of sadistic assaults. On the other hand, he may opt for the idealizing route by fetishizing and overvaluing the female body, and hence placing her on the kind of pedestal one would expect to encounter in classic chivalric legends as an object of worship.

It is hardly surprising, given these premises, that a crucial component of the transgendering process to which the protagonist of *The Passion of New Eve* is subjected should be her/his bombardment — in a style redolent of Antony Burgess' *A Clockwork Orange*—with stereotypical images of femininity of the Hollywoodian variety. At a later stage in the narrative, the character's virtual inseparability from the realm of cinematic mirage is reinforced by Eve's assertion that in recalling her existence as Evelyn, she feels that she is merely "remembering a film ... whose performances did not concern" her (Carter 2009b, p. 89). Evelyn/Eve is thus involved in ideological games wherein reality is considered a mere by-product of textuality: having grown progressively infatuated with the star Tristessa through the mediating action of celluloid, the character then proceeds to undergo a radical psychosexual transformation via the screen itself.

Furthermore, the novel can be interpreted as an allegorical commentary on Western culture's addictive entanglement with the urge described by Jean Baudrillard as "the passion for images" (Baudrillard, p. 56). In the philosopher's analysis, as in Carter's story, the term passion invokes a semiotic carousel of ambiguity which, as intimated in Chapter 1, alludes to a hybrid amalgam of intense pain and ecstatic bliss. Carter has explicitly commented on her desire to make "the cultural production of femininity" an axial element of *The Passion of New Eve* as a whole, emphasizing the specific importance, within this project, of Hollywood's fabrication of "illusions as tangible commodities" (in Haffenden 1984, p. 36). It is also necessary to acknowledge, however, that Carter does not present her fascination with Hollywood's commodification of femininity as the sole motivating factor behind *The Passion of New Eve*, as she in fact invokes other crucial aspects of American culture and history as equally instrumental in fueling her motivation to write this book. "The novel," she has stated in an interview conducted by Olga Kenyon, "was sparked off by a visit to the USA in 1969. It was the height of the Vietnam war, with violent public demos and piles of garbage in New York streets. If you remember, it was the year of gay riots in Greenwich village, when they even chucked rocks; so my scenario of uprisings isn't all that far-fetched" (in Kenyon, p. 31).

The importance of cinema as the focal theme through which Carter endeavors to mobilize her fictional speculations regarding the dynamics of the gaze deserves special consideration, in this context. As Mulvey emphasizes, despite the fact that Carter "wrote about the cinema from the perspective of its decline, she was a child of the cinema and loved it from the time she and her father used to go to the movies in South London" (Mulvey 2007, p. 243). This assertion is confirmed by the author's own reminiscences regarding the impact of cinema on her formative years. "It seemed to me," Carter writes in her Introduction to the critical collection *Expletives Deleted*, "when I first started going to the cinema intensively in the late Fifties, that Hollywood had colonised the imagination of the entire world and was turning us all into Americans. I resented it, it fascinated me" (Carter 2006c, p. 5). Hollywood's dominance in the global imaginary is emphasized even more colorfully in a review of Robert Coover's *A Night at the Movies* included in the same volume, where Carter declares: "The American cinema was born, toddled, talked, provided the furniture for all the living-rooms, and the bedrooms, too, of the imagination of the entire world.... In the days when Hollywood bestraddled the world like a colossus, its vast, brief, insubstantial empire helped to Americanise all" (p. 131).

Carter's statement concerning her early encounter with cinema clearly points to her inclination to equate that experience with the distinctive allure of Hollywood. As it happens, there is also copious evidence throughout her writings for her interest in French cinema and particularly Godard's work, which she admires as a thought-provoking alternative to the anti-intellectualist thrust of British culture. It is nonetheless undeniable that Carter is specifically drawn to Hollywood by her keen sensitivity to that culture's idealization of a unique version of feminine splendor: a construct which she recognizes as being inseparable from refined illusionism, and from the deployment of technical stratagems meant to efface the artificiality of the illusion itself. As Mulvey puts it, such ruses have enabled Hollywood cinema to foster an effective "merging of the cinema screen and feminine masquerade," as the physical reality of the actress and the filmic machinery alike have been incrementally translated "into the insubstantial" and that material substratum has come to be "subordinated to fantasy" (Mulvey 2007, p. 243). Carter raises the bar for illusionism per se by extending Tristessa's unreality beyond the dream shared by the screen and the auditorium into the novel's extracinematic environment: the star indeed "turns out to be an illusion even in her corporeal reality" (pp. 243–244).

The dynamics of the gaze and the operations of the cinematic machine — axial components of *The Passion of New Eve* in its entirety — are thrown into relief at an early stage in the narrative by two memorable scenes. The first of these pivots on the actress Tristessa de St Ange, a legendary figure deployed by Carter to celebrate cinema's penchant for magical metamorphosis. Tristessa's beauty is held to transcend both the injuries of age and the failings of technology, as her iconic image remains enshrined in celluloid even though "the film stock was old and scratched, as if the desolating passage of time were made visible in the rain upon the screen, audible in the worn stuttering of the sound track." The star's "luminous presence," paradoxically, appears to be amplified by "these erosions of temporality" (Carter 2009b, p. 1). Although the star is a spectral, virtually bodiless entity whose skin is indistinguishable from the screen on which light beams and silvery threads are projected, Tristessa accrues the corporeal density of a simulacrum: a construct so profoundly unreal as to become, uncannily, more real than the real — i.e., hyperreal. The viewer behind these remarks is the male Evelyn, the novel's protagonist in the guise in which we first make the character's acquaintance, and his stance is entirely consonant with established patriarchal conventions. In this instance, the master of the gaze is supposed to be the spectator, with the film star as its object and the cinematic screen as the mediating agency between the two. Both the star and the spectator conflate with the cinematic apparatus itself, surrendering their identities to its material mechanisms and symbolic puissance.

The second key scene focuses on the character of Leilah as she becomes gradually "absorbed in the contemplation of the figure in the mirror" without, however, appearing "to apprehend the person in the mirror as, in any degree, herself.... Leilah invoked this formal other with a gravity and ritual that recalled witchcraft; she brought into being a Leilah who lived only in the not-world of the mirror and then became her own reflection" (p. 24). In this case, Leilah would seem to operate both as the holder and as the recipient of the gaze. It is vital to appreciate, however, that beyond the individual woman's personal perceptions, there lies the gaze of a wide-reaching impersonal force: namely, the ensemble of cultural conventions, largely of patriarchal orientation, determining what ought to be expected of female beauty and of a woman in pursuit of that goal. This idea is corroborated by Evelyn's recognition that Leilah is essentially allowing herself to act as an imaginary persona in "the erotic dream" into which the looking-glass places her — and thus incarnating the figure of "the woman watching herself being watched in a mirror" on which patriarchy has traditionally relied in order to perpetuate female self-monitoring (p. 26). These Leilah-centered scenes are vividly reminiscent of an intriguing passage from Carter's 1989 essay on the Surrealist artist Frida Kahlo. Observing Kahlo's self-portraits, the writer notes: "This is the face of a woman looking into a mirror. We cannot see the mirror but we must always remember that it was there." Like Kahlo's "paintings," Leilah's actions "are a form of self-monitoring. She watches herself watching herself" (Carter 1992b, p. 100).

Addressed in tandem, the passages devoted to Tristessa's cinematic image and to Leilah's specular image obliquely point to an underlying analogy between the screen and the mirror as the two sides of the same figural coin. Tristessa's screen is also a mirror reflecting the spectator's innermost desires. This entails a two-way process of affective exchange whereby on the one hand, the spectator projects his or her desires onto the screen while on the other, he or she absorbs the images visualizing those desires and giving them provisional satisfaction. Resorting to a psychoanalytical analogy, Christian Metz contends that the act of misrecognition by which spectators may come to regard themselves as effective initiators of the cinematic sign — that is to say, the creative agents solely responsible for its emergence into being on the screen — recalls the moment of illusory self-identification with the specular image experienced by the Lacanian infant during the mirror phase (Metz). Just as Tristessa's screen can be conceived of as a mirror of sorts, so Leilah's mirror can be thought of as a metaphorical screen onto which the subject projects her own fantasies and, beyond those private endowments, a whole culture's deeply ingrained desires. Once again, we are faced with a case of bidirectional motion, insofar as at the same time as the subject projects his or her ideal self onto the mirror, he or she simultaneously incorporates — or introjects — visual evidence for the stubborn endurance of the not-so-ideal self which he or she actually embodies.

Carter subtly blurs the distinction between the screen and the mirror in the passage where the text posits the mirror as the channel through which Evelyn/Eve has encountered Tristessa: "she came and took possession of my mirror one day when I was looking at myself. She invaded the mirror like an army with banners; she entered me through my eyes" (Carter 2009b, pp. 147–148). The reader knows full well, having been introduced to the novel's world by a detailed portrayal of Tristessa's image and its inextricability from the cinematic realm, that Evelyn/Eve has actually become increasingly engrossed with the star via the screen. The mirror and the screen thus coalesce without Carter — or her narrator(s) — having to spell out their connection. In *The Passion of New Eve*, the mirror and the screen come most memorably together in the scene where Evelyn beholds for the first time the specular confirmation of his metamorphosis. At this juncture, the looking-glass delivers an image which is both him, albeit in a reconfigured guise, and hence a residually familiar sight, and a total stranger. The very notion of self, in this context, is stripped of any possible attributes of stability and coherence it might once have claimed as its legitimate possessions to become as insubstantial as a borderline hypothesis.

As David Punter observes, the character is suddenly beset by "the wrench and dislocation which is at the heart of woman's relationship with herself in a world riddled with masculine power structures: inner self forced apart from the subject of self-presentation, an awareness of hollowness, a disbelief that this self-on-view can be taken as a full representation" (Punter 1985, p. 36). However, it is also crucial to appreciate that in this poignant scene, the mirror also functions as a metaphor for the cinematic screen: as a site in which spectators encounter at once the known and the unknown — images which are capable of corroborating the fantasies which they project onto its flickering surface, and yet inevitably induce a disorientating perception of the element of excess that refuses to be accommodated within those fantasies. As a result, just as spectators may feel inclined to indulge in the feeling of having created a whole visual universe on the basis of their innermost longings, they are jerked back into reality by the screen's triumphant assertion of the autonomy of its images as vehicles for the communication of *other* desires, *other* worlds, which spectators have not quite anticipated — let alone willed into being either consciously or unconsciously.

The image of the mirror gains incontrovertible centrality in the axial portion of the narrative as the protagonist finally gets to meet Tristessa and wistfully muses: "I went to you as towards my own face in a magnetic mirror, but when, in accordance with all the laws of physics, you came towards me, I did not feel a sense of homecoming, only the forlorn premonition of loss" (Carter 2009b, p. 107). The reflection cannot grant a sense of conclusive fulfillment. In fact, it is ultimately destined to act as a harsh reminder of the inevitability of separation, disconnection and bereavement. Beholding its illusory plenitude, we seek confirmation of our own solidity but only find evidence for a splitting between subject and object which in turn replicates our internal — and incurable — self-divisions. Relatedly, Tristessa's legendary mansion itself is a tiered house of glass: this descriptive element constitutes a perfect complement for the novel's mirror-centered imagery while also providing, as Carter has stressed, "an image of a certain kind of psychic vulnerability" (in Haffenden, 1984, p. 36). Moreover, the novel's employment of the trope of specularity as a means of symbolizing the fragmentation of identity into irreconcilable shreds is sensationally reinforced by the scene in which the entire house disintegrates into a cascade of glittering slivers, chunks of once beautiful furnishings and the limbs of myriad waxworks representing Hollywood's dead idols. The latter could be seen to symbolize, like the motley body parts in Mary Shelley's *Frankenstein*, the *disjecta membra* of a whole culture and hence to operate as a memorable metaphor for the explosion not only of the individual self but also of the wider ideological formation of which it is a member.

The double movement of projection and introjection alluded to by the analogy between screen and mirror can be read as a correlative for the concurrently spatial and temporal trajectory followed by Evelyn/Eve throughout *The Passion of New Eve*. This constitutes, on the structural plane, one of the novel's most intriguing aspects. On the one hand, the protagonist progresses from New York City to California in a journey that could be seen to mimic the wave of westward expansion associated with American history and the classic myth of the Frontier as a simultaneously geographical and symbolic goal. On the other hand, the character regresses from the postapocalyptic here-and-now to the ancestral prehistory of humanity where the most potent modern mythologies find inception. These two dimensions of Evelyn/Eve's experience are brought together by the expression "Welcome to anteriority" (Carter 2009b, p. 163). As Scott Dimovitz argues, this stands out as "a curious phrase, and it highlights two primary features of Carter's narrative technique in *New Eve*. First, *welcome* implies the arrival in space from one location to another; yet *anteriority* plays upon the doubling of its spatial meaning of the 'front' of an organism with the temporal definition of 'earlier, prior to'" (Dimovitz, p. 101).

The novel's ending subtly elaborates this idea, suggesting that both connotations of anteriority come together as Eve moves forward into a new physical space and, by symbolic implication, into fresh opportunities for self-exploration and discovery, yet concomitantly reverts to a primordial reality associated with "the sombre and grandiose sea" (Carter 2009b, p. 186) — "the sea, which washes away all memory and retains it" (p. 182) This archetypal image is intensely redolent of James Joyce's description of the sea as "our great sweet mother" (Joyce 1922). This double act signals a far more authentic moment of rebirth for Carter's androgynous protagonist than her technosurgical reconstruction by Mother since the self-appointed deity is only, after all, a fabrication that could never truly presume to achieve the endlessly mutating, adaptive and sustaining capacities held by the natural environment. Accordingly, the moment of regeneration described above differs starkly from the theatrical birth, experienced by Eve earlier in the story, from the artificial womb of a flesh-walled cave symbolic of Mother. In fact, Eve's climactic embrace of the sea could be regarded as a birth not so much *from* as *into* Nature — and its promises.

In the area of characterization, Carter's demythologizing mission relies to a vital degree on strategies of graphic magnification and rhetorical exaggeration of major mythological motifs aiming to throw into relief their latently grotesque, perverse or otherwise absurd character. This project is blatantly sustained by the portrayal of Zero. A darkly amusing incarnation of the stereotypical patriarch, Zero strives to overcompensate for his multiple physical impairments — he is one eyed, one-legged and impotent — by nourishing grand aspirations of Wagnerian and Nietzschean orientation. At the same time, Leilah offers an intriguing bundle of stereotypes. Leilah, notably, doubles up as Lilith, Adam's first wife. As Robert Graves and Raphael Patai explain, this figure — the actual first woman — is reputed to have been molded out of "filth and sediment instead of pure dust" (Graves and Patai, p. 65) and to have forsaken her spouse because, considering herself his equal, she would not lie beneath him during sexual intercourse. The text repeatedly underscores Leilah/Lilith's status as an incarnation of the exotic Other — defining her as "magnificent" in a fashion redolent of Joseph Conrad's description of Kurtz's mistress in *Heart of Darkness*, and comparing her to all manner of outlandish figures, including a "siren," a "witching fox in a dark wood" (Carter 2009b, p. 16) and a "mermaid" (p. 18).

It is with the depiction of the great Mother that Carter enjoys her most adventurous foray into the domain of literary caricature. This character stands out as an embodiment of virtually every maternal figure, chthonic archetypes included, ever recorded — e.g., Cybele, Danäe, Gaea, Kali and Jocasta. In invoking such venerable mythological personages, Carter is not simply playing some clever intertextual game. In fact, she is above all endeavoring to fathom the extent to which such idols serve to fuels the myths — toward which she harbors an especially marked abhorrence — that only pretend to glorify the female principle in order to cover up and finally legitimize its cultural marginalization. Women themselves, Carter avers, have been complicit with this duplicitous ideological program.

The brand of radical feminism keen on fostering utopian idealizations of womanhood by rejecting tout court all things male is as objectionable, in Carter's perspective, as the most intolerant form of chauvinism. This message is elaborated as follows in *The Sadeian Woman*: "If women allow themselves to be consoled for their culturally determined lack of access to the modes of intellectual debate by the invocation of hypothetical great goddesses," we are warned, "they are simply flattering themselves into submission.... All the mythic versions of women, from the myth of the redeeming purity of the virgin to that of the healing, reconciling mother, are consolatory nonsenses.... Mother goddesses are just as silly a notion as father gods. If a revival of the myths of these cults gives women emotional satisfaction, it does so at the price of obscuring the real conditions of life. This is why they were invented in the first place" (Carter 1979, p. 5). Ironically, given her mythical association with life's primordial substratum, Mother is actually a freakish mélange of natural and technological ingredients: far from embodying the essence of either Nature or the Earth, she merely constitutes the "abstraction of a natural principle" (Carter 2009b, p. 46).

Portrayed as the "Castratrix of the Phallocentric Universe" (p. 64), Mother faithfully encapsulates Mikhail Bakhtin's association of the grotesque with both positive and negative impulses. On the one hand, she typifies the notion of carnivalesque excess in a brightly playful manner by suggesting not so much a person as a "wild anatomical fantasy" (Bakhtin 1984, p. 345): a utopian icon capable of subverting all sorts of patriarchal expectations concerning feminine beauty. In this regard, the character could be said to reflect the grotesque's optimistic side, by glorying in the aesthetic feast of "degradation" as a salutary "lowering of all that is high, spiritual, ideal, abstract ... to the material level" (p. 19). On the other hand, Mother's endowment with repulsive sow-like tiers of nipples and a bovine neck draws attention to the darker connotations of the grotesque. At this level, Mother's monstrosity resonates with Bakhtin's observations regarding the darker side of the grotesque as the embodiment of inhumanity, alienation, disgust and rejection. This aspect of the discourse, integral to Evelyn's initial reaction to Mother as an aberration, is replicated by his instinctive perception of his reconfigured body as an object of revulsion. Tristessa experiences a comparably dislocating sensation in response to the forced redefinition of his own sexual identity, which takes place when his female attire is wrenched away from him, and he is obliged to take cognizance of his concealed male genitals. What is brutally unhinged in these scenes is not only a character's perception of his or her gender status but also any existential certitude on the basis of which he or she might defend the self's integrity, coherence and ultimate veracity.

Carter's mixed attitude to Hollywood cinema is replicated in *The Passion of New Eve* by the images of the composite, the hybrid and the androgynous — by the man disguised as a woman who is also a specular reflection of the man reconfigured as a woman — as potent metaphors for the coalescence of two identity variations into one entity or, just as feasibly, the splitting of singularity into duality. Carter's investigation of androgyny, specifically, reaches its apotheosis as Eve, as a biological male technologically reconfigured as a woman, and Tristessa, as a male transvestite who has ironically come to be known as the most alluring woman on the planet, are joined in a parodical wedding rite, and flee together into the desert to dwell briefly in the "oasis" of their passion (Carter 2009b, p. 144). It is here that Eve is impregnated with new life and, by implication, the promise of hopeful beginnings. In full consonance with Carter's iconoclastic proclivities, the text displaces the image of the luscious garden with which conventional iconography tends to associate the mythical figure of Eve to elect a desolate wasteland as its preferred setting.

At this point, the text's contemplation of androgyny transcends the boundaries of both the discursive present in which it is being read and the dystopian future in which its story is set to soar into the ether of myth and its downtrodden utopias. Eve's reminiscences drive home such passion and sadness, in this regard, that they have the power to reverberate throughout the entire novel: "we peopled this immemorial loneliness with all we had been, or had been, or had dreamed of being, or had thought we were ... aspects of being ... that seemed, during our embraces, to be the very essence of our selves; the concentrated essence of being, as if, out of these fathomless kisses and our interpenetrating, undifferentiated sex, we had made the great Platonic hermaphrodite together" (pp. 144–145). The experiences imposed upon both Evelyn/Eve and Tristessa by the exposure of sexual identities alien to their spontaneous propensities would seem to belong to the somber end of the grotesque's spectrum as theorized by Bakhtin. Their eventual union, conversely, could be said to exemplify its jubilant and life-affirming dimension. Intriguingly, the image of Plato's hermaphrodite is also invoked by Rabelais with the symbol worn by Gargantua in *Gargantua and Pantagruel,* a key part of Bakhtin's own object of study as the epitome of carnival subversiveness.

However, the ephemerality of the idyll enjoyed by Carter's characters in the desert invests it with an aura of wistfulness and regret that ultimately emphasizes the grotesque's graver connotations. This approach is quite congruous, after all, with the fate visited upon the perfect hermaphrodite by Classical mythology, which was to be split in half by Zeus, and by the doleful task endured by each human ever since: an anxious and unappeasable search for his or her missing half. This melancholy tale is echoed by the novel's own nostalgic strain: a feature of its drama which proceeds largely from its filmic identifications. As we have seen, *The Passion of New Eve* is undoubtedly indebted to Hollywood's ideology in the elaboration of its cinematic imagery. Nevertheless, as Kate Webb suggests, it also lends itself to comparison with Marcel Carné's *Les Enfants du Paradis*, which Carter is held to have greatly cherished. Invoking the writer's own enthusiastic assessment of that work, Webb notes: "'It is the definitive film about romanticism ... in which it always seems possible to jump through the screen ... and live there, in a state of luminous anguish.' This fantasy of crossing over — and cinema's state of longing, its ingrained nostalgia for somewhere else — is explored in Carter's picaresque fantasy of the New World" (Webb).

The approach to the politics and psychology of gender adopted by Carter in *The Passion of New Eve* finds a notable correlative in the debate on sexual diversity initiated by queer theory. Seeking to foreground the multiplicity and diversity of sexual and gender identities, queer theory invites acknowledgment of pleasures not previously recognized or permitted. Its primary target is the rigidly binary classification of sexual identities and proclivities in terms of the hetero-homo opposition: a despotic formula deployed by patriarchal cultures, as Cheryl Smyth stresses, as a way of "annihilating the spectrum of sexualities that exist" (Smyth, p. 20). Insofar as sexual practices never unfold in some metaphysical void but are actually embroiled with the political and cultural realities of racial discrimination, economic inequality and educational ghettoization, sexualities can only be properly understood in relation to the broader milieux in which their own distinctive manifestations and those pressing realities coexist at all times. The concept of transgender, so pivotal to *The Passion of New Eve*, plays a particularly important role in queer theory. In this context, a transgenderist is neither a transvestite nor a transsexual and is not, therefore, defined by either cross-dressing or a sex change accomplished by recourse to medical technology. In fact, this type of individual transits fluidly across conventional gender boundaries — even, at times, in defiance of established erotic preferences — and enacts plural roles bolstered by disparate identity narratives.

A germane critical perspective of even greater relevance to *The Passion of New Eve* is Hélène Cixous' contention that the analysis of sexual desire requires a radical reevaluation of the concept of bisexuality. Resorting to psychoanalytical theory, Cixous argues that this idea has been conventionally held to designate the state of "a complete being, which replaces the fear of castration," thus keeping at bay the threat of woman as forbidding other. The mythicized bisexual entity described by Cixous is supposed to embody "a fantasy of unity" whose purpose is to erase all obvious vestiges of sexual difference — and thus efface the ongoing possibility of conflict to which sexual difference might give rise. Cixous drastically rejects the notion of bisexuality as a means of eradicating diversity, seeking instead to affirm the neglected, and indeed abhorred, value of difference. Relatedly, the critic ushers in the notion of an "*other bisexuality*" (Cixous and Clément, p. 84) able to facilitate the dissemination of heterogeneous expressions of *jouissance* and hence foster, as Toril Moi emphasizes, a sexuality that is "multiple, variable and ever-changing" (Moi, p. 109) — a sexuality precisely of the kind promoted by *The Passion of New Eve*. The scenario painted by Cixous in an evocatively luxuriant and stage-oriented register akin to Carter's own discourse is one in which "every subject, who is not shut up within the spurious Phallocentric Performing Theatre, sets up his or her erotic universe. Bisexuality — that is to say the location within oneself of the presence of both sexes, evident and insistent in different ways according to the individual, the nonexclusion of difference or of a sex, and starting with this 'permission' one gives oneself, the multiplication of the effects of desire's inscription on every part of the body and the other body" (Cixous and Clément, p. 85).

Carter's protagonist provides a perfect incarnation of Cixous' bisexual subject since her/his body and personality combine feminine and masculine characteristics both before and after the futuristically intrusive intervention of technology. Thus, Evelyn is said to exhibit somatic traits and a distinctive type of beauty that would be conventionally associated with femininity, whereas Eve occasionally evinces elements of both speech and body language that could be considered masculine. Aware of her marginal extravagance, she strives to mimic properly "feminine manners" — to *act* as a woman instead of simply *being* one. It is at this point that she fully realizes the extent to which "many women born spend their whole lives in just such imitations" (Carter 2009b, p. 97).

In *The Passion of New Eve* — and indeed across her entire output — Carter assiduously reminds us that honest dedication to the creative pluralization of sexual and gender identities, which entails a concomitant expansion of the forms of desire and pleasure potentially available to members of *all* sexes, asks us to take a questioning stance not solely toward the projects of homogenization promoted by phallocentric societies, whose principal goal is the definition of femininity as defective and errant, but also toward feminist glorifications of womanhood based on equally dogmatic generalizations. This problem is thrown into relief by Julia Kristeva in "Women's Time," where the history of modern feminism in the West is subjected to a dispassionate anatomy so as to expose the ideological perils lurking within woman's idealization as a quasi-religious ideal. The program of self-idealization pursued by Carter's Mother and her cohorts instantly springs to mind as a perfect illustration of the pernicious trends exposed by Kristeva. A fruitful alternative suggested by both Carter and Kristeva consists of a mature appropriation of the principle of difference, and a willingness to extend its conventional import to propose that each human being is fundamentally different and, as a result, that there are as many sexual and gender identities as there people.

Also relevant to Carter's engagement with issues of gender and sex-uality — and indeed to her recurrent concern with the ubiquity of specta-cle — is Judith Butler's notion of gender as a performative phenomenon. Gender, argues Butler in *Gender Trouble* (1990), is not simply a cultural construct but also a type of performance centered on the assumption and display of specific signs and on the ritualized reiteration of a certain reper-toire of conventional acts. Any sense of coherence or stability which the self might presume to achieve can only ever be a product of the repetition of particular forms of role-playing. "There is no gender identity behind the expressions of gender," argues Butler, insofar as "identity is performa-tively constituted by the very 'expressions' that are said to be its results" (Butler 1990, p. 25). This audacious inversion of traditional causality echoes Carter's own interrogation of the unexamined premises on which classical logic lamentably thrives for the purpose of perpetuating the status quo by ossifying its discursive options. Since all gender categories entail the possibility of diverse types of performance, it is ultimately absurd to defend the essentialist notion of gender identity as an ontological given. Far more constructive, according to Butler, is the conception of gender identity as "a history of identifications, parts of which can be brought into play in given contexts and which, precisely because they encode the con-tingencies of personal history, do not always point back to an internal coherence of any kind" (p. 331).

In *Bodies That Matter* (1993), Butler both expands and redefines her initial perspective on gender performativity in ways which strike even more vibrant chords with *The Passion of New Eve*. This text indeed concentrates on the practices through which the hegemony of heterosexuality comes to constitute the very matter that forms our bodies and gives shape to our genders and sexualities. Reflecting on the work, Butler has described her aims as follows: "One of the interpretations that has been made of *Gender Trouble* is that ... if gender is performative it must be radically free. And it has seemed to many that the materiality of the body is vacated or ignored or negated here — disavowed, even.... So what became important to me in writing *Bodies that Matter* was to go back to the category of sex, and to the problem of materiality, and to ask how it is that sex itself might be construed as a norm.... I wanted to work out how a norm actually materialises a body, how we might understand the materiality of the body to be not only invested with a norm, but in some sense animated by a norm, or contoured by a norm" (Butler 1994). The visible metamorphoses undergone by both Evelyn/Eve and Tristessa as they switch their gender identities and their sexual appearances, and accordingly adopt different roles within their personal relationships, could be seen as chapters of the type of mobile history which Butler posits as integral to identity formation in *Gender Trouble*.

At the same time, the intensely material quality of both characters' genders and sexualities can be read as an invitation to ponder the processes through which abstract principles assume palpable density, and through which biology becomes intertwined with ideology. In this regard, the project pursued by Carter in *The Passion of New Eve* could be said to parallel the enterprise embarked upon by Butler in *Bodies That Matter*. Furthermore, the spurious ideology promulgated by Mother and her entourage is posited as a force literally capable of constructing specific bodies according to precise technical specifications. Similarly, Zero's tyrannical regime perpetuates itself through the fashioning of distinctive corporeal identities. Mother's followers are prepared to accept the myth of the technologically sophisticated and antiphallocentric Beulah without hesitation. Zero's wives, likewise, implicitly condone their oppressor's abusive violence by wallowing in their own humiliating fantasies. Though widely different, both systems derive their power to translate abstract principles into bodily matter from their subjects' unquestioning deification of their matriarchal or patriarchal leaders.

On both counts, we are continually reminded that identity and textuality, selfhood and storytelling, psychosomatic evolution and narrative emplotment, never part company for long (if at all) in Carter's world. Gender, *The Passion of New Eve* insistently and flamboyantly reminds us, does not ensue from a set of unequivocal bodily attributes but rather results from a synthetic ensemble of narrative effects which render the physical body practically inseparable from the costumes, both literal and figurative, with which it progressively comes into contact. As noted in Chapter 2 in relation to *The Magic Toyshop*, Carter is evidently drawn to the almost magical properties of apparel as an integral component of identity. In *The Passion of New Eve*, she seeks to portray this idea in an elegantly choreographed theatrical style with the sequences in which Leilah journeys through the maze-like web of New York streets discarding items of clothing for Evelyn to collect: these are presented not as mere supplements to Leilah's body but rather as defining aspects of her person, contributing vitally to the assertion and evolution of her identity and, at the same time, punctuating the progressive burgeoning of Evelyn's desire as though it were a fragrant petal-filled rose growing intoxicated by its own scent. The importance of clothes as a critical part of the performances through which identity is constructed and communicated is again foregrounded by Eve's reflections on her past as Evelyn as she notes that her recollections of that time do not fit her any longer, as though "they were old clothes belonging to somebody else no longer living" (Carter 2009b, p. 89).

Carter returns to the theme of Hollywood's fabrication of femininity — the creation of immortal beauty that can "exist almost and only in the eye of the beholder" (Carter 2006e, p. 373) — in the spooky short story "The Merchant of Shadows": one of the most vertiginously captivating components of the collection *American Ghosts and Old World Wonders*. The tale's protagonist is an unnamed film student from London who decides to embark on a "pilgrimage" to the "Holy Grail" of Hollywood (p. 363) in order to unearth the truth about Hank Mann, a German expatriate and legendary director born Heinrich Mannheim active in pre-war Hollywood and reputed to have killed himself in 1940. Pursuing his scholarly goal for the benefit of his thesis, the student gets to meet not only Mann's widow, a star "dubbed by *Time* magazine the 'Spirit of the Cinema,'" but also her weird sister, who incongruously resembles a "superannuated lumberjack," and their pet lion Leo, once the star of the MGM movie logo and now a "geriatric feline" (p. 369). The late Mann himself comes across as a composite persona: a less sensational but no less intriguing variation on the theme of hybridity immortalized by Carter in both *The Passion of New Eve* specifically and her opus at large by recourse to all manner of chimerical, androgynous and fabulous creatures. As Webb points out, the elusive figure of "Hank Mann is clearly not Anthony Mann, director of

Westerns" but rather encompasses varyingly cryptic allusions to "Erich von Stroheim — the famously sadistic director Carter reprised in *Wise Children*...; Josef von Sternberg — who directed Dietrich in *The Blue Angel*, the German precursor of endless cross-dressing turns in Hollywood; and Heinrich Mann ... who himself washed up in California in 1940 with what was left of Germany's intelligentsia" (Webb).

Carter's protagonist is rapidly confronted with the creepiest distillation of latently malevolent uncanniness he could ever have presumed to encounter in even the most Gothic of his revelries. Enmeshed in a martini-soaked environment that resembles just a bit *too* closely the setting of some classic movie (and especially *Sunset Boulevard*), the youth is faced with an ancient star who appears to have spent several days or even weeks preparing for the interview, and to be hell-bent on having him play the part of a passive gigolo in the presence of a screen goddess. Needless to say, his desire for truth is mockingly frustrated and the entire experience leaves him feeling quite disappointed and unanchored in the grip of an alien culture. The protagonists of many of the fairy tales so dear to Carter's heart frequently misrecognize or simply fail to realize the causes of their distress as a result of their reckless interpretation of the clues at their disposal. The pathetic protagonist of "The Merchant of Shadows" resembles those traditional figures insofar as he neglects a clue thrown in his path by "the second Mrs Mann, now a retired office cleaner" though "once a starlet," as she invites him to purchase an old "spanking pic" in which the director can be seen wearing a "gym slip, suspenders and black silk stockings." In rejecting the offer in the belief that such an image "wouldn't add much to the history of film," the student does not pause to reflect on Mann's appetite for cross-dressing. In fact, this is a vital aspect of the legendary director's personality and hence holds the key to the secret which the protagonist so avidly seeks.

As it turns out, Mann's passion for self-metamorphosis, having grown to manic extremes over time, eventually led him to become the female star he had so studiously constructed for the screen, and to impersonate her so well as to actually become "a better she than she herself had ever been" (Carter 2006e, p. 375). Carter's text also hints in an elliptical fashion at the ageing star's unreality when her sister (who is, in fact, the star herself stripped of her erstwhile feminine mystique) declares that audiences "wore away her face by looking at it so much," and that "a new one" therefore had to be made for her (p. 372). The student, once again, neglects to ponder the implications of this bizarre statement and readers, too, will feasibly not grasp its full import until the end of the story. The focal point upon which the messages promulgated by both *The Passion of New Eve* and "The Merchant of Shadows" converge pertains to the very essence of Hollywood glamour. The argument pursued by Carter in both texts, Webb maintains, is that "Hollywood brought about the final denaturing of femininity in Western civilization because its eroticism was built upon the allure of the fake. The movie stars who inspired Tristessa were so manifestly queens of artifice, creatures of dream and design, they flaunted an idea only previously rumoured in books — that femininity itself was a drag act" (Webb).

As shown in Chapter 2, Carter has repeatedly invoked the image of the Baudelairean albatross in her fiction. In the cinematically disposed context of *The Passion of New Eve*, the writer herself would seem to have deliberately chosen to embody the iconic figure and, in that guise, to have hitched a glide over the swells of the unknown — a restless "ocean" that appears, as she puts in "The Merchant of Shadows," to have eternally "shattered its foamy peripheries with the sound of a thousand distant cinema organs," and "shushed and tittered like an audience when the lights dim before the main feature" and "(Carter 2006e, p. 363). In this arcane expanse, the mysteries of sexual and gender identities come to epitomize the most unfathomable conundrums with which humanity has had to contend for time immemorial and — Carter's futuristic vision suggests — may have to go on grappling for centuries to come.

CHAPTER 5

Tradition Reimagined

The Bloody Chamber and Other Stories

[Carter's] main concern is not to show us how the exact same story appears different based on what a fallible narrator perceived; rather, she longs to show us how variable and seemingly similar stories are in the first place.

— Rick Amburgey

The whole fauna of human fantasies, their marine vegetation, drifts and luxuriates in the dimly lit zones of human activity, as though plaiting thick tresses of darkness. Here, too, appear the lighthouses of the mind, with their outward resemblance to less pure symbols. The gateway to mystery swings open at the touch of human weakness and we have entered the realms of darkness. One false step, one slurred syllable together reveal a man's thoughts.

— Louis Aragon

In his introduction to Carter's *Collected Short Stories*, Salman Rushdie states that "*The Bloody Chamber* is Carter's masterwork: the book in which her high, perfervid mode is perfectly married to her stories' needs" (in Carter 2006d, p. xi). There can be little doubt that the spark-breathing prodigy of polychromous fleece and protean anatomy that is Carter's revision of the classic fairy tale yields an unsurpassed synthesis of the writer's most distinctive powers. Alternately outlandish and prosaic, sophisticated and crude, bejeweled and raucous, Carter's fairy tales repeatedly bring to the fore her inexhaustible appetite for the multifarious and the hybrid. At the same time, they also attest to her knack of alchemically joining the fanciful and the political. More often than not, these proclivities manifest themselves in the guise of a concomitantly languid and high-spirited eroticism soaked in the shadows of "the lumber room of the Western European imagination"—as Carter herself describes the verbal and visual repertoire on which her fairy tales draw (in Kenyon, p. 29). With her articulation of this enticingly dusky narrative discourse, the author is able to call attention to the most pointedly corporeal dimension of the fairy tale tradition, and thus "shatter pure and evocative imagery with the crude" so as to remind us that "there's a materiality to symbols and a materiality to imaginative life which should be taken quite seriously" (p. 33).

On the more sensational plane, Carter's fairy tales bear witness to the writer's fascination with materiality by means of stories that throw into relief with no dearth of corporeal details the countless longings and perils lurking within sexual liaisons of both familiar and bizarre kinds. There are numerous occasions, however, when Carter prefers to lay emphasis on the bodily and sensuous qualities of experience and language alike by recourse to subtle descriptive touches. A perfect example is provided by the register associated with the titular tale's heroine, whereby attention is consistently drawn to the character's temperament as a being of sensations. From the early stages in the narrative, Carter's latter-day Beauty is seen to relish the specifically physical dimension of her feelings—for instance, the "tender, delicious ecstasy of excitement" she experiences during her journey, as her "burning cheek" rests "against the impeccable linen of the pillow" (Carter 2006d, p. 111); the touch of the alarmingly animate "satin nightdress" which seems to stroke her virginal body in an "egregious, insinuating" fashion, "nudging between [her] thighs" as she moves; the "whiff of the opulent male scent of leather and spices" issuing from her spouse (p. 112).

Ultimately, in the dramatization of both their spectacular and their sedate moments, Carter's fairy tales proclaim most eloquently their unique significance within her oeuvre through the sheer dexterity with which they mingle expert knowledge and playfulness, sharp intelligence and wild fabulation, in a phantasmagoric carousel of unique energy. In this regard, the tales echo the writings of Charles Baudelaire more closely than any of Carter's other influences. As mentioned in Chapter 2, the French poet and his mistress Jeanne Duval are central to the short story "Black Venus," the titular piece in a collection published in 1985 (a.k.a. *Saints and Strangers*).

Despite its overt, self-conscious and, at times, even deliberately theatrical fictionalization of its literary historical cast and epoch, the story as a whole is especially significant in the framework of Carter's opus insofar as it exudes a quintessentially Baudelairean atmosphere. In so doing, it does not operate simply as an exercise in allusory antiquarianism — a revisionist trend in which Carter holds scarce interest anyway — but rather yields a forceful testimony to Carter's own sensibility and, most importantly, to what it specifically shares with Baudelaire's world view. In this context, Paul Valéry's description of this distinctive perspective deserves particular notice since, in providing a splendid assessment of Baudelaire's own effort, it indirectly throws light on Carter's philosophy as well.

"Critical intelligence associated with poetic proficiency" is the key to Baudelaire's unique power, according to Valéry. A "sensual and exacting" personality by nature, Baudelaire was spontaneously inclined to engage in "the most delicate formal experiments; but these gifts would doubtless have made him merely a rival to Gautier or an excellent Parisian artist, had his mental curiosity not led him to the discovery of a new intellectual world in the works of Edgar Allan Poe." Central to Valéry's portrayal, therefore, is a unique synthesis of sensuality and rigor, allied to a hearty appetite for formal experimentation and an undying intellectual inquisitiveness: the proclivities leading Carter, like Baudelaire himself, to Poe's sparklingly dark intellect. For Baudelaire and Carter alike, Poe comes to represent the ultimate incarnation of a striving for the supreme wizardly fusion of fantasy and thought, fabulation and cerebration. Poe is "a demon of lucidity," as Valéry puts it, "a genius of analysis and an inventor of the newest, most seductive combinations of logic and imagination, of mysticism and calculation, a psychologist of the exceptional, a literary engineer who studies and utilized the resources of art" (Valéry, p. 8). This is precisely the sensibility to which *The Bloody Chamber and Other Stories* unremittingly aspires with equal measures of pathos and grace from start to finish.

In approaching the fairy tale as a narrative universe, body of scholarship and, most importantly, interpretative challenge and material for creative reconceptualization, Carter will have had to confront a number of critical issues. The most conspicuous of these concerns the rambling and haphazardly recorded history of that form, which Carter indubitably recognizes as the prime trigger of its unique adaptability, pliability and versatility: the very qualities which render the fairy tale amenable to incessant metamorphosis and repositioning by other forms. One of the main reasons for that haziness is that the fairy tale as a form includes both orally disseminated narratives, supposedly attributable to anonymous and collective authorship, and literary texts with named individual authors, and that only the written variety is actually available for inspection and methodical investigation through scholarly lenses. Nevertheless, oral and written stories have promiscuously exchanged their yarns, themes and imagery with one another for time immemorial both within the scope of singular societies and across disparate cultural terrains.

As oral and literary traditions have evolved over the centuries, the fairy tale has increasingly thriven on the principle of heterogeneity, straddling numerous branches of literature and cultural history. Carter's stories bear witness to this phenomenon of structural cross-pollination insofar as her fairy tale materials are consistently integrated with elements drawn from other fields and discourses. As Sarah Gamble points out, these disparate "voices" attest to "Carter's tendency not just to rewrite or adapt such traditional narratives but to combine them with other outlawed, disreputable, or 'minor' literary forms." These include both classic folkloric matter and genres as problematic as "vampire narratives" and "pornographic texts" (Gamble 2008, p. 21). In addition, Lorna Sage reminds us, Carter's depiction of some of her more "passive" female characters is indebted to the Gothic tradition and to science fiction, genres which the writer "has always played with" (Sage 2001, p. 68).

In addition, the striking variety of approaches and styles invoked by Carter in her handling of the fairy tale consistently throws into relief this form's penchant to manifest itself virtually all over the world by recourse to archetypal tropes and motifs. Accordingly, Carter seeks to engage — both playfully and critically — not just with the development of the fairy tale tradition as such but also with the transcultural dialogue involving disparate societies in the transmission and appropriation of particular narrative components. At the same time, she obliquely prompts us to consider the degree to which this interaction might be deemed the result of an intentionally pursued plan and the extent to which fairy tales might, on the contrary, have accumulated in an accretional manner as an offshoot of the recurrent use of materials gleaned from random encounters (either among separate milieux or else of one specific civilization with a communal tradition or consciousness). Furthermore, Carter's tendency to amalgamate her fairy tale materials with ingredients derived from other genres evinces her critical awareness of the fairy tale's penchant for vivacious interplay with cognate expressions of the collective imaginary: especially, myths and legends (both with and without a foundation in historical actuality). Carter is aware that the fairy tale's imbrication with such stories has inevitably problematized the task of demarcating its generic territory and temporal scope.

Simultaneously, Carter is only too keen to join the ranks of the writers who have underscored the vital need to disassociate the fairy tale per se from the figure of the fairy. An especially eloquent proponent of this contention is J. R. R. Tolkien, who maintains that "fairy-stories are not in normal English usage stories about fairies or elves, but stories about Fairy, that is Faërie, the realm or state in which fairies have their being. Faërie contains many things besides elves and fays, and besides dwarfs, witches, trolls, giants, or dragons: it holds the seas, the sun, the moon, the sky; and the earth, and all things that are in it: tree and bird, water and stone, wine and bread, and ourselves, mortal men, when we are enchanted." By severing Faërie from the fabulous creatures reputed to inhabit it, Tolkien feels justly entitled to argue that any sensible "definition of a fairy-story — what it is, or what it should be — does not, then, depend on any definition or historical account of elf or fairy, but upon the nature of Faërie: the Perilous Realm itself, and the air that blows in that country.... Faërie cannot be caught in a net of words; for it is one of its qualities to be indescribable, though not imperceptible. It has many ingredients, but analysis will not necessarily discover the secret of the whole.... Faërie itself may perhaps most nearly be translated by Magic — but it is magic of a peculiar mood and power, at the furthest pole from the vulgar devices of the laborious, scientific, magician. There is one proviso: if there is any satire present in the tale, one thing must not be made fun of, the magic itself. That must in that story be taken seriously, neither laughed at nor explained away" (Tolkien).

Carter's fairy tales are direct heirs of Tolkien's poetic legacy. The "nature of Faërie" itself is precisely the dimension on which Carter capitalizes to evoke her distinctive fairy tale universe. In order to do her fabulistic vision the justice it deserves, it is indeed important to recognize that her characters (both those she overtly brings into play and many others pressing to enter the pages from the wings like impatient but secondary actors) gain credible personalities from their painstaking situation in apposite worlds. These are typically intended either to harmonize or to clash with the actors' individual drives and desires in the service of varying dramatic effects. Rushdie rightly identifies two principal locations as Carter's most distinctive fairy tale settings: "the fable-world" of the "sensual, malevolent forest" and "the bleak upland village" in which "wolves howl" and "many metamorphoses" take place, on the one hand, and "the fairground, the world of the gimcrack showman, the hypnotist, the trickster, the puppeteer" (in Carter 2006d, p. xi). However seemingly different, these two reality levels interact continually in the galaxy of Carter's fairy tales to evoke the unresolved — and unresolvable — tension between the sinister and the ludic, the ominous and the merry. On a broader plane, it could be argued that Carter's personal configuration of Faërie pivots on a rebellious dismissal of conventional spatial and geographical markers. This gesture serves to expose humanity's puniness in the face of realities that mock its comprehension — let alone its chances of dominance. At the same time, it unsentimentally urges us to recognize that there are places, both actual and hypothetical, which we are simply powerless to name and, in fact, should not even *attempt to* name. Were we to indulge in the naming game for which our species holds such a dubious reputation, we would be ignoring Faërie's key qualities and, paradoxically, would alienate ourselves conclusively from any hope of even approximating its mystery and its shadowy beauty.

The phrase "fairy tale" itself represents a relatively recent addition to literary discourse, having supposedly been coined in 1697 by the French fairy tale author Madame d'Aulnoy (Marie-Catherine Le Jumel de Barneville, Baroness d'Aulnoy, a.k.a. Countess d'Aulnoy, 1650/1651–1705) with the term *conte de fées*. Madame d'Aulnoy is arguably the most famous among the learned and talented women of the French aristocracy who began to gather within the *salons* of their private residences in the 1630s in order to engage in organized intellectual debates about artistic and literary matters, as well as discussions led by more pragmatic purposes on the subjects of love, married life and etiquette. Collectively known as *Les Précieuses*, these cenacles of witty ladies were drawn to the tales of wonder and magic with which they had grown up as sources of inspiration for the creation and publication of exceptionally refined narrative experiments. Frequently extensive and imbued with complicated plot developments, these narratives' "glitter and artificiality," as Elizabeth W. Harries describes their principal formal attributes, were deliberate ruses meant to "contest the emerging association of fairy tales with the primitive" (Harries, p. 153).

The *conte de fées* supplied their promoters with an ideal instrument for appraising the dominant structures of their society, and of passing judgment on their oppressiveness. The conditions of women and the dire repercussions of absolutism and iniquitous fiscal laws on virtually all strata of the population except the overprivileged few were among the key issues addressed by the *salonnières*.

Although the cocktail of humor, sparkle and horror delivered by Carter's fairy tales is undoubtedly a fruit of her individual imagination, *The Bloody Chamber and Other Stories* is in many ways indebted to the techniques ushered in by *Les Précieuses* in eighteenth-century France. Carter's consistent employment of self-reflexive tropes, in particular, is not a predilection she shares solely with postmodernist metafiction. In fact, it echoes directly one of the principal stylistic features of *contes de fées* themselves since, as Harries points out, these texts often included "self-conscious commentaries on themselves and on the genre [they were] part of" which served as thought-provoking "fairy tales about fairy tales" (p. 161). Marina Warner traces an intriguing connection between the creative enterprise undertaken by *Les Précieuses* and Carter's own engagement with the fairy tale tradition, outlining a historical trajectory which extends from the character of "the prophesying enchantress" immortalized by "the tradition of the Sibyls," through figures such as "the jolly old beldame," "Mother Goose" and "the élite *salonnière* in the old régime," right "to Angela Carter in our time" (Warner 1995, p. xx).

Whereas the phrase *conte de fées* designates a well-delimited range of narratives of a kind which many contemporary readers would instinctively identify as fairy tales, the Brothers Grimm's collected stories, published under the title of *Kinder und Hausmärchen*— i.e., *Children's and Household Tales*— in 1812, 1814 and 1822 (Grimm), evince a highly inclusive understanding of the term *Märchen*. This, as the Grimms' *Deutsches Wörterbuch* (*German Dictionary*, 1852–1960) explains, is the diminutive form of the word *Mär*, which simply means "fictional tale" (Goldberg, p. 407). Within this category, the Grimms accordingly incorporated a striking range of texts — from tales of wonder and magic to medieval moral parables, from saints' legends to animal fables — thus bringing into existence what Linda Dégh aptly describes as the "most complete [and] representative collection of miscellaneous narratives" obtainable in their days (Dégh, p. 68). Even though, as noted, the phrase "fairy tale" originated in a French context and not in the Grimms' enterprise, when *Kinder und Hausmärchen* was rendered into English, *Märchen* was often translated as "fairy tale": a term which, in fact, applied only to a comparatively limited amount of texts incorporated by the Grimms in their collected works. Occasionally, however, designations such as "wonder tale" or "popular story" were considered more apposite equivalents of the German original, which inevitably gave rise to terminological dilemmas. Carter would have been fully cognizant of these quandaries when embarking on both her fictional reinterpretation of traditional fairy tales and her scholarly task as an editor of such works.

In its devotion to the principle of inclusiveness, Carter's commodious approach to the fairy tale as a form is redolent of the Brothers Grimm's enterprise. Her stance on this issue is tersely affirmed by her introduction to *The Virago Book of Fairy Tales* (a.k.a. *The Old Wives' Fairy Tale Book*), the first publication of its ilk edited by Carter, which describes the fairy tale as a "figure of speech," freely employed to designate "the great mass of infinitely various narrative that was, once upon a time and still is, sometimes, passed on ... by word of mouth" (Carter 1990, p. ix). In this perspective, the familiar phrase would seem to have come into current usage more out of habit than out of logic or accuracy. Taking maximum advantage of the fairy tale's definitional looseness, Carter enters its field of creative possibilities with both an open mind and a hearty appetite, and hence regales her readers with a remarkable variety of narratives. These include gothic stories such as "The Bloody Chamber" and "The Lady of the House of Love," humorous adventures like "Puss-in-Boots" and tales of the macabre like "The Snow Child," romances tinged with mythical nuances such as "The Erl-King," "The Tiger's Bride" and "The Company of Wolves" and horror yarns like "Wolf-Alice."

In its elastic selection of disparate narrative molds and styles, *The Bloody Chamber and Other Stories* implicitly draws attention to the critical puzzle surrounding the nebulousness of the relationship between fairy tales and folktales. This is a dilemma which the Grimm Brothers' commodious approach to the issue of genre definition likewise urges us to acknowledge throughout *Kinder und Hausmärchen*. Carter is obviously aware of the widespread tendency to categorize fairy tales as distinctive kinds of folktales: e.g., narratives governed by the weird logic of the marvelous. Her yarns concurrently communicate an intimate familiarity with the specific repertoires of topics and symbols which are commonly identified as defining attributes of the fairy tale per se, and with the related inclination to posit the themes of metamorphosis and the quest in especially prestigious roles.

Most crucially, Carter employs throughout particular storytelling strategies which unequivocally stand out as generic markers of her stories *as* fairy tales even when she brings other genres into the narrative mix. These encompass the self-conscious employment of indeterminate, fuzzy or explicitly fantastical locations suggestive of a never-never realm as the settings within which often underprivileged heroes and heroines manage to triumph over powerful and abusive rivals against all odds. Exemplary characters and symbols are consistently brought into play to abet this classic formula, while taboos and the unpredictable repercussions of their violation furnish the teller with effective plot activators.

The narrative tissue which lends coherence to the textual cocktail typically consists of one pivotal incident and its consequences — such as the fateful encounter between a mortal and an otherworldly being likely to trigger a more or less drastic disruption of the accepted order of things. Hence, such stories tend to attribute particular prominence to extraordinary, supernatural and implausible events, while augmenting their fanciful atmosphere by recourse to sorcerous types, talking animals and magical props, as well as esoteric activities and attendant ritualized performances. In these situations, a character's flair for imaginative (and often unorthodox) problem solving often functions as a key means of advancing the action toward a varyingly spectacular or epiphanic dénouement. Although many readers and listeners have come to regard the use of happy endings and moral lessons as major aspects of the fairy tale, Carter repeatedly reminds us that these have normally issued from the toil of alacritous editors working under a disciplinary rubric. Concurrently, Carter reinforces the tradition whereby the cumulative effectiveness of the fairy tale as both a semiotic event and a dramatic structure is made dependent, to a significant degree, on the use of a distinctive discourse. Formulaic phrases, repetition, rhyming words, rhythmic compositions and cadences, archaic or regional lexis, and deft variations in the styles and registers of human characters as opposed to preternatural agents play prominent roles in this idiom.

As she adopts these ingredients, alongside many related staples and condiments of standard fairy tale fare, in the preparation of her bountiful narrative repast, Carter remains all the time alert to the speciousness of the claims to folkloristic purity advanced not only by the Grimm Brothers but also by other less famous collectors and editors of fairy tales of the same period. Above all, in restoring the fairy tale to its status as a mature form replete with dark, licentious and often downright disturbing undertones, *The Bloody Chamber and Other Stories* persistently reminds us that the stories divulged in the nineteenth century and inherited by subsequent generations as unadulterated reflections of a supposedly authentic folk spirit are actually products of substantial adaptive manipulation. The purpose of this move was to reconfigure the original materials so as to make them explicitly consonant with the moral and educational tenets treasured by a primarily bourgeois audience.

Nineteenth-century collectors and editors were especially eager to maximize the fairy tale's usefulness as an enculturing tool, aware of its unparalleled potential in the ideological shaping of children as a means of domesticating dangerous natural drives, and of inculcating the principles of moderation, docility and self-discipline as the mainstays of proper socialized conduct. The murkier and rowdier aspects of traditional fairy tales were progressively excised, softened or edulcorated while their latent Christian messages were enhanced, erotic allusions were carefully expunged, and starkly polarized gender positions were enthroned as unquestionable and immutable standards. At the same time, the degree of violence attached to the depiction of a villain's punishment was amplified — in ways, ironically, which one might not automatically deem child-friendly — to cautionary ends. As Danielle M. Roemer and Cristina Bacchilega state, it is to the Grimms that we owe the displacement of "the wicked mother figure," previously prominent in several stories, by the new-fangled notion of "a wicked stepmother character" which would not be perceived as too much of an assault on "prevailing motifs about motherhood." These modifications inevitably meant that the "resulting tales were not primarily indicative of peasant values," despite the Grimms' alleged purpose, "but of those of the German middle class" (Roemer and Bacchilega, p. 10).

In assessing the Grimms' uncontested impact on the shaping of the fairy tale's history — and, by extension, on Carter's own output in the field — it is only fair to commend the capaciousness of the Brothers' take on the *Märchen*. It is nonetheless just as crucial, for the sake of contextual accuracy, to remember that the latitude of their approach should not automatically be considered coterminous with ideological broadmindedness since their opus in fact evinces a blinkered nationalist outlook. Indeed, they were not satisfied simply to collate the folk materials at their disposal but rather endeavored to harness their choice to a very specific, and by no means liberal, ideological agenda. As the *Wikipedia* entry for the fairy tale emphasizes, the Brothers Grimm's selection criteria were not finally directed by the principle of inclusivity, insofar as their top priority was the celebration of the essence of Germanicity as embodied by the spirit of national consciousness (*Volksgeist*). "The Brothers Grimm rejected several tales for their collection though told orally to them by Germans," the article explains, "because the tales derived from Perrault, and they concluded they were thereby French and not German tales; an oral version of *Bluebeard* was thus rejected, and the tale of *Briar Rose*, clearly related to Perrault's *Sleeping Beauty*, was included only because Jacob Grimm convinced his brother that the figure of Brynhild proved that the sleeping princess was authentically German folklore" ("Fairy tale").

Paradoxically — and this bears witness to the astonishing resilience characteristic of the fairy tale as a form — the Brothers Grimm's nationalist priorities in the compilation of the *Kinder und Hausmärchen* has evidently not been conducive to the fortification of an individual and unified cultural identity. In fact, its stories have enjoyed worldwide acclaim and proved malleable to the ethical, emotional and ideological needs of disparate societies. This bears witness, on a broader plane, to the fairy tale's universal value as a narrative construct of enduring relevance and appeal, demonstrating that despite its obscure origins and tortuous dissemination, it has the power to interweave countless cultures in ongoing processes of interaction and cross-pollination. As Katherine Briggs contends, invoking the work of Hiroko Ikeda as corroboration for her hypothesis, the Grimm Brothers' "stories burst the bounds of nationality and were eagerly welcomed all over Europe. They even modified some of the folk-tale traditions in Japan" (Briggs, p. 224; Ikeda).

Maria Tatar proposes a related hypothesis, suggesting that the Grimms' nationalist vision did not prevent their work from being "denounced, in the aftermath of the Second World War, as a book that promoted 'bloodletting and violence' and that endorsed cruelty, violence, and atrocity, fear and hatred for the outsider, and virulent anti–Semitism.'" This shows that the appropriation of fairy tales within a certain social context as a means of consolidating a specific notion of cultural identity does not automatically deliver permanent results since that very identity may come to be regarded as disreputable and hence be supplanted by a different ideal. The intrinsic shakiness of the alliance between fairy tales and cultural objectives is additionally demonstrated by the "odd twist of fate" whereby the Grimms' corpus "has also become a book whose stories have been used ... to work through the horrors of the Holocaust." An outstanding exemplification of this option is the "volume of poetry entitled *Transformations* (1971)," where "the American poet Anne Sexton produced a sinister verse adaptation of 'Hansel and Gretel' that shows the parents cooking the family dog, then resolving to adopt a 'final solution,' one that leaves the children to starve in the forest." The "oven" image, moreover, is employed in such a fashion that "most readers will unfailingly connect" it "with the crematoria of Nazi Germany" (Tatar, p. xx).

These oscillations in both the Grimms' own understanding of their collection's significance and aims and in the reactions to its messages evinced by later generations persuasively corroborates Robert Darnton's suggestion that traditional stories illuminate contingent historical moments by attesting to the cultural mentalities dominant in different periods (Darnton). Therefore, universal though many of their tropes and characters are, fairy tales should never be entirely removed from their material anchorage in real human cultures, their rules, values and ideals. This clearly applies to Carter's own fairy tales no less pointedly than to any other manifestation of that form which vaunts, as Carter's stories incontrovertibly do, a cultural and historical grounding. In fact, it gains special significance in the context of Carter's fairy tale output by virtue of the writer's unflinching commitment to the material substratum from which, in her view, all art emanates and to which all art is destined to return.

In her critical assessment of the tradition which she seeks to reimagine, Carter is also sensitive to the plethora of psychoanalytic theories of both Freudian and Jungian provenance brought to bear upon the interpretation of fairy tales in the course of the past century. Readings of the psychological import of those stories circulating in the context of contemporary fairy tale scholarship are so copious and varied that positing a single psychoanalytically oriented take on the fairy tale tradition would be crudely simplistic. It does not seem preposterous to suggest, however, that the majority of the available approaches proceed from the assumption that the tales themselves are emblematic articulations of the human psyche and of its innermost events and can therefore offer some illuminating insights into people's actions and thoughts. In the context of Jungian criticism, Marie-Louise von Franz's writings are particularly worthy of notice. The fairy tales is here presented as "the purest and simplest expression of collective unconscious psychic processes" (von Franz, p. 1). Its unique discourse is held to revolve around two principal concepts: the "archetype," which refers to "the structural basic disposition to produce a certain mythologem," and the "archetypal image," which constitutes to "the specific form" assumed by the archetype within a singular narrative (p. 8).

The most renowned representative of a classic Freudian interpretation of fairy tales, and specifically of their emotional and symbolic impact on the younger generations, is undoubtedly Bruno Bettelheim. According to this august scholar, the fairy tale's murkiest motifs have the power to teach children how to cope with their own anxieties and fears in a symbolic fashion, and hence develop affective and mental resources destined to abet them in their future lives as dependable grown-ups. "Like all great art," Bettelheim maintains, "fairy tales both delight and instruct; their special genius is that they do so in terms which speak directly to children" (Bettelheim, p. 53). Concurrently, "For those who immerse themselves in what the fairy tale has to communicate, it becomes a deep, quiet pool which at first seems to reflect only our own image; but behind it we soon discover the inner turmoils of our soul — its depth, and ways to gain peace within ourselves and with the world, which is the reward of our struggles." Fairy tales, therefore, can be said to harbor capacities unknown to "any other form of literature" which enable them to "direct the child to discover his identity and calling, and they also suggest what experiences are needed to develop his character further. Fairy tales intimate that a rewarding, good life is within one's reach despite adversity — but only if one does not shy away from the hazardous struggles without which one can never achieve true identity" (p. 24).

Carter harbors serious reservations regarding the validity of Bettelheim's philosophy, arguing that fairy tales are very unlikely to be "as consoling as he suggests" (in Haffenden 1984, p. 36). Furthermore, she questions the stereotypically reductive association of the fairy tale with children by arguing that the form has, in fact, been embedded from inception in an eminently adult reality, and hence captures the very essence of our enduring bond with our ancestors — namely, the people through whose blood, sweat, tears and laughter our world gradually came into being. It is crucial to remember, in this respect, that in pre-modern societies, fairy tales would often constitute the mainstay of public performances meant to cater for the primarily adult members of disparate social classes. In such contexts, they could be flexibly adapted to the requirements of contingent circumstances in order to articulate allegorical accounts of the rhythms of the natural world, the responsibilities and demands of its supposedly supernatural activators, and the meaning of human-made institutions. These simultaneously dramatic and narrative events served the purposes of both popular entertainment and informal education. On occasion, they could also be harnessed to the communication of cautionary messages intended to inculcate not merely common wisdom but also variably stringent disciplinary rules. In all of these situations, fairy tales would frequently be expected to shape their listeners' emotional responses (or even their dominant patterns of conduct) as a means of bolstering the status quo.

Carter is well aware that the arrant philistinism besieging her culture is bound to elicit derisive aversion to the more overtly fantastic products of human imagination and creativity. "If you mention folklore in Britain, people's eyes glaze over with boredom," she comments. "They associate it with people wearing white suits with bells round their legs. It is associated with the embarrassing, with the quaint." What marks the unique power of fantasy as encapsulated specifically in the fairy tale form, according to Carter, is its unabated psychological import. To this extent, even though the writer is by no means an aficionado of psychoanalytic theory and has in fact enjoyed quite a few opportunities to poke fun at its white-bearded patriarchs, she is quite eager to stress that in the case of fairy tales, "the imagery is perpetually enchanting because a lot of the imagery is the imagery of the unconscious; beautiful and refreshing, it refreshes the imagination" (Carter 1985).

Warner suggests that Carter's own fairy tales have the power to speak to the unconscious. Describing her personal encounter with that body of fiction as a tectonic shift in her creative development, Warner has stated: "*The Bloody Chamber* wasn't the first book by Angela Carter that I read, but it was the one that turned the key for me as a writer. It opened onto a hidden room, the kind that exists in dreams, that had always somehow been there, but that I'd never entered because I'd been afraid." Extrapolating from her subjective experience of Carter's bold adaptive enterprise to address its broader cultural significance, Warner intimates that the image of the bloody chamber itself can be regarded as the implicit prototypal setting of all of Carter's narratives, functioning as "the centre of the labyrinth of desire, the eye of the stormy journey towards self-knowledge, the *ruelle* by the side of the bed where the deepest intimacies are exchanged, the cheval glass — called in French *un psyché*—of our inner selves" (Warner 2001, p. 250). "The Lady of the House of Love" is arguably the tale in which Carter indicates most explicitly that the ultimate bloody chamber is neither an outlandish location of Wallachian flavor nor a secret corridor at the heart of a Gothic manor house. In fact, far from constituting solely the province of bloodsucking or lycanthropic monsters, it is the state of haunting uncertainty of which all humans partake—whether they acknowledge it or not.

Carter's daring reorientations of the fairy tale tradition have themselves invoked critical interpretation in accordance with psychoanalytic theories of disparate orientations. An illustrative case in point is Ana María Losada Pérez' reading of "The Bloody Chamber" and "The Erl-King" in the light of Lacanian and post–Lacanian psychoanalytical perspectives. Following Slavoj Žižek, Losada Pérez proposes that those two stories usher in a world where the Lacanian concept of the Name of the Father—the fundamental signifier decreeing the subject's position within the Symbolic order with the authority of a supreme law—is subverted by the "monstrous figures" of the Marquis and the Erl-King as incarnations of "the anal father." The anal father, argues Žižek, is one of the configurations acquired by the notion of monstrosity in contemporary society, and its primary function is to express the equivocal character of "the Thing" as a meeting-point of longing and dread: "a foreign body, an intruder which disturbs the harmony of the social bond" and yet, ironically, "holds together the social edifice by means of guaranteeing its fantasmatic consistency." In other words, the monstrous as conceived of by Žižek operates simultaneously as the epitome of transgression and disruption—which is what the social order should logically abhor most profoundly—and as a cementing agency bolstering the myth of that order as an inviolable structure. The social order is not, of course, either stable or, strictly speaking, even real but as long as it is in a position to demonize an other (e.g., a monster) as its rival, it can perpetuate the fantasy of its stability and reality by ideological implication. It is hence able to enthrone itself as the legitimate model—and to go on reasserting the validity of this image—by continually revamping and continually suppressing the threat posed by its abnormal other.

"We abjure and disown the Thing," Žižek further avers, "yet it exerts an irresistible attraction on us; its proximity exposes us to mortal danger, yet it is simultaneously a source of power" (Žižek, p. 123). According to Losada Pérez, Carter's representation of her male monsters is consonant with Žižek's evaluation of the Thing's significance "as a site of fear and desire: from a distance, each monster exerts irresistible attraction; yet, as soon as he is approached his presence causes horror for it threatens to destroy the narrator's self." Concomitantly, the critic maintains, both of Carter's monsters operate "as the narrators' double, 'what is in them more than themselves,' a surplus of enjoyment that they eventually disavow to preserve their identities.... This antagonistic role of the monstrous indexes the presence of the subject as a void, as a substanceless point of pure self-relating which constitutes the ultimate source of horror in Carter's fiction" (Losada Pérez). Just as Žižek's Thing consolidates the status quo by appearing to disrupt it, Carter's monsters abet the subject's self-preservation by appearing to shatter it. Indeed, in order to shore up the shaky edifices of their selfhood, Carter's protagonists strive to distance themselves from those external manifestations of monstrosity which inevitably call attention to their own intrinsic monstrosity, their vulnerability and, ultimately, their sheer emptiness. In both instances, however, what comes to the fore is neither a strong social order nor a strong self but rather two systems equally haunted by the fear of annihilation — the raw affect underpinning all manifestations of horror at its purest.

Even though numerous critics and scholars will readily aver that fairy tales were originally meant to appeal to members of all generations, over the centuries they have incrementally come to be regarded as inextricable from a juvenile audience. *Les Précieuses* themselves were largely responsible for promoting this connection even though, as intimated, their fictional output was by and large so sophisticated and elaborate as to constitute more appropriate entertainment for adults than for kids. Since the Brothers Grimm's publication of their *Kinder und Hausmärchen*, the tie between fairy tales and kids has grown incrementally solid. This connection carries momentous ideological significance insofar as it has proved instrumental in harnessing the fairy tale to an enculturing and socializing instrument of practically unrivaled versatility: an asset which owes much to its mediatic adaptability to disparate molds and technologies.

Numerous pedagogical experts have praised the fairy tale's constructive role as an edificatory tool without bothering to ponder the darker undertones of the tradition in which it is enshrined. Laura Kready's writings typify this critical propensity, advocating that while fairy tales have the capacity to "contain" the child's "interests," they can also be approached as a beneficial "means for the expression of his instincts and for his development in purpose, in initiative, in judgement, in organization of ideas, and in the creative return possible to him." Kready would feasibly have doubted the educational kudos of fairy tales which, as Carter's do, tend to blend their literary materials with oral, popular and even sensationalist sources, insofar as she seems to regard a tale's literary worth as the prerequisite of its ethical usefulness. Indeed, Kready's principal objective is "to show what fairy tales must possess as classics, as literature and composition, and as short-stories; to trace their history, to classify the types, and to supply the sources of material" so as to determine the exact import of the "creative return" one could plausibly expect of a kid. In full consonance with these views, Kready's preface to *A Study of Fairy Tales* (1916) culminates with the cheerful announcement that "the fairy tale is also related to life standards, for it presents to the child a criticism of life. By bringing forward in high light the character of the fairy, the fairy tale furnishes a unique contribution to life. Through its repeated impression of the idea of fairyhood it may implant in the child a desire which may fructify into that pure, generous, disinterested kindness and love of the grown-up, which aims to play fairy to another, with sincere altruism to make appear before his eyes his heart's desire, or in a twinkling to cause what hitherto seemed impossible. Fairy tales thus are harbingers of that helpfulness which would make a new earth, and as such afford a contribution to the religion of life" (Kready).

As noted, Bettelheim also trusts, though perhaps less messianically than Kready, the form's nurturing and redemptive energies, imparting credence to his hypothesis by recourse to psychoanalytic doctrine. This optimistic take on the fairy tale is still current today, mainly courtesy of the sunnily simplistic versions of that form dished out over the decades by the Disney industry in the form of animated movies and of myriad spin-offs and tie-ins (including, of course, immensely lucrative theme parks). As Jack Zipes contends in the felicitously titled *Happily Ever After*, what this enterprise has methodically sought to accomplish, since the 1930s at least, is not to extend the fairy tale discourse into hitherto unexplored multimedia territory. In fact, it has aimed to maximize the influence which, as a concurrently creative and commercial force, it "could have on as large an audience as possible in order to sell a commodity and endorse ideological images that would enhance [Disney's] corporate power" (Zipes 1994a, p. 87). In so doing, the Disney empire has incessantly perpetuated stereotypical gender relations pivoting on the relegation of female characters to passive domestic roles and on the emplacement of their male counterparts as energetic action heroes.

At the same time, is has been careful to pick the simplest and best known yarns as its source material in order to ensure that the average spec-tator, not needing to face the unfamiliar or ponder plot intricacies, would be in a position to marvel at the artistic and technical quality of the images themselves and thus commend their innovative power. Although Zipes clearly does not wish to dispute Disney's excellence as an unmatched pio-neer of exciting expressive possibilities, he believes that his overall impact on the public's collective consciousness has amounted to a "domestication of the imagination" (p. 92). In *Fairy Tale as Myth, Myth as Fairy Tale*, Zipes pursues a cognate line of reasoning, suggesting that the Disney movies offering adaptations of famous fairy tales propose an "eternal return of the same" by capitalizing on formulaic cardboard characters and by promoting the values of "cleanliness, control, and organized industry" as unquestion-able ethical ideals. The cumulative result of these ruses, argues Zipes, is bound to be "non-reflective viewing" (Zipes 1994b, pp. 94–95).

The Bloody Chamber and Other Stories evidently refrains from perpetu-ating the consolatory definition of traditional fairy tales underlying the Disney-led approach by emphasizing the undercurrents of perversity and brutality coursing through both its hero(in)es and its villains' personalities. In so doing, Carter manages to bring out what she regards as "the latent content of those stories" (in Haffenden 1984, p. 36) prior to their saniti-zation and hegemonic cannibalization. Carter thus exposes the arbitrariness of the frames conventionally deployed to hem in representations of good and evil in ideologically edited versions of the fairy tale by exploding their monolithic points of reference and releasing them once more onto the slip-pery terrain of ethical, emotional and rhetorical ambiguity. Displacing the rigid structures promulgated, with obvious differences but comparable results, by both the Grimms and Disney, Carter's stories usher in a semiotic dance of endless deferral. In this respect, they constitute a radical resistance to the type of domestication described in *Happily Ever After*.

Zipes' writings have also played a groundbreaking part in questioning the fairy tale's educational worth along the lines promoted by the likes of Kready, Bettelheim and many other critics of both previous and subsequent generations. According to Zipes, even though fairy tales have been ideolog-ically embedded in history as "universal, ageless, therapeutic, miraculous, and beautiful" (Zipes 1991, p. 1), they are actually implicated in disciplinary programs governed by contingent moral and aesthetic rubrics. These strate-gies do not only impact on children — although it is undeniable that the very young are commonly their main target. In fact, they aim to determine how people from disparate generations perceive the fairy tale in ways which inevitably obscure its stupendous narrative variety and ethical ambiguity. As a result, the regimenting practices outlined by Zipes can realistically be said to have impaired the imagination and the interpretative skills of readers and listeners of all ages, inducing them to forget that fairy tales constitute an exceptionally valuable means of exploring concrete human realities (no matter how many supernatural creatures and phenomena they might instill into their yarns) by recourse to a deftly modulated balance of humor an pathos.

Carter, relatedly, is committed to a programmatic, though varicolored and exuberantly plumed, exposure of the profoundly cross-generational relevance of fairy tales old and new. In emphasizing the least savory aspects of some of the most time-honored fairy tales, she reminds us that the association of the form itself with the younger generations is not part of its natural history — let alone its inherent thematic and rhetorical constitution — but rather a corollary of post hoc ideological interventions. Relatedly, Carter knows full well that fairy tales, as Joseph Campbell contends, are often meant to operate for both boys and girls as "initiation ceremonies," or rites of passage, capable of "killing the infantile ego" (Campbell, p. 168). In addition, as L. C. Seifert maintains, both sexes are trapped in the ideological obligation to guarantee "the harmonious existence of family and society at large" (Seifert, p. 109). However, fairy tales and their fantastical figures have been elliptically exploited in even more sinister ways — most notoriously, as a means of legitimizing infantile abuse by disguising it as an expression of necessary discipline. According to Warner, this ominous proclivity finds an intriguing correlative in traditional narratives intended to rationalize the victimization of the very young or even, in the most horrendous circumstances, the practice of infanticide. In the past (a past which may seem remote and yet feels uncomfortably recent in many respects), it was not unusual to blame deaths caused by human parents or guardians on fairies. For example, a changeling, the baleful creature left by fairies in a human cradle upon snatching its legitimate occupant away for the purpose of enhancing fairy stock, "could be discreetly made to disappear, as an evil gift of the fairies, or even of the devil; to dispose of a human child on the other hand, however unwanted or damaged at birth, lay beyond the frontiers of acceptable conduct.... Infanticide, in cases where there was nothing untoward, could thus be concealed" (Warner 2000, p. 29).

G. K. Chesterton's assessment of the fairy tale is also keen to underline its involvement with the murkier dimensions of human existence in a pragmatically dispassionate fashion, emphasizing the ineluctably provisional character of success, pleasure and bliss. "It is all very well to talk of the freedom of fairyland," the writer avers, "but there was precious little freedom in fairyland by the best official accounts. Mr. W. B. Yeats and other sensitive modern souls, feeling that modern life is about as black a slavery as ever oppressed mankind (they are right enough there), have especially described elfland as a place of utter ease and abandonment." This idealistic perspective induces Chesterton to "doubt whether Mr. Yeats really knows the real philosophy of the fairies.... If you really read the fairy tales, you will observe that one idea runs from one end of them to the other — the idea that peace and happiness can only exist on some condition ... all happiness hangs on one thin veto; all positive joy depends on one negative" (Chesterton). *The Bloody Chamber and Other Stories* corroborates Chesterton's position, dispassionately reminding us at every available opportunity that in the domain of fairy tales, there is no such thing as a free lunch, so to speak. All moments of anarchic pleasure and seemingly unlimited freedom must be understood for what they are — that is, *moments*— and not be mistaken as permanent achievements. As we shall see, analogous messages are communicated, by different stylistic and structural means, in both *Nights at the Circus* and *Wise Children*.

These somber reflections no doubt demand considerate scrutiny. Nevertheless, it is vital to recognize that the fairy tale as appropriated and sculpted by Carter also retains the capacity to foster the desirability of embracing darkness as a reality which unremittingly coexists and coalesces with light. In this regard, Carter's fairy tale output is chiefly concerned with alerting us to the form's alliance with fantasy — namely, the only force endowed with an unmatched ability to energize with equal measures of vivacity and urgency both the fabric of real daily existence and the midnight masked balls of reverie at its fanciest. In so doing, it encapsulates with inspiring vigor Marcia Lane's memorable portrayal of the fairy tale in the poetically titled volume *Picturing the Rose*: "A fairy tale is a story — literary or folk — that has a sense of the numinous, the feeling or sensation of the supernatural or the mysterious. But, and this is crucial, it is a story that happens in the past tense, and a story that is not tied to any specifics. If it happens 'at the beginning of the world,' then it is a myth. A story that names a specific 'real' person is a legend (even if it contains a magical occurrence). A story that happens in the future is a fantasy. Fairy tales are sometimes spiritual, but never religious" (Lane, p. 5). Carter's fairy tales (like her writings in general) incontestably share with Lane's depiction an indomitable resolve to uphold the fairy tale's unsubmissiveness to religious doctrine.

Although Carter does not explicitly foreground this debate, there is plenty of evidence throughout her fairy tale writings of her sensitivity to a variety of interpretations surrounding the worldwide recurrence of certain narrative materials. This phenomenon could be grasped in an empirical fashion as a product of gradual improvements in global communication and the dissemination of ideas. Alternately, it could be ascribed to the existence of an underlying universal imaginary in more idealistic or even mystical terms. Whatever the causes underlying the fairy tale's culture-hopping migrations, it is patent that the adoption of recurrent factors in disparate contexts is never conducive to pure repetition. In fact, it demonstrates that there can be no such thing as straightforward and undiluted reiteration for the simple reason that meaning is notoriously prone to slippage, forever in the process of sliding, erring, taking detours and getting stuck in blind alleys. Therefore, tales produced in different geographical and historical milieux but evincing analogous ingredients should not be approached as replications or simulations of one another but rather as parallel interpretations of those core elements. Accordingly, in examining the relationship between two tales exhibiting thematic or formal affinities, we should not presume to peel away at their figurative layers and contingent culture-bound accretions in order to reach some ultimate urtext but rather accept that the materials at our disposal are only the surfaces of representation themselves, and that these very surfaces deserve credit as autonomous realities in their ability to both entertain and stimulate reflection.

A crucial aspect of *The Bloody Chamber and Other Stories* is precisely its commitment to diversification as opposed to mechanical repetition. In this respect, Carter's perspective on the fairy tale echoes Italo Calvino. This writer praises the fairy tale's studious cultivation of the minutest descriptive details as the stylistic soul of its unparalleled ability to evoke a spellbinding variety of worlds by means of carefully chosen verbal and visual touches. Besides, Calvino is deeply drawn to the "economy, rhythm and hard logic" deployed in its recounting (Calvino 1996, p. 35), according particular significance to the principle of conciseness as pivotal to a deft manipulation of time. This allows even some extreme moments of dizzying swiftness and stagnant inertia to infiltrate the action's cumulative rhythm with natural ease. No less distinctive, in Calvino's vision, is the fairy tale's flair for seeming to grow and ripple out from within by recourse to (often unpredictable) ramifications and detours.

In her reconfiguration of the fairy tale, Carter at times veers quite deliberately toward the formulaic by weaving archetypal set pieces which are instantly recognizable as narrative products of that traditional form. This proclivity is vividly typified by "The Bloody Chamber" itself. Indeed, as Rushdie points out, this story "begins as classic *grand guignol*: an innocent bride, a much-married millionaire husband, a lonely castle stood upon a melting shore, a secret room containing horrors. The helpless girl and the civilised, decadent, murderous man" (in Carter 2006d, p. xi). Furthermore, Carter does not create her characters from scratch — either in the titular tale or in the yarns which follow. In fact, she assiduously demonstrates intimate familiarity with diverse methodologies brought to bear upon the fairy tale in order to classify its contents in accordance with rigorous morphological schemata. On several occasions, her fairy tales bring to mind Vladimir Propp's mapping of fairy tales and folktales on the basis of their recurrent employment, in a supposedly immutable order or sequence, of a constant and limited set of "functions" — i.e., the actions that are endowed with vital importance within the narrative's overall development — and "spheres of action" — i.e., the character types through which the functions are acted out (Propp).

Elements of the Proppian model are undoubtedly detectable in Carter's handling of characterization. For example, while the character function designated by the Formalist critic as the "villain" finds a close correlative in the type of the male tyrant to which Carter so often — and so ironically — returns throughout her tales, Propp's "helper" is embodied by less vicious males willing to assist (though often to no avail) the protagonists' struggle for justice and freedom. While the Marquis in the titular narrative unequivocally epitomizes the former typology, the soldier in "The Lady of the House of Love" and the blind piano tuner in "The Bloody Chamber" exemplify the latter option. At the same time, several personae are intentionally constructed either as stock fairy tale characters donning new costumes and new masks or else as fusions of diverse character traits derived not solely from fairy tales but also from other narrative and dramatic forms. We thus encounter a considerable number of women defined essentially by their domestic positions regardless of whether they belong to the aristocracy, the bourgeoisie or the working classes, and no less populous a gallery of powerful men reliant on inherited wealth and authority to give free rein to their nefarious drives. Foregrounding the principles of transformation and shapeshifting so central to the fairy tale tradition as a whole, Carter additionally capitalizes on her characters' metamorphic capacities — or, should their magical flair fail them, on their masquerading and camouflaging propensities. Relatedly, even when a character does not immediately or overtly recall a traditional fairy tale type, it is sooner or later possible to identify vestigial traces of that form in its distinctive modus operandi and manipulation of alternately otherworldly and matter-of-fact wisdom.

In a sense, Carter's attraction to a miscellaneous parade of traditional stock characters — and to as many opportunities to reimagine them — is perfectly consonant with her aversion to naturalism. In an interview for *Marxism Today*, the writer describes this aesthetic peculiarity in ways which can be considered pertinent to her opus as a whole but carry special relevance to the fairy tales due to the latter's intrinsically formulaic nature: "one of the difficulties of writing fiction that's supposed to have a lot of meaning and can be read as allegory, is the tension between what people expect from the fiction, which is rounded three-dimensional characters that they can believe in, have empathy with, and the fact that that kind of character doesn't carry all that much meaning. They can't carry all that much freight of meaning." Aware that in order to impart her personae with connotations that transcend the limitations of individuality, she is bound to depart from the stylistic precepts of naturalism, Carter embraces the fairy tale as an intentionally non-naturalistic form wherein the psychological credibility of a character or situation does not emanate from their supposed full-roundedness but rather from their capacity to embody metaphorical abstractions, yet also have the power to make us laugh, cry, shudder or yawn and, most crucially, wish to contribute to the creation of the story's cumulative meaning. After all, as Carter stresses in the same piece, "reading a book is like re-writing it for yourself. And I think that all fiction should be open-ended. You bring to a novel, anything you read, all your experience of the world. You bring your history and you read it in your own terms" (Carter 1985).

In a letter to Robert Coover, relatedly, Carter further expounds her firm belief in the desire to rise above the strictures of realism as the precondition of any creative intervention which is genuinely capable of impacting on reality — its constitution, its perception, and its representation. "I'm interested, then," Carter writes, "in a fiction that takes full cognizance of its status as non-being — that is, a fiction that remains aware that it is of its own nature.... I really do believe that a fiction absolutely self-conscious of itself as a different form of human experience than reality (that is, not a logbook of events) can help to transform reality itself" (in Coover, p. 242). Authentic realism, this perspective implies, does not reside with narratives which claim to reflect reality faithfully and transparently for the sole purpose of pretending that there is such a thing as a reliable, given and immutable reality — and thus reinforce all manner of stultifying dogmas and authoritarian precepts. In fact, it is only achievable by fostering the emergence of a universe entirely *sui generis* and, having accomplished this goal, by unfailingly respecting its difference and autonomous regenerating power. Seamlessly braiding the fictional and the metafictional, chatty intimacy and studied self-reflexivity, Carter pursues this objective throughout her career but it is often in her fairy tales that she actually achieves it with magisterial aplomb.

Despite its adherence to tradition, Carter's method prioritizes the transformative powers of appropriation. While she undoubtedly recognizes the worth of critical templates which underscore the grounding of singular tales in a putatively universal deep structure, Carter also alerts us to the perilously reductionist bias intrinsic in those models. In this respect, Carter again echoes quite closely Calvino's writings on the fairy tale, where considerable emphasis is placed on the issues of recurrence and variation. While Propp recognizes the importance of each tale's singularity, his paradigm remains loyal to the overarching value of recurrence. Calvino, by contrast, lays greater emphasis on the value of diversity, arguing that focusing solely on the similarities evinced by specific stories or clusters of narratives with reference to a global matrix could ultimately amount to obscuring or even flouting the local distinctiveness of each plot. It is hence crucial to acknowledge that "reducing the tale to its unchanging skeleton contributes to highlight how many geographical and historical variables form the external casing of this skeleton; and establishing rigorously the narrative function, the place assumed within this scheme by specific instances of social existence, the objects of empirical experience, the implements available to a given culture, the plants and animals of a particular flora and fauna, can provide data which would otherwise elude us regarding the value which that particular culture ascribes to them" (Calvino 1988, p. 113).

Therefore, while fairy tales are proverbially repetitive in the manipulation of their topoi, symbols and tropes, diversity is no less axial a definer of their generic and structural cachet. The sheer sense of energy released by the individual story's heterogeneity cannot be deadened by the acknowledgment of its underlying compliance with an established repertoire. Repetition, relatedly, serves an eminently ironical purpose insofar as it contributes to the enhancement of the tale's individuality by urging us to recognize where and how difference occurs, and hence piercing the shroud of sameness. Each single story, in this scenario, can be visualized as "an arabesque of multicolored metamorphoses that issue from one another," as patterns do in an Oriental carpet (p. 146).

Calvino and Carter's perceptions regarding the fairy tale's function and goals come together most luminously in their appreciation of the inseparability of presence and absence. Insofar as any one particular plot only ever accommodates a limited number of the elements contained in the paradigm from which it draws, its significance is bound to reside not simply in what it articulates but also in the vastly more sizable parts of the paradigm which it leaves out. These untouched regions of the narratable universe can be ideated in the guise of shimmering lagoons of absence flooding the landscapes of authorial self-presence, and thus reminding us that the meaning of any human utterance, ultimately, depends on what it does not (or cannot) say no less pointedly than on what it manages to lodge. "In any tale that has a meaning," Calvino reflects, "one may recognize the first tale ever told and the last tale, beyond which the world will not let itself be narrated in a tale" (Calvino 1988, p. 126). Calvino thus reminds us with disarming honesty that the dancing "figures of darkness" (p. 137) incessantly merge with the elusive shimmer of "auroral light" (p. 129).

Carter's tendency to give precedence to diversification over mere recurrence is at all times underpinned by a keen sensitivity to the collusion of presence and absence. As a stylistic practice, moreover, it entails that even as she employs stock characters and related narrative formulae, Carter nonetheless endeavors to vary both their presentation and their impact. Thus, even though her dispossessed females are in many ways stereotypical, they are nonetheless often infused with unconventional degrees of liveliness and humor, while her rapacious males often exhibit personalities so urbanely eclectic as to transcend the monolithic category of the villain. On occasion, Carter's male villains bring to mind the demonic lovers and suitors immortalized not only by Perrault's *Beauty and the Beast* and *Blue-beard* but also by the Grimms' *Rumpelstiltskin*. These are renowned samples of a narratological category which J. C. Cooper rather amusingly describes as "the Loathly Mate" (Cooper, p. 16). At the same time, those characters blur the distinction traced by Bettelheim in his discussion of the "Animal-Groom Cycle of Fairy Tales" (Bettelheim, pp. 282–310) between the two villainous types found in *Beauty and the Beast* and *Bluebeard*. According to the Freudian critic, the former highlights the values of "gentleness and loving devotion," while the latter "has nothing whatsoever to do with love" insofar as "Bluebeard, bent on having his will and possessing his partner, cannot love anybody, but neither can anyone love him" (p. 303). Carter's male villains frequently combine the positive affects associated by Bettelheim with *Beauty and the Beast* by posing as captivatingly refined, albeit menacing, lovers and *Bluebeard*'s destructive impulses.

Concomitantly, Carter plays with subtle modulations and gradations in the depiction of both female and male figures, varying the emotional and social connotations carried by their roles so as to convey carefully individuated personalities. For instance, her mordant wit is quick to remind us, should we simplistically assume that all male villains in the fairy tale league are depraved and self-indulgent aristocrats, that some of the most negative characters are in fact middle-class fathers rendered pernicious by their petty addictions, their philistine mores or, quite simply, their absence from the scene. Be they driven by cowardice, greed or penury, bourgeois patriarchs like the bankrupt entrepreneur in "The Courtship of Mr Lyon" are finally no less dangerous than the reptilian Marquis in "The Bloody Chamber." Besides, Carter eschews the univocal portrayal of the mother figure as either a benevolent protector or a jealous competitor, drawing attention instead to the potentially infinite variety of instincts and goals coursing the maternal role.

Most importantly, even though Carter is quite prepared not merely to adopt but even to revel in typical situations and types, she simultaneously explodes conventionality and conformism by proposing varyingly audacious departures from tradition. This objective is frequently accomplished through an irreverent repositioning of established popular figures. The version of the Beauty and the Beast motif dramatized in "The Bloody Chamber" alongside the obvious Bluebeard motif, for example, proposes that the tale's crux is not Beauty as a meek daughter who consents to join the Beast for her father's sake but a courageous mother striving to save her daughter. Other versions of the same basic yarn are likewise adventurous in the treatment of classic motifs. Thus, in "Wolf-Alice," Beauty is erased from the scene altogether to leave room for two configurations of the Beast to emerge, while in "The Erl-King," Beauty and the Beast are posited as irreconcilable antagonists whose rivalry can only unleash vengeful hatred, and in "The Courtship of Mr Lyon," Beauty assumes an active and positive role as she endeavors to save the Beast's life.

"The Tiger's Bride" offers one of Carter's most inspired — and indeed inspiring — flourishes of revisionist genius as Beauty is seen to undergo an erotic awakening so intense as to cause her to morph into a superb animal in her own right. At this point, the heroine's entire being is transformed into a fluid site of *jouissance*, as all of its senses, limbs, organs and nerves appear to be working together toward a symphony of unnamable bliss: "I felt the harsh velvet of his hand against my hand, then a tongue, abrasive as sandpaper.... And each stroke of his tongue ripped off skin after successive skin, all the skins of a life in the world, and left behind a nascent patina of shining hairs. My earrings turned back to water and trickled down my shoulders; I shrugged the drops off my beautiful fur" (Carter 2006d, p. 169). "The Tiger's Bride" could be said to promulgate a view of gendered identity that is not straitjacketed by a quest for equality or parity grounded in spuriously essentialist notions of femininity and masculinity: the objective traditionally advanced by radical feminism. In fact, it posits a gendered being willing to embrace difference, and indeed the possibility of achieving harmony, mutual understanding and pleasure both *in* difference and *through* difference.

With the image of the metamorphosing heroine, Carter honors most memorably the animal nested within each and every human both as a person's intrinsic spirit (denoted by the word *anima*, or soul) and as the bestial energy that permeates and potentially connects all species on the planet in an invisible web of pulsating desire. Carter is aware that this choice on her part has upset the most ardently anthropocentric of her readers but does not appear to regret it. "Well, we are animals, after all," she passionately declares. "I said this once to somebody after I'd read *The Company of Wolves* story. She was terribly upset. She said you mean we're nasty, hairy, dirty slavering *beasts*. No, no, no, it's all right. We're mammals. Bipeds, mammals, carnivorous bipeds, primates and everything. 'It's all right,' I said. But she would not be comforted. It was as though a door had opened into hell." With characteristic irony, Carter complements her account with a biting political remark. She points out that wolves, the animals featuring most frequently in her stories, are not generally dangerous unless human beings bother them, concedes that "their social organisation is somewhat fascistic" and then immediately adds: "but who in Britain is to complain about them" (Carter 1985).

Through her unorthodox female characters, Carter is able to transcend the stereotype of the passive woman who is powerless to achieve freedom not only because of her subjection to an exploitative and selfish patriarch but also — and more ominously — because of her lack of imagination. In so doing, as Sage maintains, Carter offers her audience a chance to "take flight" from stultifying conformism by assessing the significance of women's oppression in a historically cogent and critically informed fashion (Sage 2001, p. 68). In her analysis of "The Bloody Chamber," Kathleen E. B. Manley likewise emphasizes Carter's capacity to make us see past the simplistic equation of the passive female to a victim by urging us to recognize the status of identity as a fluid and shifting endowment. Hence, the tale's heroine could be said to epitomize the figure of the "woman in process," a social creature on the verge of examining "her subject position" (Manley, p. 83). Cheryl Renfroe, relatedly, proposes that in that same tale, the subtext pivoting on the Marquis' efforts to subjugate his new spouse is counterpointed by an antithetical subtext marking the woman's gradual acquisition of an autonomous will (Renfroe).

Moreover, Carter is eager to underscore, both in the title story and in its companion pieces, the ancestral coalescence of sexual passion and monstrosity, fascination and revulsion, Eros and Thanatos. "The Tiger's Bride" conveys this message in positive, if dauntingly unorthodox, tones. With "The Lady of the House of Love," Carter paints a more explicitly forbidding picture of the collusion of blood and desire by recourse to the timeless figure of the vampire, combining horror and splendor in a creature of unearthly beauty. This is a being whose "voice is filled with distant sonorities, like reverberations in a cave" which repeat ad infinitum the baleful message "now you are at the place of annihilation" (Carter 2006d, p. 195). At times, the dynamic tension which binds conflicting forces in an atavistic embrace is expressed in eminently chromatic terms. In "The Snow Child," for example, Carter conveys the emotional conflict pivotal to this stunningly capsulated narrative almost entirely by recourse to the contrasting symbolic connotations of a few absolute hues. Thus, the "invincible, immaculate" whiteness of "midwinter" is instantly juxtaposed with the formidable Countess' darkness — starkly foregrounded by the color of the "mare" she rides and of the "glittering pelts of black foxes" she dons — and with the redness of the "blood" filling a "hole in the snow." The initial contrast gains complexity, as the Count's and Countess' irreconcilable desires become apparent, with the introduction of the titular creature: a girl born of the male lead's yearnings whose physique combines "white skin, red mouth, black hair" (p. 193) and ineluctably sparks off the Countess' intense hatred.

As Carter turns her attention to what is arguably the most cherished (and oft-adapted) of all Western fairy tales, "Little Red Riding Hood," her characters depart even more drastically from convention, and her flair for regenerating the source materials with zestful gusto declares its full caliber. Thus, "The Werewolf" outrageously intimates that the heroine's Grandmother might actually be the Wolf— as well as a witch. In "The Company of Wolves," the protagonist herself is foregrounded as the champion of unconventionality, her own sexual hunger and voracious eroticism allowing her to subjugate the lupine predator. Able to dispel the ancient threats and disrupt the obtuse customs perpetuated by superstition and lore with the disarming power of laughter, the girl firmly believes that she is "nobody's meat" and acts accordingly: "she laughed at him full in the face, she ripped off his shirt for him and flung it into the fire, in the fiery wake of her own discarded clothing. The flames danced like dead souls on Walpurgisnacht and the old bones under the bed set up a terrible clattering but she did not pay them any heed" (p. 219). As the story's final lines amusingly indicate, the girl's refusal to be intimidated — let alone submit to her intended destiny as the carnivorous male's prey — paves the way to her triumph: "See! sweet and sound she sleeps in granny's bed, between the paws of the tender wolf" (p. 220). Carter will again celebrate the unsurpassed capacities of the laughing woman in the grand finale of *Nights at the Circus*.

It is here worth noting, in appreciation of Carter's overall contribution to fairy tale history, that comparably unconventional characters also populate her fairy tales for children. The heroines of both *The Donkey Prince* (Carter 1970a) and *Miss Z, the Dark Young Lady* (Carter 1970b), for instance, foreshadow the plucky female types to be found in several of the narratives collected in *The Bloody Chamber and Other Stories* as women willing to venture into unfamiliar and perilous realities and to transgress al manner of rules, customs and prohibitions. These characters' *raison d'être* is obviously not the monolithic yearning to marry a prince with which so many fairy tale protagonists are associated in less inspired tellings of the classic yarns. In this regard, the tales in question elude strict compartmentalization as juvenile entertainment, since their duskier and graver moments actually render them appealing to a multigenerational public.

Carter's translation of Charles Perrault's eighteenth-century fairy tales likewise attests to her resolutely unconventional take on the traditional form. Carter is deeply sensitive to Perrault's ironical ambivalence, and therefore aware that his tendency to incorporate morals geared toward the ethical shaping of children does not preclude his cultivation of a refreshingly modern and playful perspective. This entails a preparedness to foster attitudes to gender relations which are by no means inimical to a feminist agenda despite the many adaptations of his work hell-bent on exploiting it as a conservative mythology. As Martine Hennard Dutheil de la Rochère emphasizes, the result of Carter's effort is a groundbreaking translation that seeks to "recover the worldly and practical purpose of Perrault's *contes*.... As in her 'Little Red Riding Hood,' the wise 'modern woman' prepared to wait for a suitable husband is opposed to the foolish 'young girls' impatient to marry and live out their empty (and self-centered) dream. The authorial voice ironizes their quest for a 'brave, rich, handsome' husband, himself commodified as a 'prize,' and cautions against the attitudes encouraged by the Sleeping Beauty myth (but certainly not by Perrault's 'La Belle au bois dormant') — namely, the desire to marry young because of the appeal of a fairy-tale marriage" (de la Rochère).

A paradigmatic illustration of Carter's approach can be found precisely in her translation of "La Belle au bois dormant," which she tersely refuses to interpret in accordance with the psychoanalytical readings influenced by Bettelheim's work in vogue in the 1970s. *Sleeping Beauty*, argues Carter, actually constitutes "a perfect parable of sexual trauma and awakening. But Perrault resolutely eschews making any such connections; and quite right, too. Never a hint that a girl's first encounter with a phallic object might shock her into a death-like trance. She's the victim of a power struggle among the heavy female fairy mafia. We're dealing with the real world, not the phantasia of the unconscious. Children get quite enough of that in the privacy of their own homes" (Carter 1998, pp. 453–454). These are the very aspects of Perrault's tale which Carter seeks to bring out in her translation — and, as we have seen, to incorporate in her subsequent appropriations of other classic stories.

In questioning all sorts of narrative stereotypes through her varyingly unorthodox or deviant personae, Carter does not only take issue with the stultifying stereotypes enforces by patriarchy but also — and no less trenchantly — with the narrow-minded brand of so-called feminism that is only too keen to blame women's predicaments on men and, by allegorical extensions, on males of all species. Prisons, cages and bloody chambers may well turn out to be of women's own making and women themselves to have caused the conditions of their physical or emotional victimization by perpetuating their definition as passive fatalities of male desire. This stance echoes the state of affairs discussed in the preceding chapter vis-à-vis Carter's ironical utilization of mythical and pseudo-mythical female figures. Simultaneously, in firmly declining to indulge in idealistic representations of either femininity or masculinity, Carter steers clear of utopian agendas promising to overturn for good the grand narratives spawned by patriarchy and feminism alike. These discourse must be examined — and, as far as humanly feasible disrupted — through imaginative counterdiscursive strategies. Yet, it would be dangerously absurd to assume that such moves can lead to a conclusive erasure of all time-honored categories or to a total dissolution of the establishment as we know it. Transgression, accordingly, must be seen as a potential resource nested within the fabric of the everyday and the legitimate — just as the carnival, as we shall see in the next two chapters, cannot be presumed to replace ordinary life permanently but should rather be understood as its dialectical challenger within prescribed boundaries.

At the same time as she imparts tantalizing variations on traditional themes for the purposes of both generic experimentation and cultural critique, Carter strives to draw attention to the very processes through which her tales are constructed and relayed by her narrators. As Steve Roberts argues, in this regard, "the question of who has the initiative at any moment in her stories is one that Carter returns to again and again. She wants to show who has the power to make things happen" (Roberts, p. 71). In the opening segment of "The Bloody Chamber," for example, the young bride revisits the events leading to the present moment in the form of an extended flashback which emplaces her point of view as the dominant narrative perspective. Carter's approach is here redolent of the stream of consciousness mode as cultivated by many modernist writers — except for the fact that the clinical lucidity with which her character's recollections are reconstructed serves to contain its dreamier elements. As a result, the girl appears so cognizant of the flow of her memories as to couch her impressions in a style which could be more appositely described as "consciousness of stream."

The protagonist's point of view remains central as she incrementally reveals her natural propensity to probe the appearance of her environment in an effort to grasp its true essence. At the same time, she is keen to decipher the meaning of her own often ambivalent responses — especially vis-à-vis the Marquis, to whom she feels willfully yet inexplicably drawn despite the ominous "absence of light" in his eyes and the "mask"-like qualities of his face (Carter 2006d, p. 112). The girl is also aware that she only ever succeeds in stealing a look at the truth behind the Marquis' actions through the many mirrors surrounding his bed — at which point, however, she is also reduced to her most passive function by being forced to act as a "multitude of girls" intended to satisfy her husband's desire to possess, albeit specularly, an entire "harem" (p. 118). In spite of her passivity, the narrator occasionally manages to appropriate and distort gender-inflected narrative conventions for her specific purpose. This is epitomized by the passage in which she imparts an ironical twist on the conventional comparison between femininity and a tender flower by equating the Marquis himself to a lily — and one of a very specific kind. "I know it must seem a curious analogy, a man with a flower," she self-consciously announces, "but sometimes he seemed to me ... like one of those cobra-headed, funereal lilies whose white sheaths are curled out of a flesh so thick and tensely yielding to the touch as vellum" (p. 113).

The heroine in "The Tiger's Bride" is portrayed as likewise conscious and critical of her circumstances from an early stage in the story, as she censures her father's self-destructive addictions and dispassionately assesses the "humiliating bargain" (p. 163) in which she has been inveigled. As the adventure progresses, to culminate in a redemptive metamorphosis that lingers in memory as one of the most spectacular yet most moving moments in Carter's entire opus, the character's reasoned approach to her ordeal increasingly bears witness not only to her possession of a resilient and resourceful personality but also to the kind of roundabout metaphysical complexity of which fairy tales alone are capable. With "Puss-in-Boots," to cite a further instance of Carter's manipulation of her narrative voices, we are presented with a flamboyantly caricatured version of male egotism embellished with overripe rhetoric, theatrical gestures, clownish humor and parodic allusions to *Hamlet* to boot.

While Carter's version of "Puss-in-Boots" cheerfully indulges in a happy ending of vaguely Disneyesque flavor, her overall take on the traditional tale evinces marked affinities with one of the more audacious of her influences, the seventeenth-century Italian fairy tale collector, poet and courtier Giambattista Basile. Accordingly, at the same time as she playfully foregrounds the anthropomorphic hero's egocentricity, Carter also seeks to emphasize the effervescent sense of vitality intrinsic in the original yarn. To abet this task, she consistently imparts the action with picaresque rhythms and imagery redolent of *The Infernal Desire Machines of Doctor Hoffman*, while also revamping Basile's penchant for blending the sublime and the ridiculous in the most unexpected ways, his talent for lewd jokes, and his aversion to conventional notions of hierarchy and order. Thus, as Roemer and Bacchilega emphasize, Carter deploys both her feline and her human heroes to disrupt "Disney's staid commitment to depictions of 'clean' living and other 'family values'" by allowing her characters to indulge in "frequent and raucous sexual escapades" (Roemer and Bacchilega, p. 14).

As they lean toward the iconoclastic end of the narrative spectrum, Carter's methods of characterization do not lose sight of the universally representative qualities held by many classic motifs enshrined in the fairy tale tradition. An especially important is accorded to the individual's development through transformative experiences of varying magnitude. In this regard, Carter's strategies often bring to mind Max Lüthi's contention that "the fairy tale is not concerned with individual destinies. Nor is it the unique process of maturation that is reflected in the fairy tale. The story of Sleeping Beauty," for example, "is more than an imaginatively stylized love story portraying the withdrawal of a girl and the breaking of the spell through the young lover. One instinctively conceives of the princess as an image for the human spirit: the story portrays the endowment, peril, paralysis, and redemption not just of one girl, but of all mankind" (Lüthi, p. 24).

In assessing the thematic dimension of the transformation trope, it is important to grasp, with Lüthi, its inherently psychological weight. Lüthi expounds this idea with reference to the time-honored trope of the hideous frog's transformation into a magnificent prince. This image symbolically encapsulates the metaphysical law which sanctions that "Lower natures are to be transformed into higher ones." On the one hand, such a process could be considered beneficial to the extension of conscious "awareness." On the other hand, it intimates that no sublimating move of this kind could ever "take place without suffering and sacrifice — and cruelty," which indicates that for consciousness to prevail, our "instincts — no matter how much they protect and nourish us — must not be left to themselves." In fact, "they must be enchanted or disenchanted, redeemed and purified by the power of the intellect," which is ultimately tantamount to an act of brute violence (Lüthi, p. 80).

The devotees of enlightened rationalism will feasibly uphold the fairy tale's power to dramatize this sanitizing moment even if they ridicule or ignore the form on every other count. Lüthi's own critique, however, suggests that interpretations of the fairy tale concerned solely with the triumph of reason are unlikely to appreciate its true significance. Most lamentably, they are powerless to comprehend the degree to which its depiction of a character's encounter with dark, amorphous and bestial energies alludes to the need to confront and embrace the human soul's own shadows. Lüthi articulates this hypothesis by recourse to Novalis' tantalizing approach to the fairy tale's use of transformation: "'In one tale a bear is transformed into a prince the moment he is loved. Perhaps a similar transformation would occur if man began to love the evil in the world.'" Lüthi's own line of reasoning opens up Novalis' perspective, stating that "the fairy tale suggests this in images which produce a much more powerful effect on the mind and heart of its hearers than do moralistic doctrines" (p. 81).

In *The Bloody Chamber and Other Stories*, the theme of metamorphosis is incontestably ubiquitous. At times, multiple implications of this phenomenon are compacted within an extremely capsulated format — most notably, in "The Snow Child," where the pivotal transformation is posited as the ephemeral product of a male fantasy fated to evaporate once its initiator has swiftly given vent to his sexual prowess. At other times, they are elaborately ritualized so as to resemble a dark parody of some solemn religious ceremony — e.g., in "The Lady of the House of Love," where the topos of transformation is ironically intertwined with its very antithesis insofar as the vampiric Countess at its center is constitutionally locked in a state of eternal youthfulness. At others still, transformation may result, as "Wolf-Alice" reminds us, from the redemptive power of selfless care and thoughtful cooperation as forces capable of imparting a sense of identity on a creature who initially lacks any genuine sense of individuality or selfhood. Transformation, most importantly, is positively portrayed as the culmination of a process of self-emancipation, as "The Tiger's Bride" proposes in a sensational fashion, to show that liberating moves may be performed within the apparently most oppressive of circumstances. In fact, Carter intimates, these are very possibly the only moves which can be considered truly liberating since anything of the kind which is staged not in a hostile environment but in a utopian realm of unrestrained freedom is always bound to amount to a vapid and useless dream. Once again, we are reminded that all transgressive experiences must be understood as events situated within the establishment and not in some wholly fantastical, untested and ultimately escapist beyond.

Bacchilega argues that the metamorphic capacities intrinsic in the fairy tale as both a narrative form and a cultural tradition are demonstrated by its unique adaptability to changing historical circumstances. "Fairy tales," according to Bacchilega, "have a history of magic transformations. Scholars of folk narrative know this well and have increasingly been interested in following the tales' trajectories not only in so-called traditional or oral settings but also into the multimedia worlds of literature and popular culture. At the same time, literary scholarship has increasingly remarked on the fairy tale's versatility in history as a genre that has ... successfully morphed to codify social norms and to nurture the desire for change" (Bacchilega, p. 181). Concurrently, the reactions evinced by contemporary readers, listeners or viewers to present-day adaptations of old narratives are bound to be shaped by their own emotional and mental journeys.

Zipes has eloquently corroborated the proposition that the fairy tale's passion for transformation as a thematic and storytelling device has a direct parallel in its evolution as a form and in its continued existence. "The notion of miraculous transformation," the critic contends, "is key to understanding most of the traditional fairy tales that have stuck in us and with us. Just as we as a species have mutated, often in wondrous ways, so has the oral folk tale transformed itself and been transformed as literary fairy tale to assist us in coming to terms with the absurdity and banality of everyday life" (Zipes 2006, p. xii). Simultaneously, the phases of incremental metamorphosis through which the fairy tale has progressed can be seen to animate the broader phenomenon of "cultural transmission" (p. xiii) at large as envisioned by Luigi Cavalli-Sforza — namely, a "mutation, or transformation that brings about the creation of a new idea" (Cavalli-Sforza, p. 68).

Zipes argues that by pondering the cultural developments through which the fairy tale has endured in ever-shifting configurations over the centuries, we can gradually identify the fascinating processes through which "the literary fairy tale has evolved from the stories of the oral tradition, piece by piece in a process of incremental adaptation," and "special forms of telling" have hence emerged as a distinctive "species" (Zipes 2006, p. 3). While it would be specious to refute that "Oral tales ... are thousands of years old and it is impossible to date and explain how they were generated," there is plenty of dependable evidence to back the argument that "they must have become vital for adapting to the environment and changes in the environment as soon as humans began to communicate through language ... those that continued to have cultural significance were 'imitated' and passed on.... Bits and pieces, what we may call motifs, characters, topoi, plots, and images, were carried on and retold.... Gradually, as tales were used to serve specific functions in court entertainment, homes, and taverns, on public squares, fields, and work places, and during rituals such as birth, marriage, death, harvest, initiation, and so on, they were distinguished by the minds of the members of a community and given special attention" (p. 13).

Carter is highly sensitive to the fairy tale's susceptibility to editing, adaptive and rewriting moves which reflect the priorities of disparate societal milieux. She is also alert to their tendency to grow increasingly multilayered over time as the old intermingling of popular and literary forms has had to find ways of integrating mass media appropriations of traditional tales in its mix. In her introduction to *The Virago Book of Fairy Tales*, Carter comments on this ongoing process as follows: "the chances are, the story was put together in the form we have it, more or less out of all sorts of bits of other stories long ago and far away, and has been tinkered with, had bits added to it, lost other bits, got mixed up with other stories, until our informant herself has tailored the story personally to suit an audience ... or, simply, to suit herself" (Carter 1990, p. x). Fairy tales meet and merge in kaleidoscopically varied constellations in a collective cauldron to which anyone, in principle, has access — not only as a reader or listener in search of entertainment but also as a creator in search of malleable expressive vehicles.

We are hence presented with a speculative universe consisting entirely of textual and narrative gestures which have been incrementally traced, displaced, distorted, reimagined and mapped on one another over several centuries or perhaps even millennia. It would indeed be difficult to deny that fairy tales have been an integral component of disparate civilizations for thousands upon thousands of years. Eminent anthropologists, folklore experts, sociologists, psychologists, literary critics, pedagogists and natural scientists would endorse this proposition and readily demonstrate its empirical verifiability despite its seemingly pretentious stance. Simultaneously, Carter strives to demonstrate how even the most disillusioned reader may learn to interact with imaginary and lore-encrusted narratives as metaphors for the hidden depths of the human animal, and hence as ancestral agencies with a potential to sustain many a human voyage of forever deferred self-discovery.

Through Carter's bold voice, the fairy tale tradition communicates its worth as a powerful allegorical correlative for the wide variety of imaginative avenues which societies motivated entirely by the imperatives of profit and glamour have been routinely blocking off for some decades on a virtually global scale. Readiness to leave such avenues open, and to allow their routes to be pursued, amounts to a commodious disposition toward the unknown and the unfathomed: the affective attitude critical to the advancement of the human imagination and to any genuine achievement of a creative kind in the domains of science and art alike.

The fairy tale's use of transformation ultimately constitutes an incontestable reminder of the existence of reality levels which humans could never presume to dominate or even, more often than not, begin to grasp. This is because the fairy tale, as Cooper persuasively argues, posits "the supernatural" as its "primary" focus, whereas "saga, and the legends derived from it, have their feet on the ground and the otherworldly, if it occurs, is a secondary consideration." Therefore, whereas in the narrative domains of "saga and legend, Man is confronted with Nature and his own kind; in the realm of faerie he encounters supernatural forces that are always a manifestation of some power beyond the normal world and beyond his control. Even if this force is manifested through some perfectly ordinary event yet it confers the power of magic and transformation." As the unmatched trigger of the marvelous occurrences resulting from such "magic and transformation," the supernatural is hence brought into play to mark our insertion in a realm governed by agencies "different from mankind, operating in a realm either above or below it" (Cooper, p. 18)—an alternate universe made profoundly mysterious, even before any weird phenomena have had a chance to unfold within its crepuscular lands, precisely by the ambiguity of its spatial positioning vis-à-vis humanity.

According to Cooper, a careful evaluation of the part played by the topos of transformation in fairy tales ought also to consider the impact upon the form of the teachings and methodologies of "alchemy, which arrived in Europe from the east and from the Arabic culture of the Middle Ages into Spain, leaving its imprint not only on scholarship but also on popular story. It gave the fairy tale the symbols of gold and silver, sol and luna, king and queen, and the concept of transmuting of base metal into silver and gold, representing the inner journey to find one's identity" (p. 21). No ancient discipline could constitute a better metaphor than alchemy for the alternately mercurial and auric worlds summoned by Carter's fairy tale sensibility with the zest and humor of a latter-day fairy godmother.

CHAPTER 6

Beyond Gravity
Nights at the Circus

This is the secret of all good storytelling: to lie, but to keep the arithmetic sound. A storyteller, like any other sort of enthusiastic liar, is on an unpredictable adventure. His initial lie, his premise, will suggest many new lies of its own. The storyteller must choose among them, seeking those which are most believable, which keep the arithmetic sound. Thus does a story generate itself.

—Kurt Vonnegut

The play therapy is designed to restore a state of health in which the reader accepts fiction for what it is: language, nothing but language, and nothing beyond language.... Literature can have nothing to do with anything that lies outside the game space of language, simply because there are no rules as to how to play those games beyond language ...

—Allen Thiher

As we have seen in the preceding chapters, Carter's writings are assiduously concerned with multifarious cultural activities revolving around the acts of seeing and looking, and accordingly utilize the images of the theater, the peep show and the screen as some of their major tropes. Carter revisits these issues in *Night at the Circus* with a focus on the virtual ubiquity of spectacle and performance as the animating forces of both its private and its public interactions. Thus, the novel proposes that dramatic and performative elements pervade with equal persistence a sensational circensian act and a personal interview, a glamorous parade and a moment of sexual intimacy. This key aspect of *Night at the Circus*, evident across its unfolding, can be seen to hold equal prominence in its inceptive segment and its climax. In the former, the narrative transits fluidly in and out of the hushed privacy of the heroine's dressing room, on the one hand, and the boisterous limelight of her professional life on the other. In both contexts, spectacle and performance are posited as integral to both the overall drama and the advancement of the protagonist's picaresque progression.

The interweaving of the private and the public is also embedded in the very nature of the autobiographical narration delivered by Fevvers with unrelenting dramatic self-awareness in the course of her interview with Walser: a performance shaded throughout by doubts regarding the reliability of her storytelling voice and hence the veracity of the facts she recounts. While her discovery as a baby in a basket on the doorstep of a brothel highlights the story's personal component, the revelation that she sprouts wings upon reaching adolescence (having only evinced lumps on her shoulders up to that point) paves the way to the heroine's public role. This dimension is reinforced by the tales surrounding her employment as a living artifact: first in the role of a statue of Cupid to adorn the brothel's reception area, and then as an icon of the Winged Victory holding a sword treasured by the madam herself, Ma Nelson. The public role held by Fevvers not just as a budding performer but also — and far more ominously — as a theatrical prop of sorts gains weight with the stories revolving around her appropriation by the formidable Madame Schreck, who places the girl on display alongside other female captives endowed with bizarre physiques and qualities in a sinister business combination of freak show and whorehouse, and subsequent sale to Christian Rosencreutz, a regular client, who is hell-bent on sacrificing a winged virgin as a means of achieving immortality. This sequence of performance-oriented events escalate to full spectacle with Fevvers' decision to join Colonel Kearney's circus as an aerialist and her swift rise to immense fame.

In the climactic portion of the story, likewise, Carter moves seamlessly across scenes of communal interplay so populous and noisy as to appear to swamp the personal dimension altogether, and textual pockets of sensuous proximity while highlighting, once again, the centrality of spectacle and performance to both realities. The spectacular element progressively acquires momentum as we move from the scenes charting the entire circus' Eastward train journey across the continent, the train's attack by a band of runaway convicts and apocalyptic destruction, to the removal to the convicts' camp of the whole troupe except Walser, who ends up as a shaman's apprentice. The multi-setting portion of the narrative following these sensational moments provides Carter with further opportunities for theatrical exuberance. Most notable, in this respect, are the sequences in which Fevvers asks the clowns to entertain the despondent convicts and both the entertainers and their audience end up being blown away into the night by a mighty blizzard. The pace of the action gradually begins to mellow — though by no means to slacken — as the remnants of the company, seeking to return to civilization, find refuge in a derelict music school, while Fevvers and Lizzie resolve to look for Walser. The personal element would seem to win the day as Fevvers and Walser, reunited at last, greet the new century together amid fond embraces.

In the final analysis, the ascendancy of spectacle and performance is emplaced by Carter as a logical corollary of a basic human propensity — so basic, in fact, as to be categorizable as an atavistic need or instinctual drive — which the prismatic cast of *Night at the Circus* embodies to paradigmatic degrees. This refers to the human tendency to orchestrate existence around the endless staging of acts capable of providing settings and opportunities for the narration of stories. It is through these acts and the narratives they are made to accommodate that identities may be forged and sustained. Thus, Carter proposes that we are constantly spinning narrative weaves *about* ourselves and other people as well as *to* ourselves and other people. In telling such stories, we perform specific narrative moves that are ineluctably endowed with theatrical connotations (even at their quietest and least obtrusive), insofar as the act of narration is inseparable from performance.

As we journey through life, we are forced to face variable enigmas: hence, we are enjoined by circumstances to adapt our performances and our yarns to those changing scenarios so as to address different questions — and, no less crucially, learn how to question different facets of both our personal situations and our collective engagements in light of those shifts. Carter's focus on these issues is, in a sense, a direct offshoot of her ludic sensibility. Indeed, as R. A. Lanham reminds us, the Latin concept of *ludus* "pulls together the public and the private domains; public spectacle or game, stage-playing, joke, private amusement.... Above all, it reflects what all share ... all are self-conscious about language and literary form, making all language a *ludus*, a knowing public display of rhetoric, a game" (Lanham, p. 29).

An especially important image in Carter's articulation of the politics of visuality in *Nights at the Circus* is the panopticon. This image is inspired by the writings of Michel Foucault, no less close a traveling companion for Carter in the area of poststructuralist thought than Roland Barthes. Investigating the multifold strategies deployed by disparate cultures and ideologies in order to render their subjects docile, and thus secure their compliance with the status quo, Foucault posits the human body as a primary site of monitoring, policing and all-around regimentation. An especially important role is played, within the philosopher's writings on this topic, by the concept of dividing practices — namely, the ensemble of activities and measures designed to isolate putatively deviant and disruptive individuals. Such practices include the confinement of the mentally afflicted to asylums — the very same facilities, incidentally, once used for the segregation of lepers — and the concurrently physiological and psychiatric penetration of medical patients by the scrutinizing gaze of omnipotent professionals.

Schools, factories, barracks and armies, argues Foucault, can be seen to depend on analogous ruses for the emplacement and maintenance of their authority. They accordingly depend on rigid hierarchies and timetables, repetitive tasks, normalizing criteria, and a meticulously spatialized modus operandi whereby every subject is expected to perform (and behave) within a carefully prescribed place. As Foucault emphasizes, "one finds in the program of the Panopticon a ... concern with individualizing observation, with characterization and classification, with the analytical arrangement of space" (Foucault, p. 203). In this perspective, the panopticon comes into play as an ideal correctional tool meant to maximize the effectiveness of solitary confinement on all manner of offenders. Foucault's discussion of this specific dividing practice presumes a recognition of the gradual evolution of the relationship between power and visuality in Western societies. Foucault is particularly concerned with the shift, alluded to in Chapter 3, from the principle of spectacle — abetting the control of the masses through opulent display — to the principle of surveillance — based on the observer's ability to see all while remaining unseen — as the key mechanisms supporting the machinery of government and animating its ubiquitous deterrents.

Derived from the utilitarian philosopher Jeremy Bentham, the image of the panopticon epitomizes the transition to the modern concept of surveillance: a corollary, according to Foucault, of the erosion of feudal and agrarian dispensations triggered by the Industrial Revolution, and related unanchoring of traditional notions of identity, community and belonging. On a broader plane, the panopticon also operates as a potent metaphor for the pervasively carceral nature of human society at large. Within this diabolically planned architectural configuration, each convict is confined to a small cell and unrelentingly watched by the invisible, yet all-seeing, eye of a single being — an Orwellian Big Brother of sorts. The panopticon's principal goal, Foucault maintains, is "to induce in the inmate a state of consciousness and permanent visibility that assures the automatic functioning of power" and thus ensure that each prisoner becomes his or her own jailer (p. 201).

Panoptical vision carries immense relevance to contemporary technologized societies, as indicated by the exponential growth of surveillance-oriented apparatuses, and is hence telling evidence of the ongoing pertinence of Carter's fiction to today's world even as it seems to fly off into the wildest realms of fantasy and fable. The ascendancy of that phenomenon today is attested to by the specific context of Carter's own culture. "The British have become more closely watched," Henry Porter explains in the *Afterword* to his novel *The Dying Light*, "than any other people in the West — maybe in the entire world. We have more CCTV cameras than the rest of Europe put together. CCTV infests not only streets and shopping centres, but restaurants, cinemas and pubs where, with the encouragement of the police and local officials, cameras record the head and shoulders of every individual who enters. People are watched the whole time" (Porter, p. 514). An assessment of contemporary reality which only a few years ago would have smacked of Orwellian dystopianism, and many people would have derisively dismissed as a case of conspiracy theory syndrome writ large, is now hard to refute by anybody who has cared to look at the world dispassionately — as Carter was unremittingly wont to do.

The panopticon might at first come across as a relatively marginal textual presence in *Nights at the Circus* but actually proves crucial to the world picture informing its narrative fabric. The image makes its spectacular appearance with the women's penitentiary conceived by the Countess P. This constitutes both an embodiment of the perfect prison ideated by Bentham as a putatively progressive penal structure, and an exemplification of Foucault's notion of the panopticon as a means of optimizing discipline through relentless surveillance — a system in which, somewhat perversely, the privilege of concealment is totally denied and "visibility" itself becomes "a trap" (Foucault, p. 200). The Countess' prison is configured with the same degree of demonic punctiliousness as the template commended by Bentham: "it was a panopticon she forced them to build, a hollow circle of cells shaped like a doughnut, the inward-facing wall of which was composed of grids of steel and, in the middle of the roofed, central courtyard, there was a round room surrounded by windows" (Carter 2006e, p. 247). Each prisoner is constantly visible to the monitor situated in the center of the doughnut, which secures their uninterrupted exposure to the warden's probing gaze, and invisible both to the other convicts and to the guards. No less significantly, the women are deprived not solely of the sight but also of the touch of other humans.

The Countess is supposedly motivated by charitable intentions, her goal being the creation of an institution in which various women who have killed their husbands might regret their crimes, accept responsibility for their deeds, and thus reenter human society as properly normalized subjects. Her panopticon, therefore, is essentially conceived of as a disciplinary machine intended to inculcate contrition as the prerequisite of genuine atonement. The prison revolves around an introspective practice which its artificer regards as "a therapy of meditation" designed to follow a disarmingly simple route: "the women in the bare cells, in which was neither privacy nor distraction, cells formulated on the principle of those in a nunnery where all was visible to the eye of God, would live alone with the memory of their crime until they acknowledged, not their guilt — most of them had done that, already — but their responsibility. And she was sure that with responsibility would come remorse" (p. 248). For the Countess' prisoners, as for the docile subject theorized by Foucault, punishment pivots on the internalization of the law, whereby the guilty party's own conscience, as we have seen, becomes the supreme custodian.

In outlining this process, Carter engages in a characteristically tongue-in-cheek critique of the collusion, or perhaps collision, of gender politics and inherited ethics. She thus highlights an unresolved tension between how the murderesses actually feel about their crimes and how they are supposed to perceive those acts by the Countess — and, by extension, the discourse of power she unquestioningly promotes through her putatively reforming initiative. Ironically, the Countess herself is guilty of mariticide and would seem never to have got over her guilt: hence, her unacknowledged keenness to displace her sin onto others by having them participate in its expiation — or indeed carry her burden on her behalf. Her plan is destined to boomerang, however, for the flimsily idealistic vessel of her vision is eventually capsized by the reality of the convicts' personalities, emotions and true aspirations. As Joanne M. Gass points out, "unfortunately for the Countess P., her victims are nothing like her, and in all the years of the prison's existence not one woman has come forward to receive the Countess's benediction. Not one of the inmates feels responsibility, much less remorse; each of them views her act as one in which she has freed herself from the intolerable tyranny of a husband whose every cruel act is justified and legitimized by the state."

At the same time, the centrality of the panoptical model to the novel as a whole is borne out by the ubiquity of strategies of inspection and compartmentalization governed by visual criteria. Walser, for instance, "is in London ... to observe, to objectify, to subject Fevvers to his scrutiny, to define her. Jack is part of a system that defines others by labeling, naming, and describing what they are — a 'hoax' or a humbug, perhaps, but never an individual human being. Knowing someone in this system means classifying her" (Gass). Analogous priorities underpin the establishments progressively occupied by the heroine in the course her saga (the brothel, the freak show, the circus). All of these domains are shaped by the principles of spectacle and performance, routinely fashioning their subjects as items on display to be either ocularly or manually consumed by a viewing public in search of relatively safe thrills. Like the panopticon's inmates in Foucault's own description, these entities are akin to performers relegated to a studiously delimited stage: hemmed in by the impervious walls of "small theatres, in which each actor is alone, perfectly individualized and constantly visible." Such spaces are, by virtue of their very architecture, capable of inculcating "in the inmate a state of consciousness and permanent visibility that assures the automatic functioning of power" (Foucault, p. 201).

It is also vital to appreciate both the image of panopticon itself and Carter's reflections concerning possible ways of counterbalancing its tyrannical ascendancy not only as discrete aspects of the novel but also in terms of the prison's dialectical relationship with seemingly carnivalesque and disruptive discourses. These include, in especially prominent roles, the world of the circus and the tradition of shamanism. In the sphere of the circus, conventional notions of order, hierarchy and stability appear to fall apart, as wild beasts behave like thoroughly encultured humans and humans, in turn, are placed in animalistic roles. At the same time, Carter is determined to impart its circensian vision with a cogent sense of history.

Without for an instant indulging in gratuitous name dropping, *Nights at the Circus* accordingly abounds with subtle hints at several major figures in the annals of clowning. Thus, even as the text repeatedly alludes to canonical authors and artists such as Shakespeare, Swift, Blake, Poe, Baudelaire, Goethe and Mozart, it is no less profoundly indebted to disparate actors: from Charles Adrien Wettach (*Grock*) to Ernie Burch (*Blinko*), from the Fratellinis to Buster Keaton, from Charlie Chaplin to Tony Hancock, from Abbot and Costello to Jacques Tati, from the Marx Brothers to Laurel and Hardy — and the list could no doubt stretch on considerably, particularly in the hands of a clown aficionado. At the same time, the novel's cast frequently brings to mind several of the major stock roles found in popular traditions closely related to clowning, notably *Commedia dell'Arte* and germane mask-oriented theatrical forms. These include the witty and nimble Harlequin, the unscrupulous Scaramouche, the slow-witted but honest Pierrot, the braggart Captain, the arrogant yet gullible merchant Pantaloon: all of them characters whose salient traits may be found, upon careful inspection, to underlie Carter's characterization through the text.

In the shaman's world, as in the sphere of the circus and particularly the clowning component thereof, established patterns of logic and reason are ruptured by the subversive interpenetration of the spirit and human domains. Regarded as mediators or messengers enabling the human dimension and the spirit dimension to interact, shamans are held capable of treating all manner of ailments, traumas and psychosomatic imbalances by purging the soul or spirit of the afflicted and hence restoring the physical body's integrity and natural equilibrium. In order to abet the human world and alleviate problems held to emanate from the infiltration of alien elements into the human body, the shaman operates principally within the spiritual realm, repeatedly visiting its alternate realities with the intention of solving, or at least mitigating, the problems that trouble both the individual and the community. Carter's choice of location for her shamanic adventures is fully explained by the relevant *Wikipedia* entry: "Siberia is regarded as the *locus classicus* of shamanism. It is inhabited by many different ethnic groups. Many of its Uralic, Altaic, and Paleosiberian peoples observe shamanistic practices even in modern times. Many classical ethnographic sources of 'shamanism' were recorded among Siberian peoples" ("Shamanism").

Despite their subversive undercurrents, the sites of creative anarchy released by both the circus and the shamanic realm are presented by *Nights at the Circus* as cultural discourses contained within well-defined milieux and regulated by their own internal logic and architecture — the literally encircling and containing spaces of the ring and the village. In neither case is the disorder allowed to contaminate the reality stretching beyond the designated zones of performance and spectacle. At the same time, the world of clowning — the epitome of circensian practice at its rowdiest — is compared to a carceral dimension. "Clown Alley, the generic name of all lodgings of all clowns," is described as "a place where reigned the lugubrious atmosphere of a prison or a madhouse" (Carter 2006e, p. 134). The state of affairs here depicted offers a perfect analogy for Foucault's disciplinary template. Additionally, clowns are not unproblematically categorizable as ludic agents of unrestrained fun: the medical profession in fact recognizes the pathological fear of clowns (*coulrophobia*) as a well-documented and not particularly unusual syndrome.

As the entry for "Clown" in Wikipedia comments, "many people find clowns disturbing rather than amusing. It is common for children to be afraid of disguised, exaggerated, or costumed figures — even Santa Claus. Ute myths feature a cannibalistic clown monster called the Siats." This phobia can be attributed to several factors but seems most likely to stem from either the clown's corporeal and sartorial attributes, which invariably signal a troubling deviation from conventional notions of propriety, harmony and docility, or the contexts in which they are encountered. "Clowns' costumes," the article continues, "tend to exaggerate the facial features and some body parts, such as hands and feet and noses. This can be read as monstrous or deformed as easily as it can be read as comical." Yet, it has also been suggested that these figures' somatic characteristics are not necessarily unsettling per se but only acquire menacing connotations as a result of "early childhood experience, when infants begin to process and make sense of facial features. The significant aberrations in a clown's face may frighten a child so much that they carry this phobia throughout their adult life." Moreover, even grown-ups who do not carry the legacy of infantile traumas of this type may still be disconcerted by the appearance of a clown in an unexpected context and consider uncanny and latently ominous images which they would easily dismiss as innocent fun in different circumstances. Therefore, whereas "at a circus or a party, a clown is normal and may easily be funny," the very "same clown knocking on one's front door at sunset or sitting in a diner ... is more likely to generate fear or distress than laughter or amusement. This effect is summed up in a quote often attributed to actor Lon Chaney, Sr.: 'There is nothing funny about a clown in the moonlight'" ("Clown").

The world of the circus, of which clowning could be regarded as the epitome, cannot be regarded, in the light of these reflections, as an unequivocal wellhead of amusement, laughter and relaxation — let alone unlimited freedom. Likewise, the cosmos disclosed by shamanism is necessarily restricted, despite its ostensible infinity and spell-binding fluidity. As Carter emphasizes, however far and wide it might extend in its oneiric and hallucinatory peregrinations, it is powerless to "extend laterally" and cannot, therefore, "take into account any other interpretation of the world." This implies that in principle, that universe of apparently inestimable vastness and never-ending opportunities for exploration and experiment may ultimately degenerate into a vision as monolithic or dogmatic as the strictest rationalist ideology. Its "cosmogony, for all its complexity of forms, impulses and states of being perpetually in flux," proves finally and irrevocably "finite" for the simple reason that it constitutes, like any other ideology, "a human invention" (p. 299). Most vitally, the transgressive acts associated with the cultural domains of both the circus and shamanism are shown by Carter to be provisional, and order to be reinstated as soon as the carnivalesque moment is over. As Gass observes, "The circus provides a forum whereby society may indulge itself without, in fact, exposing itself to the dangers that the clowns represent. We must not forget that carnival is a legitimized event 'allowed' by the power structure" (Gass).

Night at the Circus corroborates this proposition in its utterly unsentimental depiction of the subversive energy of clowning as a cultural force which is accorded a legitimate place and scope of influence within society only on condition that it is kept within recognizable boundaries. The garish performers are thus "permitted the most ferocious piracies as long as, just so long as, they maintain the bizarrerie of their appearance, so that their violent exposition of manners stays on the safe side of terror." However, even as the clowns' stylized performance is drained of its more malign connotations, their viewers are aware, deep down, that "laughter" does not emanate from carefree enjoyment so much as from a "successful suppression of fear" (Carter 2006e, p. 176). Clowns are ghettoized as subjects entitled to perform within spaces that allow for the legitimate deployment of their aberrant appearance and behavior for the purposes of entertainment or possibly playful shock. Should they transgress the carefully demarcated line separating their territory from so-called proper society, which is precisely what happens when Buffo the Great loses his mind to murderous effect, they will be automatically silenced or even, if the magnitude of their felony were to require it, punished by the most ruthless of means. The clown's carnivalesque pranks are never, therefore, completely divorced from the disciplining measures which their conduct is bound to invoke as soon as the sanctioned limits of their freedom are disrupted. Even when clowns behave entirely in accordance with normal expectations, the elements of violence and terror inherent in their manners serve as implicit reminders of the policing forces ready to seize upon virtually anything supposed to be abnormal.

The idea that the carnival is not only a liberating but also a regulatory discourse is persuasively upheld by Jonathan Dollimore in his analysis of the concepts of containment and subversion, where he contends that the carnival does not upset the social order but actually contributes to its bolstering. Central to Dollimore's argument is "the anthropological version which sees allegedly transgressive practices like carnival as not at all disturbing of dominant values but rather as their guarantor — a licensed release of social tension, a kind of safety-valve effect which far from undermining the existing order, actually contributes to its survival" (Dollimore, p. 82). The anarchic and invigorating impact of carnival occasions in which the authorities ruling the everyday world are "uncrowned" and power is usurped by the masses are also underscored by Mikhail Bakhtin. In *Rabelais and His World* and in *The Dialogic Imagination*, in particular, the philosopher maintains that such festive events, with their outbursts of satirical vulgarity and sensual looseness, provide an opportunity to interrogate and mock society's treasured mores. For Bakhtin, François Rabelais's book *Gargantua and Pantagruel*, emblematizes this frank carnivalesque expression of earthiness, indecency and irreverence.

Expounding Bakhtin's perspective on the carnival with direct reference to *The Dialogic Imagination*, Michael D. Bristol proffers insights of immediate relevance to Carter's opus at large, and specifically to the topsy-turvy reality portrayed in *Nights at the Circus*. Bristol is especially concerned with the historical evolution of the phenomenon, noting that "Bakhtin describes Carnival as a 'second life' or 'second culture' sustained by the common people or plebeian community throughout the Middle Ages and well into the early modern period." With the transition to the Renaissance age, "this culture engages with and directly opposes the 'official' culture, both in literature and in the public life of the marketplace and city square.

The 'ennobled language' of official ideology, official religion and high literature becomes saturated with the language of everyday productive life." The carnival's gradual infiltration of cultural practices extending well beyond the context of the festive moment — and especially writing and textuality — can be regarded as the historical substratum of Carter's own unique forays into carnivalesque pastiche. As the "genres of literature become 'Carnivalised,'" Bristol explains, and "their structures 'permeated with laughter, irony, humour, elements of self-parody,'" the discourse ultimately manages to infuse "into these structures an indeterminacy, a certain semantic open-endedness, a living contact with unfinished, still-evolving contemporary reality" (Bristol, p. 22; Bakhtin 2004).

The carnival as such does not de facto represent "a literary phenomenon," Bakhtin emphasizes in *Problems of Dostoevsky's Poetics*, but rather "a pageant without footlights and without a division into performers and spectators" which is convivial, instinctive, dynamic, averse to serious reflection and therefore, in principle, incompatible with the novel form itself. Nevertheless, novels with particular experimental leanings have the potential to yield "a carnival sense of the world." Bakhtin identifies various features as distinctive of the type of text which he deems informed by a characteristically carnivalesque sensibility. Especially pertinent to Carter's oeuvre is the contention that the carnival is primarily interested in suspending "hierarchical structure and all the forms of terror, reverence, piety, and etiquette connected with it" (Bakhtin 2003, p. 123). The flouting of hierarchies of all kinds — be they based on class, gender, race, species or wealth — is a trait of Carter's style which could be said to permeate virtually every syllable of the sumptuous tapestry she weaves through the pages of *Nights at the Circus*. Through this ruse, the writer harnesses the carnival's corporeal and festive excess to the articulation of a resolutely anti-binary universe in which dualities, dichotomies and ambivalences are everywhere palpable but never neatly resolved in the service of unity: that is to say, the highest goal of Western logocentrism in all its manifestations. In fact, each of the members of any one dual relationship choreographed by Carter's writing is continually engaged in a dialectical exchange with its adversary — an interminable, perpetually shifting and spiraling dialogue in which neither element is ever in a position to declare itself triumphant over the other.

Writing specifically about the type of carnivalesque play inherent in eighteenth-century English culture and fiction, Terry Castle has thrown into relief this tradition's latent association with ancient rites redolent of the other principal discourse brought into play by Carter to expose the limitations of rationalism and order, shamanism. Castle indeed maintains that in that context, "a distinctly ungenteel liberty was the goal: liberty from every social, erotic, and psychological constraint. In this search after perfect freedom — a state of intoxication, ecstasy, and free-floating sensual pleasure — the eighteenth-century masquerade demonstrated its kinship, however distant, with those rituals of possession and collective frenzy found in traditional societies" such as "shamanic rites" themselves (Castle, p. 53). Thus, "masquerade metamorphosis insinuated a new global fluidity, not only between bodies but between states of being," overthrowing the conventional "hierarchy of rank and class, destroying distinctions between masters and servants, consumers and producers" (p. 77). It would be quite inaccurate, however, to claim that the masquerade's assault on accepted notions of decorum was totally free and untamed. As Castle emphasizes, despite "all the multiplicity of costumes from which to choose, the masquerader was never entirely at liberty." In fact, "a set of implicit collective prescriptions served as a guide." Accordingly, in seeking to shock, enthrall or unsettle others, the masquerader had no choice but to adhere to "several anti-conventions" defining "how such a visual éclat was to be achieved" (p. 75).

The vestmentary codes intrinsic in the eighteenth-century masquerade can therefore be seen as eloquent evidence for the inevitable imbrication of the carnival's seemingly unrestrained world view with underlying structures of regimentation and regulation. This ambiguity is fully corroborated, in Castle's view, by the essentially paradoxical nature of the particular manifestation of carnivalesque upheaval entailed by the eighteenth-century masquerade. "On the one hand," the critic maintains, "it satisfied archaic, irrational cultural dreams — for new bodies, new pleasures, new worlds.... But on the other hand, it was a phenomenon already belated. The masquerade was the last brilliant, even brittle eruption of an impulse inexorably on its way to extinction." This fate was rendered certain by the obvious incompatibility of that whole discourse with the ideological requirements of the rising bourgeoisie, which saw it as a menace to propriety and "rationalist taxonomies," and was especially hostile to its animating icons, "mask and costume," as the dangerous "signs of a joyful exchange between self and other" which "had to be laid aside" for the sake of "more sober pursuits" (p. 107). Hence, it would appear that over history, the spirit of carnival has systematically been held at bay either by forces seeking to exploit its temporary freedom as a safety valve and to allow people to let off steam without endangering the status quo, or else by agencies actively dedicated to its progressive marginalization from society as a means of inducing its eclipse without having to bloody their hands.

While apparently transgressive discourses such as the circus and shamanism may prove repressive, the prison, conversely, could be seen as potentially empowering. Carter's emphasis on the positively disruptive agency of love and bodily contact as instrumental in the panoptical inmates' self-emancipation deserves close consideration in this respect. On the surface, the Countess' fortress is configured as a site of rigorous control and order — these are emblematized, as hinted earlier, by the hardness of "steel." Yet, that same universe also harbors, within its very architectural texture, elements of looseness and softness — which the image of the "doughnut" immediately conveys. According to Ruth Robbins, it is vital to grasp the metaphorical significance of Colonel Kearney's circus and the Countess' prison alike as twin expressions of their society's mores. "The circus and the prison," according to the critic, "share both a context (they are in the same novel) and a geometry (they are the same circular shape). We are invited to read them as connected structures, and our expectations about their meanings (prisons bad, circuses good) are subverted, though not evenly so — our expectations are not simply overturned because, in the end, both prisons and circuses are shown as bad, in different ways and for different reasons." This contention is fully validated by Carter's ironical portrayal of her clowns as "more unnatural and perverse than the murderesses," which entails that the "world of entertainment has more serious and disturbing implications than the world of the prison" (Robbins, p. 115).

Given the centrality of spectacle and performance — i.e., the mainstays of the world of entertainment — to *Nights at the Circus* as a whole, this means that its action is continually implicated with elements of turbulence and gravity despite the carnivalesque levity to which its friskiest scenes tend to allude. The key phrase in Robbins' commentary is arguably "not evenly so." The proposition that Carter is eager to undermine the reader's conformist opinions by recourse to subtle modulations of the ethical scale is indeed axial to the author's entire output, bearing witness to her impatience with stark binary oppositions and univocal attributions of good and evil, and attendant inclination to intimate that even the most cathartic and uplifting structure may host wicked residents and disreputable guests.

This concurrently moral and political ambiguity is repeatedly encapsulated, across the prismatic fabric of *Nights at the Circus* in its entirety, by the image of the grotesque body. Peter Stallybrass and Allom White's comments on corporeal grotesqueness are pointedly relevant to Carter's articulation of this quintessentially carnivalesque motif in *Nights at the Circus*, as will be evident to even those readers who have barely dipped into Fevvers' mock epic saga, and even more blatantly clear to those who have had a chance to meet the novel's numerous curiosities and weirdos. "Grotesque realism," Stallybrass and White argue in the evocatively entitled volume *The Politics and Poetics of Transgression*, "images the human body as multiple, bulging, over- or under-sized, protuberant and incomplete. The openings and orifices of this carnival body are emphasized, not its closure and finish. It is an image of impure corporeal bulk with its orifices (mouth, flared nostrils, anus) yawning wide and its lower regions (belly, legs, feet, buttocks and genitals) given priority over its upper regions (head, 'spirit,' reason)" (Stallybrass and White, p. 9).

Practically every detail of Fevvers' own physique appears to contravene the classical formula for somatic balance and beauty, to the point that it actually spells out grotesque excess. Her size is unusual for a woman of her times: being "six feet two in her stockings," it is hardly surprising that "at close quarters ... she looked more like a dray mare than an angel" (Carter 2006e, p. 9). Furthermore, she is the first to admit that her body lacks proper proportions: "my legs don't tally with the upper part of my body from the point of view of pure aesthetics.... Were I to be the true copy of Venus, one built on *my* scale ought to have legs like tree-trunks" (p. 44). Fevvers' "face," for its part, is said to be "as broad and oval as a meat dish" (p. 9), and the shape and dimensions of her features are likewise immoderate by classical standards, as attested to by "a pair of vast, blue, indecorous eyes." The heroine's voice, relatedly, strikes bizarrely cacophonous chords in that it resounds "like dustbin lids" (p. 3).

Fevvers is clearly not ashamed of her grotesqueness — even though there can be little doubt that it has made her the victim of exploitation and abuse (e.g., by Madame Schreck and Rosenkreutz) and that further dangers triggered by her wingedness lie ahead (e.g., the Grand Duke's immolatory appetite). In fact, she endeavors to appropriate it as an asset and even, when the opportunity arises, extend its influence to the world around her by electing it as a guiding principle. This is made evident, in the novel's opening lines, by the character's flamboyantly unconventional attitude to narrative performance: a stance marked by her ludic adaptation of the idea that a proper epic work ought to begin *ab ovo*, whereby the classic metaphor is irreverently literalized and embodied as Fevvers recounts her own birth as an outcome of being "hatched out of a bloody great egg" (p. 3).

Where canonical literature strives to assert and perpetuate the sanctity of its tropes by etherealizing them, Fevvers adopts a viscerally subversive approach by corporealizing them instead. In this regard, the aerialist's attitude exudes the very kind of carnivalesque verve ascribed by Bakhtin to grotesque realism: a genre whose principal objective is the "degradation ... of all that is high, spiritual, abstract" to "the material level, to the sphere of earth and body in their indissoluble unity," allied to a desire to "turn their subject into flesh." The response induced by this textual tactic is the "laughter that degrades and materializes" by displacing "every high ceremonial gesture or ritual to the material sphere" (Bakhtin 1984, pp. 19–20). As argued in this book's opening chapter, and substantiated through specific examples in subsequent chapters, Carter never loses sight of the material conditions in which even the most fantastical creative flourishes strike their roots.

In intensifying its fictional angel's physicality to almost unpalatable, even obscene, extremes, *Nights at the Circus* finds a pair of close narrative relations in Patrick McGrath's short story "The Angel" and Anne Rice's *Vittorio, the Vampire*, where the idea of angelicness is also invested with intensely corporeal, and often unsavory, connotations. McGrath strips his angel of all possible vestiges of romanticized immaculateness not solely by underlining the creature's bodiliness but also by exposing his susceptibility to unstoppable corruption, disease and decay — to the point that the winged ranks' immortality becomes a curse. Thus, the short story methodically debunks conventional notions of spirituality through an uncanny defamiliarization of the preternatural organism. The following extract neatly encapsulates the text's overall tenor: "there was, first of all, the smell: a wave of unspeakable foulness was released with the removal of the corset.... Harry [the angel's] flesh had rotted off his lower ribs and belly, and the clotted skin still clinging to the ribs and hipbones that bordered the hole was in a state of gelatinous putrescence. In the hole I caught the faint gleam of his spine, and amid the indistinct bundle of piping the forms of shadowy organs.... He should have been dead, and I suppose I must have whispered as much, for I heard him say that he could not die" (McGrath, p. 17).

In Rice's novel, angels are likewise depicted as both physically and epistemologically deficient in spite of the stunning abilities with which they are concurrently invested. Though "monumentally solid," they evince a "wide-eyed simplicity," and beneath the splendid plumage of their wings, one can glimpse the pathetic shape of "shoulders ... sloped like those of a young boy" (Rice, p. 215). In addition, confronted with fundamental questions about God's plans, they pitifully admit that they "are only angels" and, as such, simply "don't know" (p. 285). The unpleasant elements associated by these authors with the angelic breed are not entirely surprising when one considers the primeval iconography associated with both angels generally and, specifically, with the entity connected by Rosenkreutz with Fevvers' fate, Azrael. As Miranda Fellows explains, Azrael is the "Angel of Death, who draws the soul out and steals it away.... In classical mythology, he has four faces and four pairs of wings, and his body is covered with eyes. It is said that when one blinks, a soul dies." Throughout history, even the sweetest and cutest of angelic typologies have at some point been the object of baleful artistic representations. "Cherubs," for example, were once perceived as "terrifying creatures — vile in appearance with many heads and bodies — who stood at the entrance of Paradise and guarded celestial palaces and kingdoms" (Fellows, p. 3).

What is most notable about Fevvers' specific case is Carter's wish to emphasize at every available opportunity that the attribution of angelicness does not serve to refine or purify the woman's essential being: her wings, in fact, are inseparable from bodily attributes that starkly contradict all conventional notions of either sophistication or purity. An eerie blend of glamour and coarseness, feminine allure and masculine bulk, Fevvers stands out as "a being on the borderline of the species" (Carter 2006e, p. 92), a quintessentially "ambivalent body" (p. 93) capable of eliciting equal doses of fascination and disgust at one and the same time. Comparably ambivalent responses are triggered by several of the other threshold creatures who people the text: from the mouthless Toussaint to the inert Sleeping Beauty, from the androgynous Albert/Albertina to the Human Chicken impersonated by Walser, from clowns whose faces are inextricable from their pained masks to shamans afloat in the ecstatic contemplation of undifferentiated flux.

By engaging with these various personae both as individuals and as facets of a complex intersubjective constellation, *Nights at the Circus* strives to achieve a precarious balance between the personal and the communal. At the same time, it seeks to weave a mediating fabric between the socially accepted self and the impenetrably and sacrilegiously other. In the process, the text touchingly draws attention to the inevitability of loneliness in a world marked by intolerant definitions of the normal and the abnormal, the sacred and the profane. Therefore, even as it celebrates the value of gregariousness in a typically carnivalesque fashion, *Nights at the Circus* takes it upon itself also to intimate that learning to survive and learning the art of being alone may ultimately amount to one and the same thing. Characters such as Toussaint, the Sleeping Beauty, Albert/Albertina and — most crucially — Fevvers herself serve to remind us that throughout history, hybrid and deformed entities have proved remarkably versatile tools for expressing widespread cultural anxieties. Their ruthless exploitation as fairground material, epitomized by the Victorian cases of the "Elephant Man" Robert Merrick (1862–1890) and the "Sicilian Fairy" Caroline Crachami (1815–1824) illustrate those creatures' domestication for the purposes of spectacle and recreation. Nonetheless, the grotesque body insistently returns to haunt the communal imaginary, its insistent resurgence reflecting the ubiquity of feelings of insecurity, dislocation and dread as deeply rooted existential conditions.

Carter invites us to reflect on this onerous legacy by drawing attention to a thought-provoking pair of oxymorons: that of the monster as an amusing threat, and that of the monster as frightening entertainment. Monstrously grotesque entities may be ideated as hideous foes or thrilling playmates. Yet, they can never be conclusively categorized insofar as they keep reminding us of the existence of troubling pockets of experience which have somehow eluded the processes of socialization and enculturement to which children are typically exposed in putatively civilized societies. These interstitial realities cannot be safely accommodated either in the domain of the normal and the familiar or in that of the abnormal and the uncanny. As a result, they point to the stubborn persistence of heterogeneous slivers of being which the grown-up world is powerless to name and address — let alone incorporate into its ratified systems of signification. Lurching between comedy and agony, yet never fully assimilable by either, these realities ultimately testify to the unfathomability of language and meaning.

Julia Kristeva's writings on abjection illuminate this nexus of ideas, implicitly providing an inspiring lens through which Carter's own work may be inspected. Kristeva resorts to the notion of abjection to describe the ways in which we violently reject and cast off all those aspects of our nature which society brands as impure or improper, asocial or antisocial. "*Abjection*," argues Kristeva, "is something that disgusts you, for example, you see something rotting and you want to vomit — it is an extremely strong feeling that is at once somatic and symbolic, which is above all a revolt against an external menace from which one wants to distance oneself, but of which one has the impression that it may menace us from the inside" (Kristeva, p. 118). Most threatening, in this scenario, are those threshold parts of the body which preside over the elimination of supposedly undesirable (i.e., abject) substances, such as blood, semen, urine, feces, tears, milk, and sweat.

Abjection, therefore, can be read as a drastic violation of the presumed sanctity of the self's integrity. *Nights at the Circus* experiments with numerous variations on this theme. In the Petersburg part of the novel, in particular, Carter offers several instances of interactions that entail the collapse of bodily boundaries. The dividing line between humans and other animals is repeatedly crossed, as the Princess of Abyssinia, a silent tiger tamer, incorporates the character of Mignon, the Ape-Man's abused partner, into her act with dancing cats, and Walser is employed as the waltzing companion of a now redundant tigress. This reshuffling of the established cast unleashes chaos, as the tigress whose mate has been matched with Mignon grows insanely jealous and becomes a threat to the girl's very life, and the Princess is left with no choice but to shoot her.

These incidents indicate that the disruption of the border presumed to separate human and feline performers becomes tantamount, in the logic of the narrative, to a blasphemous disruption of the natural order of things bound to lead to devastation and, finally, death. The gravity of the situation is reinforced by the events running in parallel to its unfolding: the attempted murders of Walser by the clown Buffo the Great when the latter loses his mind, and of Fevvers by the Charivari family of acrobats. Carter is not saying, at this juncture, that boundaries are sacrosanct and should go unquestioned. Rather, she is eager to remind us that to challenge culturally sanctioned compartments is not a move to be performed with levity but rather an onerous political act — however humorously we might choose to play it out. The circus, like the carnival, is averse to the release of undiluted fun: we engage in its heady rituals at great risk and should always be prepared for the possibility of random occurrences and even calamities. Carter, we are reminded, has no time or patience for gratuitously utopian gestures. If Fevvers incarnates the concept of the grotesque body through her hybrid and excessive bodiliness, she simultaneously epitomizes the idea of abjection by insistently drawing attention to the lower strata of corporeality. As Sarah Waters aptly remarks, "Fevvers is a wonderfully fleshly creation, a creature of sweats and appetites, of belches and farts" (Waters, p. ix). This contention is vividly confirmed by Walser's perception of the smell permeating Fevvers' personal space in the course of the interview: a "hot, solid compost of perfume, sweat, greasepaint and raw, leaking gas" (Carter 2006e, p. 4), augmented by "a powerful note of stale feet" as the "final ingredient in the highly personal aroma, 'essence of Fevvers,' that clogged the room" (p. 5).

The hybrid, grotesque and aberrant bodies populating Carter's menagerie are often portrayed as objects of perverse exploitation. Madame Schreck's museum of female monsters, for example, capitalizes on the lucrative reification of disparate female bodies brought together by hybrid and anomalous physiques or bizarre habits. Its core is a crypt-like chamber employed as the exhibition ground for the callous woman's precious merchandize. The earthy and jocular tone used by the narrator to describe the dismal location does not lighten the darkness of the perversity inherent in Madame Schreck's venture — as indeed in other cases of analogous exploitation of the grotesque body — but rather accentuates it by means of defamiliarization. As Gina Wisker notes, on this point, the "everyday Cockney tone of the winged, iconic aerialiste Fevvers renders these traditionally gothic horrors almost domestic" (Wisker 1993, p. 167), yet there is something unequivocally harrowing about the gallery of necrophiliac, sadistic and masochistic clients whom the museum routinely attracts. This mood is intensified by the presence of props and tools of the least savory kind imaginable, intended to cater for the fetishistic urges of Madame Schreck's depraved clients. The carnival exuberance of *Nights at the Circus* never seeks to efface altogether the tenebrous appetites coursing human sexuality. This affective tension points to Carter's deliberate cultivation of a galvanizing sense of ambivalence. As Marina Warner comments, in this matter, "humour in Carter's fiction signals her defiant hold on 'heroic optimism,' the mood she singled out as characteristic of fairy tales, the principle which sustained the idea of a happy ending." Nonetheless, "laughter never unburdens itself from knowledge of its own pessimism" and therefore "remains intrinsically ironic" (Warner 1995, p. 197).

The image of the appalling hole, having featured prominently in the segment of the narrative devoted to Madame Schreck's museum to designate its key setting, reasserts itself at a later stage in the story through Rosenkreutz's ominous description of female anatomy. This strives to foreground femininity's association with a sense of intolerable lack, equating the female genitals to an "atrocious hole, or dreadful chasm" and comparing their function to that of a "vortex that sucks everything dreadfully down, down where Terror rules." The insane Rosicrucian objectifies the heroine herself as a distillation of mythological figures that simultaneously fascinate and disgust him — "Flora; Azrael; Venus Pandemos!" (p. 88) — and avers that by engineering the portentous fusion of his own body with that of Fevvers as Azrael, he is bound to achieve immortality. Fevvers is again exposed to the threat of ritual immolation by a deranged patriarch upon meeting the Grand Duke, another manic collector ruling a world of balefully crystallized forms. Fevvers indeed perceives his fabulous mansion as the kingdom of "vitrification," depicting as a domain haunted by an overbearing atmosphere of "frigidity" and "sterility" (p. 217). In the middle of his elegantly laid dining-table stands a "life size" sculpture of Fevvers made wholly of "ice" (p. 218).

As the aforecited examples indicate, Carter presents us with varyingly acute desecrations of the female body not in order to excuse sexual abuse but rather to throw into relief the hypocrisy inherent in whole societies that strive to conceal the omnipresence of both literal and figurative drives to maim, tear and dissect through iniquitous power relations. In advancing this message, Carter highlights the ongoing interplay of bliss and horror, excitement and pain, desire and apathy, in a typically gothic mode. This is not to say that Carter could ever be regarded merely as an accomplished Gothic Revival author: something she could easily have become had she univocally developed the style and rhetoric found in the early novels, and especially *Shadow Dance* and *Love* (here discussed in Chapter 2). In fact, Carter's gothic vision assiduously coalesces with her flair for handling grotesquery with magisterial self-control, with unpredictable rhetorical flourishes rooted in a passion for the minutest facets of language and rhythm, and with an imagist elegance nourished by her inveterate commitment to the concrete and the ordinary. In *Nights at the Circus*, the utterly original voice orchestrated by this expressive ensemble, allied to an intuitive taste for likewise original thematics, enables Carter to transcend the gothic formula as such in order to engage with the existential ordeals of our times with unparalleled degrees of both intimacy and intensity.

According to William Patrick Day, gothic fiction seeks to translate "the anxiety of fear" into "pleasure" (Day, W. P., pp. 10–11), whereas Judith Halberstam views it as a sustained metamorphosis of desire into dread triggered by libidinal anxieties (Halberstam). Whichever line one may opt for, it seems clear that Carter's take on gothic darkness presupposes the coexistence of baleful and hopeful possibilities in a genuinely apocalyptic vein, the concepts of doom and regeneration being inextricably entangled in the notion (and etymology) of the word "apocalypse" itself. Fevvers herself could be seen to embody this ambivalence, insofar as her ineradicable difference functions both as a devastating wave and as a promise of fresh beginnings. Redolent at once of Bakhtin's carnivalized bodies and of Kristeva's abject, Fevvers indeed deploys her corporeal concreteness, both intentionally and instinctively, to undermine the abstract and intellectually aseptic values upheld by her culture as a means of keeping individual creativity at bay and, relatedly, maximizing the subject's productivity and ontological stability.

Fevvers' destabilizing role is most convincingly foregrounded in Gass' analysis of *Nights at the Circus*, where the critic underscores the character's power to "provide the means by which the panopticons of the whorehouse, the freak show, and the circus are ruptured. Her presence in an institution seems to invite its disastrous demise.... Fevvers' heroic role, it seems, is to be the instrument of destruction of panopticons." At the same time, however, the critic hails the character's constructive agency as no less vital a component of her being, arguing that Fevvers "is not just a destroyer; she is a mender, a builder, a unifier. What she destroys are the cages that confine the socially oppressed.... What she builds are human relationships" (Gass). Waters embraces an analogous interpretation of the novel's finale, arguing that "the narrative ultimately celebrates liberation, the casting off of myth and mind forg'd manacles, the discovery of voice, empathy, conscience, the making of a 'new kind of music.' The novel ends with Fevvers' laughter, with an affirmation of life" (Waters, p. x). The apotheosis of this productive energy lies with the project upon which Fevvers and Walser embark together at the end of the novel: the chronicling of the dormant "histories of those women who would otherwise go down nameless and forgotten, erased from history as if they had never been" (Carter 2006e,

p. 338). Walser will act as the heroine's scribe, and Fevvers will play the role of the muse — rather a more active type of muse, it should be noted, than the stereotypical version of this classical figure fantasized about by Melanie in the opening part of *The Magic Toyshop*.

Most crucially, Carter is eager to show that the grotesque body is the receptacle of a strident aporia. On the one hand, it can be read as a subversive site of resistance seeking to challenge time-honored aesthetic tenets and operating as a powerful metaphor for a radical decentralization of power from the abstract mind to the corporeal periphery. On the other hand, it is persistently posited by the dominant structures of power as the target of disciplinary control: as a disruptive phenomenon which implicitly legitimizes, by dint of its very existence, the invention and deployment of repressive and containing strategies. The grotesque body thus confronts us with a logical conflict akin to the one we encountered vis-à-vis the circus/prison dialectic. As a result, as Michelle Nelmarie Buchel emphasizes, Carter's ideation of Fevvers as a New Woman can be interpreted simultaneously as a "demythologizing" move, by means of which she "secularizes" the "idealized image of femininity" promulgated specifically by Guillaume Apollinaire and hence advances "a redefined feminine identity," and a "remythologizing" ruse which unhinges existing stereotypes at the cost of emplacing yet another archetypal image (Buchel, p. 180).

While it would be arduous to refute that Carter's literally larger-than-life heroine carries the credentials of a mythical entity, it is important to recognize that her creator is not unequivocally committed to the ideation of myths. In fact, while traditional myths are first and foremost defined by their determination to propound supposedly universal and immutable values, Carter grounds both Fevvers herself and the events in which she becomes embroiled in tangible historical milieux riven by political tensions and undercurrents of turmoil. This contention is validated by the writer's response to Anna Katsavos' question as to whether her protagonist "is out to create her own myth": "No," Carter tersely ripostes, "Fevvers is out to earn a living" (in Katsavos, p. 3).

As Buchel maintains, in accordance with Barthes' proposition that "the best weapon against myth is perhaps to mythify it in its turn, and to produce an *artificial myth*" (Barthes 1993, p. 135), Carter's winged woman can be interpreted as an "artificial myth" intent on "debunking essentialist notions of the feminine identity as biologically determined, rather than culturally variable. In this sense Carter does remythologize, but not by creating another feminine archetype." By extension, it is possible to argue that through this pseudo-myth that tenaciously refuses to be read as either timeless or universally applicable, the writer supplies an allegorical commentary on "the artifice of gendered identity" at large "as culturally determined." Therefore, *Nights at the Circus* does not passively reinscribe the ancestral myth of the winged female but rather appropriates and reimagines it with provocative glee. In so doing, the text again enthrones the principles of spectacle and performance as pivotal to its fabulistic weave. Even as Carter's heroine "temporarily incarnates an archetypal femininity," we are all the time reminded that "this is just a performance, a production, a publicity stunt, for Fevvers is also a spectator, an agent of self-representation whose public persona is a finely judged act" (Buchel, p. 183).

Relatedly, as Lorna Sage proposes, Carter's preoccupation with origin myths — or "the past's debris" — is not so much a form of nostalgia as a "mopping up" strategy, proposing that if human identity is fashioned through the accumulation of the past's "ready-made meanings," then perhaps there also dwells the opportunity "to piece together your own myths" (Sage 1994, pp. 9–11). Carter is not satisfied just to dismantle the myths that have been transmitted to us across the generations but actually compels us to acknowledge the extent to which we are all responsible for sculpting our own myths from the past's gradual accretion of meanings, clues and symbols akin to *object trouvées*. In Carter's demythologizing enterprise, myth is thus endlessly — and vigorously — renewed at every turn: her stories never cease to unleash magical worlds of possibilities as existing tales spawn new tales practically ad infinitum.

Furthermore, *Nights at the Circus* is sustained throughout, albeit inconspicuously at times, by a serious and salubrious engagement with issues of history and historicity. As Helen Stoddart argues, this textual dimension resonates with Walter Benjamin's reflections on Paul Klee's "Angelus Novus" (1920), so much so that "Fevvers begins to look very like a fictional (and female) articulation of Benjamin's imagined 'angel of history'" (Stoddart, p. 22). Given its uncannily pointed bearing on Carter's novel, the relevant passage deserves extensive citation: "Klee's painting named 'Angelus Novus' shows an angel looking as though he is about to move away from something he is fixedly contemplating. His eyes are staring, his mouth is open, his wings are spread. This is how one pictures the angel of history. His face is turned toward the past. Where we perceive a chain of events, he sees one single catastrophe which keeps piling wreckage upon wreckage and hurls it in front of his feet. The angel would like to stay, awaken the dead, and make whole what has been smashed. But a storm is blowing from Paradise; it has got caught in his wings with such violence that the angel can no longer close them. The storm irresistibly propels him into the future to which his back is turned, while the pile of debris before him grows skyward. This storm is what we call progress" (Benjamin 1992, p. 259).

It would be difficult to deny that the curve of Fevvers' picaresque epic consists of a sequence of interconnected events which climaxes with the catastrophic train crash from which the protagonist receives the critical prompt to move on and grow into a truly autonomous and self-determining creature. The links in this chain are held together, it must be emphasized, neither by causality nor by determinism but rather by a consummately ludic sense of chance. The strength which Fevvers thus acquires is immediately channeled, as noted, into a textual project of unquestionable ideological significance: the insertion of unknown or neglected women into the network of history with the assistance of Walser, an individual who has also experienced a drastic awakening and thereby transcended his initially stereotypical patriarchal outlook. In this respect, *Nights at the Circus* could be said to extend to unprecedented degrees Carter's commitment to material reality by embracing the mission of historical materialism as conceived of by Benjamin himself: that is to say, a methodical effort "to brush history against the grain" and displace "the victor" as the class to which canonical historiography has invariably accorded centrality so as to focus instead on "the anonymous toil of his contemporaries" (p. 248).

Carter's own vision of the angel of history as abundantly embodied by Fevvers acts as a powerful reminder of the ineluctability of historical transformation. "Even women who imagine they have 'wings,'" Stoddart avers, "could not escape the wind" blown by the formidable storms which Benjamin describes "because to avoid the storm would mean being removed from the momentum of historical change and therefore altogether without power" (Stoddart, p. 23). Fevvers is able to avoid becoming transfixed by the murky lure of the past and to contemplate the future *not*, it must be stressed, by actually *forgetting* the past but rather by rewriting it. In other words, having acknowledged her own humanity to the fullest by accepting her physical and emotional vulnerabilities and by contemplating frankly the possibility of love, Carter's heroine resolves to face the storm in order to grasp and reconfigure the concatenations of events that have led to it and the reasons for its occurrence.

Walser's evolution is no less remarkable, in this respect. At the beginning of the novel, the American reporter is seen to depend on ossified normative conventions decreeing what is real or inauthentic, valuable or worthless. Hell-bent on answering the question utilized by Carter as a narrative leitmotif—"Is she fact or is she fiction?" (Carter 2006e, p. 3)—Walser seeks the truth about Fevvers in order to be able to classify her conclusively and appropriate her as a suitable case in his series of stories titled "'Great Humbugs of the World'" (p. 8). These pretensions—and, by implication, those of the patriarchal value system Walser abides by—are sensationally exploded as he is "bamboozled" by the Siberian shaman (p. 348) and figuratively reborn by Fevvers. Carter hence exposes the stereotypical vacuity of the massaged fairy tale formula in which persecuted heroines are invariably saved by courageous princes, and heterosexual fulfillment is automatically advertised as the supreme goal. Walser is clearly the antithesis of the classic hero: in fact, even prior to his subjection to the shaman's bizarre world view, the suggestions that there is "something a little unfinished about him" (p. 6) and that his very self is somewhat akin to a found object serve to paint him in rather pathetic hues. It is not altogether surprising, therefore, that having set out as a strict rationalizer unwilling to accept that Fevvers could be naturally equipped with both wings and arms, he should precipitate, courtesy of the bossy shaman, into a chronic state of ecstatic lunacy prior to his rescue by the Cockney Venus. What Walser finally learns, most importantly, is the necessity of adopting a more cautious stance toward history and its recording than he has thus far been wont to do.

The character of Lizzie, whose Marxist ideals are never in question throughout the novel, provides an indirect commentary on the importance of the lesson learned by both Fevvers and Walser. She does so by emphasizing that embracing the future in total disregard of the past is, quite simply, foolish. Relying on Lizzie as a mouthpiece of sorts, Carter implies that it is only by acknowledging the ascendancy of the "past historic" (p. 240) that we may also arrive at some understanding of the multifold processes through which, as she puts it in *The Sadeian Woman*, "our flesh arrives to us out of history" (Carter 1979, p. 9). Historical materialism, as encapsulated in Lizzie's perorations, represents an approach to history capable of conceiving of the past as a sequence of events that do not hold autonomous meaning, since their actual significance lies with their potential to give rise to the present and the future. In this perspective, the task of the historian is principally to fathom the concrete conditions in which historical events have unfolded by unearthing and reconstellating their authentic contents so as to rectify the methodically distorted rendition of facts dished out by official historiography. *Nights at the Circus* could be said to capture the essential spirit of historical materialism as a brave preparedness to see the past — and indeed history at large — as a process of constant metamorphosis with an unremitting flair for triggering abrupt and random commotions.

As the arguments pursued in the preceding paragraphs intimate, the cumulative message proffered by *Nights at the Circus* can be deemed positive on two counts. On the one hand, the novel proposes a fruitfully destabilizing power dynamics, conducive to a tantalizing reconceptualization of gender roles and positions. On the other hand, it inaugurates a fresh perspective on our understanding of facts, and of both their official and their unofficial recording. In the process, it rarely refrains from bathing both aspects of its discourse in the exhilarating balm of fulsome, yet defiant, laughter. This message is unflinchingly bolstered by the text's invitation to question everything, and attendant insistence that such a project is a source of affirmative strength unto itself— however dispiriting its outcomes might seem to be — insofar as we have the ultimate freedom to entertain it in an ironical, festive and irreverent mood. This, Carter reminds us at practically every turn of Fevvers' flighty history, is an inalienable right which nobody can take away from us. If fail we must, it is at least possible to fail laughing — or at least, as Samuel Beckett famously suggests in *Worstward Ho*, to go on trying to "fail better" (Beckett 1983).

CHAPTER 7

Mirror Identities
Wise Children

It is a wise child that knows its own father.
— Late Sixteenth-Century Proverb
It is a wise father that knows his own child.
— William Shakespeare

If textuality is about weaving, as intimated by the Latin root *texere*, "to weave," then intertextuality can be legitimately thought of as being about interweaving: a creative process of blending, braiding or twining whereby existing textual strands do not merely come together but incrementally shape one another until new identities — and hence new fictions — are born. Therefore, intertextuality cannot be shallowly dismissed (or derided for that matter) as a mechanistic act of adaptation, citation or emulation of an existing source. In fact, it constitutes an incessantly evolving dialectic predicated on the idea that every text can be open to the creative influence of other texts and, most importantly, willing to invite them to participate actively in its coming into being. In *Wise Children*, intertextuality proclaims itself most sonorously even upon cursory sampling of its elating ride with the novel's plural generic identity. This, as Michael Duffy emphasizes, brings together "simultaneously a romance, memoir, intended autobiography extending to family history, dramatic monologue, fairy tale, parody, farce, pantomime, carnival, satire" (Duffy, p. 102). Echoing the novel's narrator, one could do worse than complement this provisional list with a wholesomely inconclusive "etc. etc. etc." (Carter 2006f, p. 158).

When it comes to the actual texts invoked by Carter in the writing of *Wise Children*, it would be preposterous to refute that these are both numerous and kaleidoscopically varied, insofar as they encompass not only venerable classics and acclaimed representatives of the canon of English letters and globally recognized world literature — such as John Milton, Laurence Sterne, William Wordsworth, Jane Austen, Charles Dickens, Lewis Carroll, Bertolt Brecht, Bernard Shaw, William Faulkner, Nathanael West, Dylan Thomas, Francis Scott Fitzgerald, Graham Greene — but also Hollywood stars and popular entertainers such as Charlie Chaplin, Fred Astaire and Ginger Rogers, Gloria Swanson, Lana Turner, Jean Harlow and Nöel Coward (and beyond), alongside a plethora of movies, songs, musicals, fairy tales, proverbs, old and new jokes, aphorisms, quips, citations and traditional verbal riddles. In addition, *Wise Children* echoes structurally two of the most acclaimed masterpieces of literary modernism, James Joyce's *Ulysses* and Virginia Woolf's *Mrs. Dalloway*, by locating the entire scope of its action within a single day. Dora's references to the so-called Fall of the House of Hazard, moreover, are a clear echo of Edgar Allan Poe's famous story "The Fall of the House of Usher."

It would be hard to deny, however, that these interstitial allusions feel relatively underplayed in comparison with Shakespeare's opus, which in fact comes to the fore as an indisputably major player. Variably explicit references to that body of works pepper Carter's fabulatory bill of fare so profusely as to transcend the status of optional seasoning and rise instead to the level of key gastronomic ingredients. The Bard's corpus is evoked on practically every page but often makes its appearances (in lead roles and through cameo visitations by turns) in unpredictable ways. A paradigmatic instance of this ruse is supplied by the portion of the narrative in which the narrator reminisces about her time in Hollywood, participating in a cinematic adaptation of *A Midsummer Night's Dream*. This context gives Carter a perfect opportunity to engage in a playful reinvention of Hollywood history and lore. As Abigail Nussbaum points out, the main characters involved in the film and the events surrounding its production evince "an obvious parallel to Richard Burton and Elizabeth Taylor," since the male lead "falls passionately in love with his leading lady, the producer's wife, and they abandon their respective spouses for a tempestuous and short-lived marriage as the film goes to pieces around them" (Nussbaum).

No less frequently, the text's manipulation of some of Shakespeare's most famous lines reaches straight into the domain of clownish mockery.

This is attested to, for example, by the scene in which the protagonists don "bellhop costumes" to perform their "*Hamlet* skit"—in this context, the Prince of Denmark's metaphysical reflections are jocularly turned in a hotel address ("2b or not 2b"), and the performers, in a peculiar intertextual leap of dramatic logic whereby *Macbeth* suddenly comes into play, "burst out of a giant haggis in a number based on the banquet scene" (Carter 2006f, p. 90). Hamlet's legendary line becomes the butt of an even more irreverent gibe in the context of a TV commercial enacted by "My Lady Margarine," who stands "on a rampart" wearing "a long yellow frock" and, "gazing sternly at a half-pound pack on a dish before her," poignantly intones: "To butter or not to butter..." (pp. 37–38). In addition, the narrator seems instinctively drawn to word play and, in indulging this proclivity, frequently echoes well-known Shakespeareans lines in parodic form. A good example is her progressive distortion of the subtitle of *Twelfth Night*, culminating with the absurd line "*What? You Will?!*" (p. 217).

The novel consistently weaves into its own yarn and its own thematic concerns a wide range of motifs, tropes and character types traditionally associated with Shakespeare's corpus, while also pondering its significance and ostensibly undying influence as a social phenomenon. Carter herself has stated that communicating "the idea of Shakespeare as a cultural ideology" was one of her chief priorities in the creation of *Wise Children* (in Sage 1992, p. 188). In her fictional examination of the ideological import of the Shakespeare phenomenon, Carter will have been well aware of certain classic studies of Elizabethan society concerned with highlighting the Bard's relationship with a particular Zeitgeist, and of materialist responses to those texts. Especially prominent among the former are undoubtedly E. M. W. Tillyard's *The Elizabethan World Picture: A Study of the Idea of Order in the Age of Shakespeare, Donne & Milton* (1942) and *Shakespeare's History Plays* (1944), Theodore Spencer's *Shakespeare and the Nature of Man* (1951), Lily B. Campbell's *Shakespeare's Histories* (1964), and C. S. Lewis' *The Discarded Image* (1964).

These studies tend to assume the existence of a shared cultural and political conception of order in the Elizabethan age which is supposedly grounded in a cosmic conception of balance, and therefore holds universal validity. The august notions of the Great Chain of Being, the Music of the Spheres and the cosmos' Corresponding Planes constitute the primary building blocks of this system, and are indeed invoked to bolster the proposition that the universe is essentially an expression of God's plans. More recent materialist criticism, conversely, has emphasized the ideologically contingent character of the Elizabethan world view, approaching the cultural, political and cosmological principles depicted in those seminal studies as specific expressions of a dominant ideology — and clearly not the sole ideology implied by Shakespeare's plays. Materialist critics such as Jonathan Dollimore and Alan Sinfield, for instance, argue that Shakespeare's writings no doubt reflect various aspects of the dominant ideology but not in order to legitimize unequivocally an established social order as Tillyard and other critics insistently contend (Dollimore and Sinfield). Fostering the genius of ambiguity and paradox, and giving it characteristic articulation in a charade of ironies and ambivalences, Shakespeare's work eschews reductive resolutions even as it claims to deliver neat endings in which all loose ends are apparently tied together. In fact, the artificiality of such endings persistently reminds us of the inherently insoluble and open-ended nature of the conflicts which they seem to settle.

In order to accomplish her critical objective as intended, and thus convey the idea of Shakespeare as a cultural ideology, without incurring the risk of dishing out a turgid political manifesto devoid of either passion or humor, Carter enables her impish narrator to assume the role of a chronicler not only of her dynasty's intricately wacky history but also of British history itself. It is at this level of the textual weave that Shakespeare's ideological significance comes to the fore most overtly. This is borne out by the family's depiction as a veritable titan of British theater and by the presentation of its patriarchs, specifically, as figures who have derived their regal status directly from their impersonation of various Shakespearean royals, and endeavored to disseminate the Bard's presumed wisdom around the world with an ardor reminiscent of missionaries driven by evangelical ambitions in the heyday of the British Empire's colonial expansion.

The family's self-righteous bulwarks appear to believe unquestioningly in the sanctity of their assignment, and to consider their cultural purity as an automatic marker of moral integrity that effectively legitimizes its undertaking in any context they choose as their stage. Yet, despite their dignified public image, these characters are ultimately powerless to efface their imbrication in a web of murky relationships which renders their line far from homogeneous — let alone pure. By laying bare this fundamental aporia, Carter's narrator implicitly calls attention to the nature of Britishness and British culture — as concepts which those patriarchal figures are supposed to incarnate — as hybrid realities whose attempts to establish neat partitions between disparate aspects of their makeup cannot finally suppress their inherent plurality.

A potent leitmotif throughout the text is the exposure of dangerously doxastic distinctions between "high" and "low" cultures with which Shakespeare's name is so often, and so misleadingly, associated, and of their no less blinkered coupling with broader notions of legitimacy and illegitimacy. The protagonists' experiences as performers within that portion of the entertainment industry which their culture regards not only as popular but also as morally polluted (such as music halls and gaudy vaudeville venues) tersely encapsulates the whole issue. Relatedly, their rejection by the allegedly legitimate dramatic establishment personified by their father, an eminent Shakespearean actor, exemplifies the destiny meted out to those who are deemed to challenge the otherwise unexamined ascendancy of the canon. This is not to say that Carter, in *Wise Children*, embarks on a critique of cultural prejudices so serious as to induce her as to abstain from humor altogether. For one thing, all of the activities and venues associated with the showbiz of the decades she engages with (or merely touches upon) are treated with an amiably satirical voice. At no juncture in the story's multilayered mnemonic cavalcade is there any suggestion that Carter militates openly in favor of a specific sector of the entertainment industry and, by extension, of a singular ideological position. In fact, *Wise Children* is eager to sprinkle each of its speckled surfaces with just enough fairy dust of carnivalesque vintage to impart it by turns with visceral joy, sardonic wit and lustful punning. As Ali Smith contends, this novel is quite feasibly "the most cheerfully orgiastic and generous and comic and fulfilled of her books, a celebration of birth, life and continuance, ... a book all about Will, and will, and legacy, and the legacy of entertainment" (Smith 2007, p. 16).

Although the boards — and the vicissitudes of the world of public entertainment at large — constitute the principal lens through which *Wise Children* advances (and sustains) its puckish social critique, the tension between high and low cultures is not communicated solely through those themes. In fact, one of its least overt, yet poignant, manifestations can be found in Carter's characterization of Grandma Chance, the woman who assumes responsibility for the protagonists' upbringing following paternal rejection. This figure brings to mind the fairy tale tradition as a discourse which may occasionally assume a peripheral position in Carter's heart but seldom leaves the narrative scene altogether when this writer is involved.

Indeed, Grandma Chance elliptically echoes the traditional female story-tellers recognized by the author as pivotal presences in the evolution of that discourse and in its cross-cultural perpetuation over the centuries.

Female figures such as the French *commère* and the Italian *comare* are typical representatives of a broader transtemporal web that can be seen as largely responsible for the production and propagation of the sorts of narratives we have come to regard as fairy tales. This discursive network is documented by Marina Warner with equal measures of scholarly scrupulousness and textual vitality in *From the Beast to the Blonde*. As argued in Chapter 5, the analysis conducted by Warner traces the figure of the traditional female narrator back to the character of the female diviner epitomized by the figure of the Sibyl, and then proceeds to assess its evolution over history through types such as Mother Goose to elucidate the significance of its ongoing ascendancy in contemporary culture. When the storyteller's presence was eventually "established as legitimate for certain purposes — the instruction of the young — writers co-opted it as their own," the critic explains, "using it as a mask for their own thoughts, their own mocking games and even sedition" (Warner 1995, p. xx). Italo Calvino has likewise stressed the axial role played by women in the dissemination of fairy tales over time in the context of his evaluation of the Brothers Grimm's opus, noting that "the fairy tales the Grimms were writing down were those told to kids by German mamas and grandmas which they, in turn, had learnt from their own mamas and grandmas" (Calvino 1988, p. 83).

Given the intensely kinetic quality of Dora's textual voyage, the relationship between traditional narrators and dynamism requires some attention in this context. It is first of all crucial to acknowledge, in this matter, that neither Sibyls nor crones by the hearth nor alleyway tattletales evince any obvious proclivity toward motion, two of their defining cultural traits being, in fact, physical confinement to very restricted locations and the state of sedentariness which such spatial restriction inevitably entails. In the context of seventeenth-century France, where many of the narratives we still enjoy today originated, the actual locations witnessing the genesis and dissemination of fairy tales were the *ruelles* — literally, "alleys." A term employed to describe the type of venue in which aristocratic *salonniéres* would meet to exchange and discuss both contemporary issues and fantastic yarns, the word *ruelle* was initially appropriated as part of her coterie's lexicon by the Marquise de Rambouillet (1588–1665). For the Marquise, the *ruelle* consisted of "the space between her bed and the wall" (Warner 1995,

p. 50) in the chamber where she would welcome her female guests and chair the proceedings from "her show bed" (p. 49). *Ruelles,* most significantly, were places "established by noblewomen in the image of the humbler, more chaotic gathering, the gossiping" (p. 50). In spite of their pointedly sedentary lifestyle, these female narrators, like Sibyls and grannies before them, are traveling companions in an unending creative journey, and hence stand out, ironically, as dynamic figures. The storytelling verve exhibited by Dora is heir to this extensive semiotic voyage.

The association of the figure of the traditional storyteller with women and female occupations is sustained by Dora's narrative through a recurrent emphasis on the influence exerted on her and her sister' development by their split and potholed family's matrilineal component. The only "fixed point" in their "fathers' genealogy," she observes in the course of an extensive digression into the past, is provided by a "paternal grandmother" they have never actually met except through the medium of archaic photography. Their "maternal side," conversely, "founders in a wilderness of unknowability" but makes its lingering energy felt in a displaced guise with the one person who actually assumes responsibility for the protagonists' upbringing, the aforementioned Grandma Chance. Their departed mother's landlady, this character is said to have raised her charges "not out of duty, or due to history, but because of pure love." Echoing one of Freud's most famous phrases but also, and more inspiringly, the spirit of Shakespeare's late plays, Dora describes the outcome of this disposition as "a genuine family romance" (Carter 2006f, p. 12).

It is worth noting, on this point, that several aspects of the novel's thematics lend themselves simultaneously to Freudian and Shakespearean readings. This contention is sonorously corroborated by the text's ongoing emphasis on incestuous passion, Oedipal resentment and narcissism as motifs which can be regarded as quintessentially Freudian and quintessentially Shakespearean in equal measures. Dora's own name, incidentally, recalls the subject of one of Freud's most famous (or perhaps notorious) case histories — though the positive outcome of the learning curve traced by Carter's narrator evidently opposes the fate met by Freud's fictionalized patient. (Nora's denomination, for its part, could be read as a distant allusion to the protagonist's of Henrik Ibsen's *A Doll's House.*)

Dora's brand of jestful wisdom is also akin to the voice of the traditional oral teller of the kind one could expect to encounter not only in a *ruelle* or by the fireside but also in a market square in days gone by — vanished, no doubt, and yet not so remote as to have been altogether forgotten in some of the older communities of rural Europe. Concomitantly, Dora's stance brings to mind the related figure of the traveling magician. A vibrant instance of this type is provided by Carter's portrayal of Perry: a character whose presence on the scene is invariably enshrouded by a potent aura of enchantment, revelry and ludic disorder. Perry has the power to conjure white doves out of his handkerchief (Carter 2006f, p. 31), to cause all of the crockery and cutlery employed in the course of an afternoon picnic to vanish in one fell swoop (p. 62), to summon a couple of cream buns out of Grandma's cleavage along with a cloud of talcum powder (p. 73) and, most sensationally, to remove "a scarlet macaw" (p. 133) from Melchior's theatrical tights and thus put an end to the embarrassment occasioned by the actor's "offending parts" (p. 132).

Another character endowed with credentials reminiscent of the traditional itinerant entertainer is Gorgeous George — a typical holyday club comedian, seaside resort clown or even fairground performer well-versed at doling out generous portions of humor laced with inevitable sexual innuendos. Repeatedly ridiculing conventional principles of integrity and decorum, Gorgeous George delivers his most memorable performance when, having sung a number of hymns traditionally associated with the apotheosis of Britishness, British valor and Britain's God-given entitlement to worldwide authority (e.g., "God Save the Queen" and "Rule Britannia"), he strips off to expose a torso sporting a tattoo of the map of the world. This scene no doubt supplies us with an enthusiastic celebration of the image of the iconoclastic and rootless carnival reveler as a literal citizen of the world unrestrained by insular criteria and values. It is also noteworthy, however, that Carter honors her anti-utopian pragmatism by ultimately disclosing Gorgeous George's decline to the status of a wretched tramp. As argued in more depth later in this chapter, Carter never loses sight of the carnival's darker side.

While echoing the figures of the traditional storyteller and the nomadic entertainer, Dora also brings to mind Shakespeare's fools in her ability to recognize and laugh at the absurd, and thus puncture unremittingly from beginning to end the self-inflated mystique enfolding social hierarchy and the pretensions to depth and purity advanced by so-called high culture. Carter's narrator encapsulates with paradigmatic accuracy some of the time-honored figure's most distinctive traits, as vividly portrayed in *foolsforhire*: "'Fools enact the raw material of a culture, ceremo-

niously demonstrating and articulating what becomes of a society if it forsakes the 'burden' of tradition.... The fool displays a folly which is just as
important as rationalized wisdom, a construct of magical quality and ambiguity which accurately counterbalances the rationalism of both medieval
and renaissance systems.... The fool constantly questions our perceptions
of wisdom and truth and their relationship to everyday experience.... S/he
gives us the opportunity to humorously look at our own values and judge-
ments as the powerful socio-cultural structures of power [which] pull,
push, and shape our identity" ("History of the Fool").

Furthermore, in her stance toward the establishment, Dora is more
akin to the sharp-tongued Beatrice than the meek Hero (*Much Ado About
Nothing*), the resourceful Edmund than the naive Edgar (*King Lear*), the
rootless Antipholus of Syracuse than the reputable Antipholus of Ephesus
(*The Comedy of Errors*), the enterprisingly streetwise Mercutio than the
conventionally level-headed Benvolio (*Romeo and Juliet*). In elliptically
mimicking such well-known Shakespearean personae, Dora consciously
embraces her own alternative status, reveling in her concurrently spatial
and ethical wrong-sidedness not so much to declare her resistance to
authority as to emphasize with fool-like inverted wisdom that the culture
and society she inhabits are not sites of rigid demarcation but rather med-
leys of diversity and hybridity. Shakespeare himself comes to typify this
proposition as *Wise Children* progressively exposes the latent absurdity of
the playwright's idolization as the supreme emblem of legitimate and
unadulterated culture, when his opus is actually pervaded by bastardry,
plurality and polymorphousness — and this is arguably what attracts Carter
most potently to his prismatic multiverse. The House of Hazard, likewise,
may strive to represent tradition and convention but is ultimately a motley
crew of dispossessed, errant, promiscuous, decadent and quirky souls.

"Good morning! Let me introduce myself. My name is Dora Chance,"
the narrator exuberantly announces on the opening page of *Wise Children*,
thus presenting herself explicitly as the narrative focus. Informing the
reader straightaway that this is meant to be an unconventional text, she
then proceeds to inform us that her dwelling is situated in South London,
the traditionally less cultured and affluent portion of the metropolis. "Welcome to the wrong side of the tracks," Dora proclaims. "Put is another
way. If you're from the States, think of Manhattan. Then think of Brook-
lyn. See what I mean? Or, for a Parisian, it might be a question of *rive
gauche, rive droite*. With London, it's the North and South divide" (Carter

2006f, p. 1). In comparing her experience of local English geography with relevant foreign analogs, Dora evinces a distinctively cosmopolitan disposition that accompanies her throughout the text — which is somewhat paradoxical when one considers that the immediate context in which her life story unfolds is relatively narrow, and that the pragmatic outlook which both her intrinsic personality and empirical evidence have enjoined her to adopt could easily have been conducive to a stolidly parochial perspective.

At the same time, in designating her part of London "the *bastard* side of Old Father Thames," Dora ushers in a theme bound to play so pivotal a role throughout the entire text as to rise to the level of an autonomous, fully rounded protagonist: the dynamic tension between legitimacy and illegitimacy. *Wise Children* indeed capitalizes on deftly modulated variations on this theme by focusing on a social, emotional and psychological parallel: namely, the correspondence between dynastic and cultural forms of illegitimacy. The barrier supposedly separating high and low cultures, symbolized by the geographical boundary traced through London by the river Thames, is paralleled by the divide between legitimate and illegitimate members of the Hazard family. The narrator's enthusiastic tone, moreover, foreshadows an aspect of her makeup destined to shape the whole narrative. This consists of an unshakable determination to embrace and celebrate her indeterminate standing as a woman of illegitimate parentage while concurrently embracing the murky periphery of official culture as preferable to its mainstream manifestations — or, at any rate, no less desirable. At the same time, Carter harnesses Dora's storytelling verve to the articulation of a crucial component of her philosophy: the adamant rejection of binary oppositions. Hence, Dora's relationship with her society eschews all neat demarcations. As it turns out, Dora's art itself straddles the two sides of the river, charting a history of segregation and antagonism, yet also recording the apotheosis of the marginal and the unorthodox.

Therefore, even as the novel's tasty *entrée* foregrounds the clash between legitimacy and illegitimacy as a concurrently private and collective phenomenon, cracks soon appear in this dualistic social apparatus to evoke a tangled multi-culture. It is also noteworthy, in this respect, that Carter's portrayal of cultural partitioning again reveals the influence of Michel Foucault, and specifically his contention that the binary structures embedded in the seemingly distant the past — such as religious doctrine, imperialism, colonialism and patriarchal dominance — are still immensely influential today. Carter applies this lesson to her own text by repeatedly intimating that the societal circumstances unfolding through *Wise Children* over several generations are shaped by past dogmas no less than by contingent events. Multiplicity and dividedness, Carter reminds us via the loquacious Dora, are not exclusive markers of the modern world but have actually permeated history as fundamental definers of humanity as such.

The geographical split outlined by the narrator in the novel's opening segment is echoed across the textual fabric by the interplay of what Duffy aptly describes as "contrasting semantic fields." Thus, the reader experiences "on the one hand, the tone and vocabulary of the South London showgirl; and, on the other, the more refined, literate, philosophical, perhaps conscious, elevation of language" (Duffy, p. 102). At times, Dora makes deliberate use of a literate or even literary voice, especially in her intertextual references to Shakespeare's oeuvre. On such occasions, Carter gives her penchant for ambiguity a chance to swell up unchallenged as she abstains from overtly disclosing whether Dora is actually paying homage to the Bard's genius or rather mocking both him and her pompous father. There are even hints that Dora might be acting primarily, in circumstances of this kind, as Carter's vehicle for poking fun at the intertextual game generally. In lingering affectionately on her narrator's scholarly affectations, the writer might therefore be exposing that ploy' liability to degenerate into vapid feats of self-importance. It is noteworthy, on this point, that Dora never takes a person's literary education for granted — she comes across as genuinely surprised, for instance, when she discovers that her sister is familiar with Oscar Wilde's work (Carter 2006f, p. 192).

The novel's tantalizing blend of low and high cultures is assiduously interwoven with no less stirring a mixture of time levels in Dora's chronicling of her tortuous family history. Past and present interlock in wild dances and mellow embraces by turns as the narrative progressively maps out its characters' lives in the guise of meandering, zigzagging, looping, buckling and world-hopping trajectories redolent of the oneiric domain at its most riotous. At times, Dora abruptly brings her account to a halt slap in the middle of a scene to shift several generations back into her family's history and dwell on events concerning peripheral dramatis personae which bear precious little relevance to the scene in hand. The narrator exploits this technique in a markedly self-reflexive and self-conscious fashion, emphasizing its theatrical and cinematic connotations with unmistakable glee. This is evinced, for instance, by the following passage: "freeze-frame. Let us pause awhile in the unfolding story of Tristram and

Tiffany so that I can fill you in on the background. High time! you must be saying" (p. 11). The reader is then treated to a detailed portrayal of Dora and Nora's paternal grandmother.

Although, as noted, digressions of this ilk are not thematically or dynamically pertinent to the events they freeze in mid-frame, they are nonetheless notable in the overall context of *Wise Children* insofar as they capture with aphoristic pithiness crucial facets of both Dora's stance and Carter's own world view. In this particular case, for example, the description of the narrator's paternal grandmother turns out to be based on an image: one of the many "antique picture postcards" she and Nora treasure as something of a playfully makeshift version of a genealogical archive. As Dora explains, the Chance girls have never encountered their "*real* grandmother and only know her as you see her here, captured in the eternal youth of the publicity photo" (p. 12). These reflections are important, in communicating the novel's existential message, because they serve to remind us of the extent to which people only ever know one another not only *through* images but also, more disturbingly still, *as* images: synthetic portraits based on the discordant — and, by and large, inexorably prejudiced — perceptions of their being experienced by myriad other eyes. As argued in previous chapters, this proposition is pivotal to Carter's philosophy and finds varied expression in both her novels and her short stories across her career.

There can be little doubt that Carter's fascination with the virtually infinite potentialities of colloquial language and slang at their most prosaic — a trait of her style already triumphant in Fevvers' register — reaches new heights in *Wise Children*, where they assert themselves as a pivotal contribution to her overall verbal vivacity and passion for baroquely ornate tropes. The preference for conversational and markedly informal language impacts on practically all levels of Dora's discourse, affecting her diction, grammar, syntax, figurative language and verbal rhythm in equal measures. "Her English is frequently flawed," as Duffy aptly observes, and its overall tenor therefore feels "profane in both its narrow and broader sense. Colloquialisms appear often in the choice of a word, a colourful simile, her freedom with grammar and sentence structures, movements between tenses often using the historical present. There are sudden shifts to address, question — even challenge — the reader ... and sudden shifts in time as a word or an image triggers a memory" (Duffy, p. 103). Dora even enjoys infusing her use of French with a distinctively London-inspired flavor, as exemplified by the following observation: "some superannuated hoofers put on the avoirdupois like nobody's business" (Carter 2006f, p. 6).

Most notable, as a veritable mainstay of Dora's colloquial discourse, is a consistent reliance on bathos pivoting on the tendency to plummet from an elevated tenor to a prosaic or even bawdy voice. Essentially comical in a genuinely carnivalesque sense of the term, this ruse is systematically deployed to dethrone the precious accents and inflections traditionally associated high culture and its champions. Once again, Mikhail Bakhtin's writings on the carnival assert their relevance to Carter's world view — in this context, with specific reference to language. As Tom Sobshack explains in his discussion of the Bakhtinian principle vis-à-vis 1950s British comedy (a form in itself relevant to *Wise Children*'s temporal situation, "the carnivalesque spirit which turned everything topsy turvy, led eventually to a change in language. The difference between street language (the colloquial) and the language of the ruling class (the formal tongue of court and church) was narrowed when aristocrat and commoner mingled during the carnival" (Sobshack, p. 183).

In his valuable and meticulous study of *Wise Children*, S. L. Deefholts contends that "the spirit of the carnivalesque" veritably "permeates" the text, manifesting itself most fervidly in its narrator's attitude to hierarchy: "Dora has absolutely no reverence for the more exalted characters in the novel. The Lady Atlanta Hazard, first wife to Dora's father, Melchior, affectionately becomes 'Wheelchair' when she is confined to the aforementioned apparatus after an unfortunate fall left her with spinal damage.... Time and time again, Dora refuses to pay homage to her social 'superiors.' Instead, she is more than ready to pull away the veil of mystique that enshrouds those who are higher up in the social hierarchy." Dora's formidable father does not escape her appetite for irreverent critique, her priority being "to remind us that for all his high-flown language and ambitions, he's as human and as flawed as the rest of us" (Deefholts 2003c).

Toward the end of the novel, Dora invokes one of the Shakespeare plays in which hierarchy is most boisterously flouted in a genuine carnival spirit, *Henry IV, Part Two*, and considers the possibility of a finale in which "the young king," when he "meets up again with Jack Falstaff," does not "send him packing but digs him in the ribs" and merrily announces: "Have I got a job for you!" (Carter 2006f, p. 222). The world here imagined by Dora is one in which the carnival goes on beyond the appointed limits to spill over into the everyday and redefine its coordinates. However, as argued in the preceding chapter, no carnival is ever meant to become permanent or total, insofar as the fundamental function assigned to disruptive moments of excess is to celebrate disorder, flux and chaotic energy in order to demonstrate the desirability — and inexorability — of the return to the norm, and thus help the status quo to consolidate itself. It is intrinsic in the very nature of carnival transgression, therefore, to come to an end in a cloud of nostalgia: a somber pall which is ironically intensified by its juxtaposition with the wave of sheer joy exuded by its climactic jokes, acrobatics and fireworks.

This darker side of the carnivalesque sensibility is powerfully conveyed by the scene recording the party held after the shooting of the film *The Dream*, where the set of the Athenian wood undergoes a radical metamorphosis to transit fluidly from the domain of dramatic artifice into reality — a menacing, dark and bewildering reality: "there was a real, black sky above us.... And I no longer remember that set as a set, but as a real wood, dangerous, uncomfortable." In this disorientating quasi-reality, Hollywood itself becomes coterminous with "the enchanted forest ... the wood where you go mad; the wood where the shadows live longer than you do" (pp. 157–158).

Although Carter never loses sight of this pragmatic dimension, Dora's approach to both history and storytelling could be said to offer an alternate take on the classic cultural matrix underpinning the relationship between the carnival and the establishment. Thus, while the latter appears to feel entitled to exploit the former for the purpose of self-perpetuation, carnival, in turn, is at liberty to use the status quo as the target of ongoing random assaults which stubbornly refuse containment by the calendarized arrangement of social existence. This message is persistently communicated by Dora's voice through her refusal to feel stunted or humiliated by her illegitimacy and by the marginalized social standing attendant upon it. Endowed with the born survivor's rubber resilience, she keep bouncing right through to the end — or, in actual fact, *beyond*. Thus, she brings her effervescent ride through history to an end declaring that neither she nor her sister can "afford to die for at least another twenty years" now that they have been entrusted by Peregrine with the welfare of twin babies (a boy and a girl, to be precise) — creatures, she stresses, bound to grow into "wise children" indeed (p. 230). It is only appropriate, therefore, that the novel's closing line should reiterate the message interspersed throughout the narrative as a refrain: "What a joy it is to dance and sing!" (p. 232).

Dora is able to accept her inscription in a world shaped by rational-ized — if not actually rational — mores, disciplinary constraints and hege-monic demands. Yet, she never gives up conclusively the Dionysian energy coursing through the carnival world of magic, rowdy pleasure, fantasy, revelry and visceral disorder. Dora knows full well that the disruptive force of laughter is neither boundless nor unconditional and that the world, relatedly, cannot be radically reconfigured in accordance with a carniva-lesque ethos. Such a perspective, however tantalizing and refreshing it might be, is ultimately powerless to eradicate the horrors of war, economic inequality, the evils of discrimination and persecution, and the iniquities of power at large. In other words, the material conditions of the actual world cannot be transcended or evaded through riotous play alone. Nev-ertheless, the carnival spirit has the power to provide a provocative glimpse into *other* realities — not as visions of the future, which would feasibly remain utopian and hence unattainable, but rather as possibilities which lurk in the underbelly of the here-and-now, in the occluded folds and cre-vices of official culture, and in unforeseen moments of both hyperkinetic elation and tranquil reflection, in the guise of *as ifs* wherein creativity may find, albeit temporarily, free and legitimate rein.

If Dora echoes Fevvers through her employment of a markedly col-loquial tone and register, she is no less close a relative of the legendary aerialist in the region of narrativity. She knows full well that in the face of a first-person narrative, readers will inevitably place their trust in the tale itself rather than in its teller, and indeed recognizes the intrinsic unre-liability and partiality of this form at numerous junctures. Dora is also disarmingly willing from the start to acknowledge the extent to which her materialistic priorities outstrip any aesthetic considerations: "romantic ille-gitimacy, always a seller." She is hence quite prepared to exploit her cul-ture's commercial preferences even though she is aware that "to tell the truth, there was sod all romantic about" her and her twin sister's "illegit-imacy. At best, it was a farce, at worst, a tragedy, and a chronic inconven-ience the rest of the time" (p. 11). Like Fevvers, therefore, Dora stands out as a flamboyantly unreliable narrator. With Dora, Carter relies to unsur-passed dramatic effect on an especially marked sense of intimacy stemming from the establishment from the start of the narrator's direct dialogue with the reader. The communicational dialectics between addresser and addres-see is not, in this instance, filtered by the presence of an intermediary or interviewer as is the case in *Nights at the Circus*. This entails that even if

Dora's account contains an element of distortion (or even mendacity for that matter), we cannot blame her incontrovertibly because by the time we discover for sure that this is the case, we have become her accomplices — and plausibly begun to relish this rascally status.

However, though unreliable, Dora does not despotically impose a single voice — and, by implication, a univocal perspective — on the narrative in the style of a classic realist narrator: an entity that is also, despite appearances, an inevitably biased teller but effaces this status under a hypocritical cloak of objectivity. In fact, Dora is all the time keen to draw attention to her narratorial identity and to the inherent artificiality of this role. At the same time, she strives to embrace a disparity of tongues, perspectives and sensibilities within her commodious narratorial wings and, most vitally from a psychological angle, to remind us that no narrative which tries to revisit the past could ever be expected to yield accurate results due to its dependence on the most fluctuating of human powers. As Deefholts emphasizes, "the concession that memory is fallible is realistic — more realistic than those first-person narratives where the tellers recall exact dialogue from twenty years past.... Yet, the convention of filmic accuracy in first-person narration is so well established that we rarely question the seamlessness of the narrative" (Deefholts 2003b). Especially tantalizing are the passages in which the first-person narrator candidly admits to the fallibility of her mnemonic powers and then proceeds to spin a most implausible narrative web. At such moments, any reader equipped with a modicum of curiosity is bound to wonder what might have truly taken place instead. Relatedly, when Dora alerts us to the fact that practically all of the anecdotes she relates find inception in the more or less distant past, and have therefore been progressively overlaid by the fanciful veil of multigenerational reminiscences, we are urged to ask ourselves how many of the particulars she dishes out as so-called facts she is likely — or willing — to recollect correctly.

If it is important to acknowledge that Dora's narrative is distorted by her ineluctably subjective perceptions of events and her role in them, it is no less vital to recognize that she, too, is a product of fictional distortions resulting from her representations both by individuals she encounters at various stages in her colorful life and by her cultural milieu at large — images which, in keeping with Carter's kaleidoscopic imagination, are embedded in diverse media and formats, including sculpture, fiction and cinema. The first instance of this textual trend worth noting in this context consists of Dora's use as the template underlying the physical molding of another woman. This is pivotal to the mock fairy tale scene set in the "artificial woods" where art and life unexpectedly confront each other in the persons of Dora and her fiancé's ex-wife. Reflecting on this disorientating experience, the narrator recalls: "I saw my double ... and then I saw it was a replica. A hand-made, custom-built replica" (Carter 2006f, p. 155). It rapidly transpires that the fiancé's ex-wife has translated herself into an approximate mock-up of Dora by surgical means, enduring the torments of multiple cosmetic interventions and strict dieting to end up with a slightly pathetic slapdash version of its model. The woman's ordeal recalls Ghislaine's facial reinvention following her insane lover's assault as dramatized in *Shadow Dance*. No less crucially, Carter declares her dislike of stark binaries by alluding to the element of artificiality underlying Dora's own reality. If Dora's rival is merely a second-rate imitation of a supposedly worthy original, there is also a sense in which Dora herself is no more real than a vaporous eidolon, in this context. Indeed, her engagement is just a travesty devoid of any trace of genuine affection even though it is publicly paraded as the apotheosis of true love.

The second notable case of identity construction with Dora at its center consists of her reinvention through literature. This occurs when one of her many lovers, Irish, realizes that she is losing interest in him and resolves to channel his disappointment into the creation of *Hollywood Elegies*, a volume which goes on to win him a "posthumous Pulitzer" (p. 154). Attempting to assess the work's representation of her character and appearance in relation to what she sees as her true self, Dora states that her ex-lover's portrayal merely indulges in the obscene construction of a "treacherous, lecherous chorus girl" blighted by a "chronic insensitivity to a poet's heart" (pp. 119–120): in other words, a fictional creature who bears no resemblance to the woman she perceives herself to be. Even the ostensibly factual aspects of Dora's liaison with Irish appear to have been twisted and displaced. Having experienced artistic inscription first as a painterly and sculptural artifact and then as a novelistic caricature, Dora's character is further *processed*, so to speak, as a cinematic product when *Hollywood Elegies* undergoes adaptation to the screen — an invention of which she merely harbors the vaguest recollections: "I forget who it was played me. Some painted harlot" (p. 154).

In dwelling on the successive stages of her narrator's metamorphosis into arbitrarily deformed art objects, Carter is able to engage directly with one of her deepest philosophical preoccupations. This consists of the proposition, already promulgated in *The Infernal Desire Machines of Doctor Hoffman*, that we only know other people as images of them forged out of our impressions — and misconceptions — of their being, not as they genuinely are. Carter is also eager to remind us that we are inclined to misconstrue and misrepresent ourselves, through both literal and figurative forms of storytelling, as much as others warp our identity by recourse to their own imaginary projections. Hence, *Wise Children* makes it incontrovertibly clear that Dora has concocted a self-image which is alternately crude, clownish, gentle, loving, generous and forthright but this representation might not ultimately coincide with anybody else's perception of her character — either among her fellow dramatis personae or among Carter's readers.

Furthermore — and this is the climactic joke played by the text at both its narrator and its reader's expense — the narrative voice, the events it reconstructs and Dora herself, if regarded from a standpoint external to the fictional web itself, are essentially fictional constructs ideated by a writer, and not empirically verifiable entities or events. The progressive deferral of any degree of veracity plausibly attributable to Dora's account is comparable to the incessant slippage of meaning in language. First, we realize that Dora is the object of imaginary representations; second, we come to appreciate that these distorted visions have been further warped before being consigned to the page and offered to us through Dora's filtering of their import, impact and color; and finally, we have no choice but to accept that all of those images — both Dora's and other characters' — are fictional representations ideated by the invisible (yet mockingly powerful) writer behind them all. As Carter's narrator becomes more and more engulfed in a universe of representations authored by either her textual companions or the writer herself, the novel's documentary authenticity recedes into a flickering mirage.

In juggling both its symbolic and its philosophical speculations, the novel epitomizes the operations of intertextuality as described in the opening part of this chapter. Indeed, the novel proceeds throughout, albeit unobtrusively and with engaging variations, according to the principle that neither Carter's personal insights nor the Bard's messages can, or indeed *should*, emerge unaltered from their narrative-dramatic encounter. It could be argued, in fact, that both parties undergo a sea change of veritably tempestuous magnitude. Given its allegiances to art and magic more than science proper, the storytelling event staged through this interoperability has more in common with an alchemical metamorphosis than a chemical reaction. In its productive dialogue with the Shakespearean corpus, *Wise Children* approaches that body of works as a paradigmatic exemplification of the type of text which Roland Barthes designates as "writerly" (*scriptible*). Such a text is not "replete" with meanings conducive to unproblematically transparent interpretations but is actually traversed by plural and even discordant messages whose "goal is to make the reader no longer a consumer but a producer of the text" (Barthes 1974, p. 4). Whereas the "readerly" (*lisible*) text posits itself as a closed and finished "product," the "writerly text is ourselves writing, before the infinite play of the world is ... plasticized by some singular system (Ideology, Genius, Criticism) which reduces the plurality of entrances, the opening of networks, the infinity of languages" (p. 5). Contributing actively to the text's production turns interpretation from "a parasitical act" into a "form of work" (p. 10). In endeavoring to engage dynamically with the verbal and visual signs of a plethora of Shakespeare plays, Carter — placing herself in the position of a reader as well a writer — fully acknowledges their plurality and resistance to monolithic readings and, in the process, strives to elaborate a distinctive "form of work" from her own perceptions, observations and responses.

Furthermore, by working in tandem with Shakespeare's plays instead of presuming to act upon them from a standpoint of critical mastery, Carter draws attention to the genesis of both her own novel and the works with which she is intertextually involved, presenting them as parallel discourses — or, to appeal to one of *Wise Children*'s axial tropes, as semiotic *twins*. According to Barthes, the writerly text combines numerous codes, each of which represents "one of the voices out of which the text is woven," and none of which can ultimately claim incontrovertible precedence over the others. Even when one particular code appears dominant, one should never forget that "alongside each utterance, one might say that off-stage voices can be heard" (p. 21). The adoption of reading strategies prepared to forgo the prerogative of mastery enable us to play the role of one of those off-stage voices, and hence to write or speak not so much about a text as alongside it. The interpretative approaches embraced by Carter vis-à-vis Shakespeare are precisely of this order.

In this respect, Carter's enterprise could also be said to echo Jacques Derrida's description of the deconstructive gesture as a matter of writing with *both hands* — by which the philosopher means that in advancing any one view or conviction, one should never neglect the simultaneous tenability of at least one other alternative perspective. In working with one possible reading of her intertextual partner, Carter, like Derrida, is always aware of the possibility of the implicit presence of other entirely different readings — traces of which may sporadically make themselves felt as ghostly actors even if they are not pursued and developed. *Wise Children* works with one, albeit prismatic, set of interpretations of the Bard's oeuvre but never loses sight of the welter of alternate options potentially available to both Carter herself and other readers. Thus, like the text ideated by Derrida, it stands out as an inherently double reality: a fleeting alliance of "two texts, two hands, two visions, two ways of listening. Together simultaneously and separately" (Derrida, pp. 75–6).

Considering the novel's imbrication with Shakespeare's oeuvre, it is not especially surprising that one of its principal textual energizers should be the mechanism of wild coincidence and that the rhetorical force at its core — its discursive generator, so to speak — should be irony. The coalescence of chance and irony is most potently conveyed by the novel's structure: its key occurrences are almost invariably presented, right from the beginning, as fortuitous products of coincidence or accident. Yet, ironically, they are studiously and wittily distributed over the novel's fabric in a fashion that leaves precious little to sheer happenstance. The result is a stunning oxymoron: a carousel of balanced chaos. The sense of balance ensues from Carter's careful coupling and juxtaposition of myriad personae, while chaos springs from the heady complications caused by several cases of mistaken identity, by sudden outbursts of carnival inversion, and by the unexpected psychological and emotional developments undergone by the characters as time rolls by. The reader's awareness of Carter's careful orchestration of seemingly random experiences and data becomes increasingly palpable as the number of identical and fraternal twins harbored by the story among its personae grows to vertiginous proportions. The tortuous and occasionally incestuous relationships in which both these and other characters are insistently engaged enhances the text's aura of deliberately cultivated implausibility, raising the bar for what can be legitimately presented as credible, possible or acceptable within any story.

Wise Children plays with the power of chance in an ironically self-conscious manner from the beginning, as it transpires that twin sisters Dora and Nora Chance have reached their seventy-fifth birthday and that this, by a weird coincidence, concurs with the one-hundredth birthday of their natural father, Sir Melchior Hazard, and his putatively deceased twin brother, Peregrine. The date, as though this were not enough of a bizarre touch on the part of fate, further coincides with Shakespeare's own birthday, 23 April. Dora and Nora's birthday enjoys an appropriately dramatic start as their half-brother Tristram Hazard unexpectedly descends upon them to announce that his girlfriend Tiffany, the twins' goddaughter, has gone missing. It is not long before Dora and Nora find out that Tiffany is pregnant with Tristram's baby and learn that he is by no means prepared to accept the responsibility. The drama escalates as it is revealed that a body believed to be Tiffany's has been discovered.

As anticipated in Chapter 1, *Wise Children* pivots on the interdependent topoi of repetition and difference. Doublings and replications of all imaginable sorts assiduously collude to suggest prismatic similarities between the reciprocally mirroring sides of a dyad. At the same time, Carter brings into play no less varied a range of contrasts and disparities which cause those paired elements to stand out as diametrically opposed polarities. Building her cast around a veritable host of both actual and figurative twins, Carter thus projects a world picture in which self and other are inextricably intertwined and the concept of personal identity itself dissolves in the dizzying geometry of a hall of mirrors. According to Deefholts, "the profusion of pairs allows the implied author to play with all manner of dualities. Hence, the comic and tragic faces of the theatre, represented in Peregrine and Melchior. The motif of the good and evil twin is common enough, but in this case, the author has added an engaging twist to the popular trope that allows it to evade being overfamiliar" (Deefholts 2003a).

Concurrently, Dora and Nora themselves are portrayed as specular images of each other, while their twin cousins Saskia and Imogen can be seen as the Chance sisters' inverted doubles. Thus, if Dora and Nora mirror each other as individuals, Saskia and Imogen mirror both as a pair. Socially and economically privileged from birth, Saskia and Imogen are presented not merely as unsympathetic but also, at times, as overtly malevolent. They do not hesitate, for example, to throw their own mother out of her family abode. It is the Chance twins, who may be unrefined, licentious and blasphemous but are also immensely generous and affectionate, who offer the woman a substitute home. The two sets of sisters are also contrasted, often to considerable humorous effect, at the somatic level. Thus, Saskia and Imogen are said to have typified pretty, red-haired English Roses in their youth, whereas the young Dora and Nora, as the narrator regretfully concedes, were "more coquette than finishing school.... Nymphettes, I suppose they'd call us now" (Carter 2006f, p. 70).

The image of the mirror famously plays a major part in the fairy tale tradition so dear to Carter's heart and mind — suffice it to mention its ascendancy in Charles Perrault's *Snow White* as the essence of a narcissistic power trip, in Hans Christian Andersen's *The Snow Queen* as the means of infiltration by the familiar world of a radically alien reality, and in the Japanese tale *The Mirror of Matsuyama* as a vehicle for the celebration of the creative power of maternal and daughterly love. The most renowned use of the mirror in fantasy literature of all times arguably consists of Lewis Carroll's *Through the Looking-Glass, and What Alice Found There*. Of special relevance to *Wise Children*, in this connection, is Luce Irigaray's analysis of the specular trope in the Alice story in the context of *This Sex Which Is Not One*.

It is first worth mentioning that Irigaray's most comprehensive assessment of the rich metaphorical luggage carried by the concept of the mirror occurs in the earlier volume titled *Speculum of the Other Woman*— a designation in itself worthy of inspection as pertinent to Carter's mirror-oriented imagery. The "speculum" invoked by Irigaray is an eminently multiaccentual term, referring at once to the medical, and primarily gynecological, instrument used to penetrate the female body in a fashion that renders it a passive object of the professional gaze; to the mirror of the world (*speculum mundi*) constructed by patriarchy to project its particular world picture and intended to bear the image of man as a cosmic ruler; to the concept of woman as the specular antithesis of man, a surface reflecting the value of virility by defect through the attributes she is deemed to lack (Irigaray 1985). The realization that the concept of the mirror abounds with figurative connotations varyingly articulating woman's marginalization within patriarchy should invite a judicious interrogation of its currency. Both Irigaray and Carter know full well that it would be utterly spurious to yield to the facile assumption that the mirror can simply be shattered. *Wise Children* indeed emphasizes that specular images, deceptive and disfiguring though they might be, are instrumental in the genesis of subjectivity and identity. Concurrently, it enriches and problematizes a perspective already explored by Carter in the context of *The Magic Toyshop* with a focus on Melanie's rite of passage, to show that whatever we may choose to call reality is not a realm of transparent and self-evident truths but rather a murky edifice riddled with occluded passageways, ghost-infested closets and secret (possibly even bloody) chambers.

In the chapter of *This Sex Which Is Not One* headed "The Looking Glass, from the Other Side," Irigaray provides a kind of parable indicating that attempts to discard the specular dimension in a culture where meanings are inseparable from illusory representations is far from desirable: Alice is paralyzed within a life where her reflections in the mirror exist entirely for others. In cutting though the specular surface and thus escaping the eyes that follow her wherever she goes, Alice may seem to achieve a modicum of freedom. In fact, Irigaray contends, this is clearly not the case since no identity, name or substance is ultimately available outside the network of representation: the moment the images that impart Alice with a recognizable self cease to obtain, her very being evaporates (Irigaray 2000). *Wise Children* conveys a comparably sobering message by persistently reminding us that no trip into the carnival realm of playfulness and freedom is anything other than temporary — and that any escape from the symbolic network by which adult socialized existence is defined can never, accordingly, constitute a permanent achievement. The only consistent opportunities for play are those provided by the self-consciously artificial domains of spectacle, theater, enactment and role-playing — and these are indeed the areas of human interaction to which Carter's novel insistently returns. As Smith emphasizes, "*Wise Children* is, from start to finish, a performance — an act" (in Carter 2006f, p. xvii). In this regard, the novel could be regarded as both an intensification and a recapitulation of the scenarios painted by Carter — with sumptuously polychromatic variations — in *The Magic Toyshop*, *The Infernal Desire Machines of Doctor Hoffman*, *The Passion of New Eve* and *Nights at the Circus*.

What distinguishes *Wise Children* is its unprecedented emphasis on the sheer art of regeneration and rebirth. Thus, in spite of its unsentimental take on the ineluctability of humanity's inscription in a tenacious web of representations and symbols, the novel is nonetheless able to celebrate the possibility of fresh horizons and new prospects at practically every turn of the page. *Wise Children*, as Smith lyrically puts it, "lets the lost be found and the old be young. It invents impossible fertilities. It renews everything it touches. It bursts with energy, passion, wit, hilarity, hope, skill, art and love. Resurrective in so many ways, it's Carter's final legacy, and it's a legacy of good, fierce, raucous potential. What a wisdom. What a joy" (p. xviii). It is noteworthy, in this respect, that the text's emphasis on renewal carries the dramatic flavor typical of Shakespeare's late plays. These works' compositional style is explicitly reflected in the novel's use of a redemptive storyline crowned by a happy ending. In the climactic gala intended to celebrate Dora and Nora's father's birthday, long-separated family members are reunited and reconciled, the paternity of several children is revealed, a wronged woman is given the chance to denounce her fickle lover in public, an errant husband is forced to acknowledge his true spouse, selfish children meet their punishment and magnanimous ones are dispensed their legitimate rewards. The novel's blend of mellow and sensational moments, moreover, could be said to echo the Bard's own tone in the final stages of his career as a playwright.

Wise Children is concerned throughout with the quest for identity as the ultimate mission animating singular individual and whole cultural formations. In elaborating this theme, it never loses sight of the virtue which it implicitly posits as supreme in its opening paragraphs: namely, the ability and the necessity to reinvent oneself afresh at a moment's notice. Having spent their entire lives in the midst of thespian types so keenly self-dramatizing as to perceive every instant of their lives as a link in a chain of stagy climaxes or tragic downfalls, the Chance twins are the first to acknowledge the importance of that virtue and to realize that the only way to develop it is to accept that real life itself, when the histrionics are over and the curtains are drawn, is merely a series of moments with no clear plot — let alone resolution. Nussbaum captures this idea in simple yet memorable words: "the secret, the sisters know, is to hope for the best, prepare for the worst, and always be ready for a new beginning" (Nussbaum). Mimicking Dora's unflinching passion for word play, it could be argued that the novel ultimately proclaims its optimistic disposition through its very characters, for Carter's *wise children* act as allegorical personifications of the *wisecracks* of which both its author and its narrator are so fond, as *whiz-kids* proficient at the art of resilient self-reinvention, as iconoclastic incarnations of the *wise men* of old, and even as ironical embodiments of the principle of *wysiwyg* that leave us continually — and teasingly — in doubt as to the sheer trustworthiness of their utterances.

Whether she draws on the fairy tale or the pantomime, Shakespeare or Hollywood, Sterne or Baudelaire, Carter wears her sources on her sleeve, never submerging them in the secretive mist summoned by more elitist authors to present their influences as hints and whispers for the chosen few to recognize and locate. In fact, she is at all times a frank deconstructionist in the most genuine sense of the word — that is to say, a writer concerned not with destroying or presuming to erase what has gone before (a role frequently and erroneously ascribed to the practitioner of the deconstructive art) but rather with concurrently sabotaging and invigorating the past and its legacy by showing that all texts are inherently self-dismantling and hence incessantly open to reconceptualization. In the process, Carter's idiosyncratic pen discloses a realm of Russian nesting dolls and Chinese boxes: a vibrant celebration of the principle of *mise en abîme* wherein a story always harbors another story. While this narrative galaxy is unquestionably ornate, or even flamboyant, it never evinces a crassly gem-encrusted semblance. The richness of Carter's fictions, in fact, is akin neither to the ostentatious glitter of diamonds nor to the complacent smartness of emeralds but rather to the subtle, gently stardusted glory of lapis lazuli.

Bibliography

Please note that all online materials were available at the time of the book's execution. Their enduring accessibility cannot, of course, be assured.

Amburgey, R. 2006. "Angela Carter's Revision of Popular Fairy Tales." *Associated Content.* http://www.associatedcontent.com/article/61923/angela_carters_revision_of_popular.html?cat=38.

Aragon, L. 1980. *Paris Peasant.* Trans. S. Watson Taylor. London: Pan.

_____. "Fantasy." *Love Quotes.* http://www.1-love-quotes.com/cgi-bin/viewquotes.cgi?action=search&Category=FANTASY.

Atwood, M. 1992. "Angela Carter Obituary." *The Observer* 23 February.

_____. 2004. *Lady Oracle.* London: Virago.

Bacchilega, C. 2008. "Extrapolating from Nalo Hopkinson's *Skin Folk*: Reflections on Transformation and Recent English-Language Fairy-Tale Fiction by Women." In *Contemporary Fiction and the Fairy Tale*, ed. S. Benson. Detroit: Wayne State University Press.

Bakhtin, M. [1965.] 1984. *Rabelais and His World.* Trans. H. Iswolsky. Bloomington: Indiana University Press.

_____. [1929.] 2003. *Problems of Dostoevsky's Poetics.* Trans. C. Emerson. Minneapolis: University of Minnesota Press.

_____. [1981.] 2004. *The Dialogic Imagination: Four Essays.* Trans. C. Emerson and M. Holquist. Austin: University of Texas Press.

Barthes, R. 1974. *S/Z: An Essay.* Trans. R. Miller. New York: Hill and Wang.

_____. 1990. *A Lover's Discourse.* Trans. R. Howard. London: Penguin.

_____. [1972.] 1993. *Mythologies.* Trans. A. Lavers. London: Vintage.

_____. [1980.] 1996. *Sade/Fourier/Loyola.* Trans. R. Miller. Baltimore: Johns Hopkins University Press.

Baudelaire, C. [1861.] 2010. "L'albatros." *Fleursdumal.org.* http://fleursdumal.org/poem/200.

Baudrillard, J. 1988. *America.* London: Verso.

Beckett, S. 1983. *Worstward Ho.* New York: Grove.

_____. [1946–1950.] 2009. *Three Novels: Molloy, Malone Dies, The Unnamable.* New York: Grove.

Belsey, C., and J. Moore. 1997. *The Feminist Reader.* London: Macmillan.

Benjamin, W. 1982. "Letter to Rilke." Cited in R. Wolin. *Walter Benjamin: An Aesthetic of Redemption*. New York: Columbia University Press.

_____. [1938.] 1983. "The *flâneur*." From "The Paris of the Second Empire in Baudelaire." In *Charles Baudelaire: A Lyric Poet in the Era of High Capitalism*. London: Verso.

_____. 1985. "Central Park." *New German Critique*, no. 34 (Winter). Trans. L. Spencer and M. Harrington.

_____. 1992. "Theses on the Philosophy of History." In *Illuminations*, ed. H. Arendt. Trans. H. Zohn. London: Fontana.

_____. [1914.] 1996. "The Metaphysics of Youth." In *Walter Benjamin: Selected Writings Volume 1: 1913–1926*, eds. M. Bullock and M.W. Jennings. Cambridge, MA: Belknap Press, Harvard University Press.

_____. 1999a. "Dream Kitsch." In *Walter Benjamin: Selected Writings Volume 2: 1927–1934*, eds. M.W. Jennings, H. Eiland and G. Smith. Cambridge, MA: Belknap Press, Harvard University Press.

_____. 1999b. *The Arcades Project*. Trans. H. Eiland and K. McLaughlin. Cambridge, MA: Belknap Press, Harvard University Press.

Bergson, H. 1900. "Laughter: An Essay on the Meaning of the Comic." *Project Gutenberg*. http://www.gutenberg.org/etext/4352.

Bettelheim, B. [1976.] 1991. *The Uses of Enchantment: The Meaning and Importance of Fairy Tales*. London: Penguin.

Bonca, C. 1994. "In Despair of the Old Adams: Angela Carter's 'The Infernal Desire Machines of Dr. Hoffman.'" *The Review of Contemporary Fiction. FindArticles.com.* 2 September 2010. http://findarticles.com/p/articles/mi_hb3544/is_n3_vl4/ai_n 28644336/.

Boston, R. 1970. "They Survived a Nuclear War." *The New York Times,* 13 September. http://www.nytimes.com/books/98/12/27/specials/carter-villains.html.

Boyer, M.C. 1996. *CyberCities: Visual Perception in the Age of Electronic Communication*. New York: Princeton Architectural Press.

Briggs, K. 2002. *The Fairies in Tradition and Literature*. London: Routledge.

Bristol, M.D. 1985. *Carnival and Theatre: Plebeian Culture and the Structure of Authority in Renaissance England*. London: Methuen.

Brite, P.Z. 1997. *Exquisite Corpse*. London: Phoenix.

Bryson, N. 1988. "The Gaze in the Expanded Field." In *Vision and Visuality*, ed. H. Foster. Seattle, WA: Bay.

Buchel, M.N. 2003. "'Bankrupt Enchantments' and 'Fraudulent Magic': Demythologising in Angela Carter's *The Bloody Chamber* and *Nights at the Circus*." University of Pretoria etd. <http://upetd.up.ac.za/thesis/available/etd-10282004-103512/unrestricted/00dissertation.pdf>

Bürger, P. 2004. *Theory of the Avant-Garde*. Trans. M. Shaw. Minneapolis: University of Minnesota Press.

Butcher, H. 2008. "'Desiderio in Search of a Master': Desire and the Quest for Recognition in Angela Carter's *The Infernal Desire Machines of Doctor Hoffman*." *Forum: University of Edinburgh Postgraduate Journal of Culture and the Arts* 6 (Spring). http://forum.llc.ed.ac.uk/archive/06/butcher.pdf.

Butler, J. 1990. *Gender Trouble*. London and New York: Routledge.

_____. 1993. *Bodies That Matter*. London and New York: Routledge.

_____. 1994. "Gender as Performance." *Radical Philosophy* 67. http://www.theory.org.uk/but-intl.htm.

Callil, C. 1992. "Flying Jewellery." *Sunday Times*, 23 February.

Calvino, I. 1988. *Sulla Fiaba*, Turin: Giulio Einaudi.

_____. 1996. *Six Memos for the Next Millennium*. Trans. P. Creagh. London: Vintage.

Campbell, J. 1988. *The Power of Myth*. New York: Doubleday.

Caplan, F. *ThinkExist.com*. http://thinkexist.com/quotes/frank_caplan/.

Carter, A. 1969. *Heroes and Villains*. New York: Pocket.

_____. 1970a. *The Donkey Prince*. New York: Simon and Schuster.

_____. 1970b. *Miss Z, the Dark Young Lady*. London: Heinemann.

_____. 1979. *The Sadeian Woman: An Exercise in Cultural History*. London: Virago.

_____. 1985. "The Company of Angela Carter: An Interview." *Marxism Today*. http://www.amielandmelburn.org.uk/collections/mt/pdf/85_01_20.pdf.

_____. 1990. *The Virago Press Book of Fairy Tales* (a.k.a. *The Old Wives' Fairy Tale Book*). London: Virago.

_____. 1992a. "Omnibus: Angela Carter's Curious Room." BBC transmission script, 15 September.

_____. [1982.] 1992b. *Nothing Sacred — Selected Writings*. London: Virago.

_____. 1998. *Shaking a Leg: Collected Writings by Angela Carter*. London: Vintage.

_____. [1968.] 2005. *Several Perceptions*. London: Virago.

_____. [1967.] 2006a. *The Magic Toyshop*. London: Virago.

_____. [1971; 1987.] 2006b. *Love*. London: Vintage.

_____. [1992.] 2006c. *Expletives Deleted*. London: Picador.

_____. [1998.] 2006d. *Burning Your Boats — Collected Short Stories*. London: Vintage.

_____. [1984.] 2006e. *Nights at the Circus*. London: Vintage.

_____. [1991.] 2006f. *Wise Children*. London: Vintage.

_____. [1966.] 2009a. *Shadow Dance* (a.k.a. *Honeybuzzard*). London: Virago.

_____. [1977.] 2009b. *The Passion of New Eve*. London: Virago.

_____. [1972.] 2010. *The Infernal Desire Machines of Doctor Hoffman*. London: Penguin.

Castle, T. 1986. *Masquerade and Civilization — The Carnivalesque in Eighteenth-Century English Culture and Fiction*. Stanford, CA: Stanford University Press.

Cavalli-Sforza, L. 2004. *L'evoluzione della cultura: Proposte concrete per studi futuri*. Turin: Codice.

Caws, M.A. 1971. *André Breton*. New York: Twayne.

Chesterton, G.K. 1908/1915. *All Things Considered*. Extract. In "G.K. Chesterton's Fairy Tales." *SurLaLune*. <tp://www.surlalunefairytales.com/introduction/gkch esterton.html>.

Christensen, P. 1994. "The Hoffmann Connection: Demystification in Angela Carter's 'The Infernal Desire Machines of Dr. Hoffman.'" *The Review of Contemporary Fiction*. *FindArticles.com*. 1 September 2010. http://findarticles.com/p/articles/mi_hb3544/is_n3_v14/ai_n28644337/.

Cixous, H., and C. Clément. 1987. *The Newly Born Woman*. Trans. B. Wing. Manchester: Manchester University Press.

"Clown." Wikipedia. http://en.wikipedia.org/wiki/Clown#Fear_of_clowns.

Coleridge, S.T. 1817. *Biographia Literaria. The Literature Network*. http://www.online-literature.com/coleridge/biographia-literaria/13/.

Cooper, J.C. 1983. *Fairy Tales: Allegories of the Inner Life — Archetypal Patterns and Symbols in Classic Fairy Stories*. Wellingborough, Northamptonshire: Aquarian.

Coover, R. 2001. "Entering *Ghost Town*." In *Angela Carter and the Fairy Tale*, eds. D. Roemer and C. Bacchilega. Detroit, MI: Wayne State University Press.

Dalí, S. "Salvador Dalí Quotes." *Brainy Quote*. <http://www.brainyquote.com/quotes/authors/s/salvador_dali.html> and http://www.brainyquote.com/quotes/quotes/s/salvadorda139255.html.

Darnton, R. 1984. "Peasants Tell Tales: The Meaning of Mother Goose." In *The Great Cat Massacre and Other Episodes in French Cultural History*. New York: Basic.

Day, A. 1998. *Angela Carter: The Rational Glass*. Trans. R. Hurley, M. Seem and H.R. Lane. London and New York: Continuum.

Day, W.P. 1985. *In the Circles of Fear and Desire*. Chicago: University of Chicago Press.

Deefholts, S.L. 2003a. "Interpretive Reading—Hazarding Chance: Reading Angela Carter's *Wise Children*: Part One." *Margin—exploring modern magical realism*. http://www.angelfire.com/wa2/margin/nonficSLD2.html.

_____. 2003b. "Interpretive Reading—Hazarding Chance: Reading Angela Carter's *Wise Children*: Part Two." *Margin—exploring modern magical realism*. http://www.angelfire.com/wa2/margin/nonficSLD3.html.

_____. 2003c. "Interpretive Reading—Hazarding Chance: Reading Angela Carter's *Wise Children*: Part Three." *Margin—exploring modern magical realism*. http://www.angelfire.com/wa2/margin/nonficSLD4.html.

Dégh, L. 1988. "What Did the Grimm Brothers Give to and Take from the Folk?" In *The Brothers Grimm and Folktale*, ed. J.M. McGlathery. Urbana: University of Illinois Press.

de la Rochère, M.H.D. 2010. "'But Marriage Itself Is No Party': Angela Carter's Translation of Charles Perrault's 'La Belle au bois dormant'; or, Pitting the Politics of Experience against the Sleeping Beauty Myth." http://www.faqs.org/periodicals/201001/2061407101.html.

Deleuze, G., and F. Guattari. [1972.] 1984. *Anti-Oedipus: Capitalism and Schizophrenia*. Trans. R. Hurley, M. Seem and H.R. Lane. London: Athlone.

Derrida, J. 1982. *Margins of Philosophy*. Trans. A. Bass. Chicago: Chicago University Press.

_____, and A. Ronell. 1980. "The Law of Genre." *Critical Inquiry*, vol. 7, no. 1 (Autumn). Chicago: University of Chicago Press.

Dimovitz, S. 2009. "Angela Carter's Narrative Chiasmus: *The Infernal Desire Machines of Doctor Hoffman* and *The Passion of New Eve*." *Genre* XVII. http://www.regis.edu/content/fac/pdf/Scott_Dimovitz_Carter2.pdf.

Dollimore, J. 1991. *Sexual Dissidence: Augustine to Wilde, Freud to Foucault*. Oxford: Oxford University Press.

_____, and A. Sinfield. 1994. *Political Shakespeare*. Manchester: Manchester University Press.

Duffy, M. 2006. *Wise Children*. York Notes. London: Longman, York.

Eliot, T.S. [1944.] 2000. "Burnt Norton." *Four Quartets*. http://www.tristan.icom43.net/quartets/norton.html.

"Fairy tale." Wikipedia. http://en.wikipedia.org/wiki/Fairy_tale.

Fellows, M. 1998. *The Art of Angels and Cherubs*. London: Parragon.

Foucault, M. 1979. *Discipline and Punish: The Birth of the Prison*. Trans. A. Sheridan. New York: Vintage.

Frazer, J.G. [1913–1920.] 1992. *The Golden Bough: A Study in Magic and Religion*, 3d ed. New York: Macmillan. Electronic Edition: *Bartleby.com*. 2000. http://www.bartleby.com/196.

Freud, S. 1919. "Das Unheimliche." http://www-rohan.sdsu.edu/~amtower/uncanny.html.

Gamble, S. 1997. *Angela Carter: Writing from the Front Line*. Edinburgh: Edinburgh University Press.

_____. 2008. "Penetrating to the Heart of the Bloody Chamber—Angela Carter and the Fairy Tale." In *Contemporary Fiction and the Fairy Tale*, ed. S. Benson. Detroit, MI: Wayne State University Press.

Gasiorek, A. 1995. *Post-War British Fiction: Realism and After.* London: Edward Arnold.

Gass, J.M. 1994. "Panopticism in 'Nights at the Circus.'" *The Review of Contemporary Fiction. FindArticles.com.* 27 September 2010. http://findarticles.com/p/articles/mi_hb3544/is_n3_v14/ai_n28644338/?tag=content;c011.

Gerrard, N. 1995. "Getting Carter." *The Observer* Life, 9 July.

Goldberg, C. 1998. *"Märchen."* In *Encyclopedia of Folklore and Literature,* eds. M.E. Brown and B.A. Rosenberg. Santa Barbara, CA: ABC-CLIO.

Graves, R., and R. Patai. 1983. *Hebrew Myths: The Book of Genesis.* New York: Greenwich House.

Grimm, J., and W. Grimm [1812/1814/1822.] 1909. *Grimm's Fairy Tales.* Trans. E. Lucas. London: Constable.

Haffenden, J. 1984. "Magical Mannerist." *The Literary Review,* November.

_____. 1985. "Interview with Angela Carter." In *Novelists in Interview,* ed. J. Haffenden. London and New York: Methuen.

Halberstam, J. 1995. *Skin Shows: Gothic Horror and the Technology of Monsters.* Durham, NC: Duke University Press.

Harries, E.W. 1997. "Fairy Tales About Fairy Tales: Notes on Canon Formation." In *Out of the Woods: Origins of the Literary Fairy Tale in Italy and France,* ed. N.L. Canepa. Detroit, MI: Wayne State University Press.

Hegel, G.W.F. 1977. *Phenomenology of Spirit.* Trans. A.V. Miller. Oxford: Oxford University Press.

"History of the Fool." *foolsforhire.* http://www.foolsforhire.com/info/history.html.

Hoffmann, E.T.A. "E.T.A. Hoffmann Quotes." *Brainy Quote.* http://www.brainyquote.com/quotes/authors/e/e_t_a_hoffmann.html.

Holmes, O.W. *ThinkExist.com.* http://thinkexist.com/quotes/with/keyword/iconoclasm/.

Huizinga, J. 1955. *Homo Ludens: A Study of the Play-Element in Culture.* Boston: Beacon.

Hutcheon, L. 2006. *A Theory of Adaptation.* London and New York: Routledge.

Ikeda, H. 1963. *The Introduction of Foreign Influences on Japanese Children's Literature through Grimm's Household Tales.* In *Brüder Grimm Gedenken.* Marburg: Elwert.

Irigaray, L. [1974.] 1985. *Speculum of the Other Woman.* Trans. G.C. Gill. Ithaca, NY: Cornell University Press.

_____. [1977.] 2000. *This Sex Which Is Not One.* Trans. C. Porter. In *French Feminism Reader,* ed. K. Oliver. Oxford and New York: Rowman and Littlefield.

Jay, M. 1987. "Scopic Regimes of Modernity." In *Vision and Visuality,* ed. H. Foster. Seattle, WA: Bay.

Joyce, J. 1922. *Ulysses.* http://www.online-literature.com/james_joyce/ulysses/1/.

_____. 1957. *Letters.* New York: Viking.

Karpinski, E.C. 2000. "Signifying Passion: Angela Carter's *Heroes and Villains* as a Dystopian Romance." *Utopian Studies. FindArticles.com.* 14 September 2010. http://findarticles.com/p/articles/mi_7051/is_2_11/ai_n28819172/.

Katsavos, A. 1994. "An Interview with Angela Carter." *Review of Contemporary Fiction* vol. 14, no. 3 (Fall).

Kenyon, O. 1992. *The Writer's Imagination: Interviews with Major International Women Novelists.* Bradford, England: University of Bradford.

Ker, W.P. [1931.] 1957. *Epic and Romance: Essays on Medieval Literature.* New York: Dover.

Kready, L. 1916. *A Study of Fairy Tales.* Boston: Houghton Mifflin. http://www.sacred-texts.com/etc/sft/sft01.htm.

Kristeva, J. 1996. "Feminism and Psychoanalysis." (Interview with E. Hoffman Baruch.) In *Julia Kristeva: Interviews,* edited by R. Mitchell Guberman. New York: Columbia University Press.

Lacan, J. 1991. *The Seminar of Jacques Lacan: Book II: The Ego in Freud's Theory and in the Technique of Psychoanalysis 1954–1955.* London: W.W. Norton.

Lane, M. 1993. *Picturing the Rose: A Way of Looking at Fairy Tales.* New York: H.W. Wilson.

Lanham, R.A. 1973. *Tristram Shandy: The Games of Pleasure.* Berkeley: University of California Press.

Lautréamont, I.D. 2001. *Les chants de maldoror et autres oeuvres.* London: LGF.

Laxton, S. 2003. "The Guarantor of Chance: Surrealism's Ludic Practices." In *Papers of Surrealism* 1 (Winter). http://www.surrealismcentre.ac.uk/papersofsurrealism/journal1/acrobat_files/laxton.pdf.

Lefebvre, H. 1991. *The Production of Space.* Oxford: Blackwell.

Lodge, D. 1985. *Small World: An Academic Romance.* London: Penguin.

Losada Pérez, A.M. "'In Me More Than Myself': The Monstrous as a Site of Fear and Desire in Angela Carter's 'The Bloody Chamber' and 'The Erl-King.'" http://www.inter-disciplinary.net/wp-content/uploads/2009/08/draft_m7_analosada1.pdf.

Lüthi, M. 1976. *Once Upon a Time: On the Nature of Fairy Tales.* Trans. L. Chadeayne and P. Gottwald. Bloomington: Indiana University Press.

McGrath, P. 1995. *The Angel and Other Stories.* London: Penguin.

Manley, K.E.B. 2001. "The Woman in Process in Angela Carter's 'The Bloody Chamber.'" In *Angela Carter and the Fairy Tale*, eds. D. Roemer and C. Bacchilega. Detroit, MI: Wayne State University Press.

Metz, C. 1982. *The Imaginary Signifier: Psychoanalysis and the Cinema.* Trans. C. Britton, et al. Bloomington: Indiana University Press.

Moi, T. 1985. *Sexual/Textual Politics.* London and New York: Methuen.

Mulvey, L. 1975. "Visual Pleasure and Narrative Cinema." *Screen* 16.3 (Autumn). http://imlportfolio.usc.edu/ctcs505/mulveyVisualPleasureNarrativeCinema.pdf.

_____. 2007. "Cinema Magic and the Old Monsters: Angela Carter's Cinema." In *The Flesh and the Mirror: Essays on the Art of Angela Carter*, ed. L. Sage. London: Virago.

Munford, R. 2006. "Introduction: Angela Carter and the Politics of Intertextuality." In *Re-Visiting Angela Carter: Texts, Contexts, Intertexts*, ed. R. Munford. New York: Palgrave Macmillan.

Narváez, P. 1991. *The Good People: New Fairylore Essays.* Garland Reference Library of the Humanities, vol. 1376. New York: Garland.

Nussbaum, A. 2005. "*Wise Children* by Angela Carter." *Asking the Wrong Questions.* http://wrongquestions.blogspot.com/2005/08/wise-children-by-angela-carter.html.

Perrault, C. 1977. *The Fairy Tales of Charles Perrault.* Trans. A. Carter. London: Victor Gollancz.

Pile, S. 1996. *The Body and the City: Psychoanalysis, Space and Subjectivity.* London: Routledge.

Pireddu, N. 1997. "CaRterbury Tales: Romances of Disenchantment in Geoffrey Chaucer and Angela Carter." *The Comparatist* 21. http://www.themodernword.com/scriptorium/carter_pireddu.pdf.

Plato. [360 B.C.] 2004. *Symposium.* In *Plato Unmasked: The Dialogues Made New.* Trans. K. Quincy. Cheney, WA: Eastern Washington University Press. http://keithquincy.com/books/platounmasked/WhyReadPlato.html.

Porter, H. 2009. *The Dying Light.* London: Phoenix.

Propp, V. [1928]. 1969. *Morphology of the Folk Tale.* Austin: University of Texas Press.

Punter, D. 1984. "Angela Carter: Supersessions of the Masculine." In *Critique: Studies in Modern Fiction*, vol. 25, no. 4 (Summer).

_____. 1985. *The Hidden Script: Writing and the Unconscious.* London: Routledge.

Purkiss, D. 2000. *Troublesome Things: A History of Fairies and Fairy Stories.* London: Penguin.

Renfroe, C. 2001. "Initiation and Disobedience: Liminal Experience in Angela Carter's 'The Bloody Chamber.'" In *Angela Carter and the Fairy Tale*, eds. D. Roemer and C. Bacchilega. Detroit, MI: Wayne State University Press.

Rice, A. 2000. *Vittorio, the Vampire.* London: Arrow.

Robbins, R. 2000. *Nights at the Circus.* York Notes. London: Longman, York.

Roberts, S. 2008. *The Bloody Chamber.* York Notes. London: Longman, York.

Roemer, D., and C. Bacchilega. 2001. "Introduction." In *Angela Carter and the Fairy Tale*, eds. D. Roemer and C. Bacchilega. Detroit, MI: Wayne State University Press.

Rushdie, S. 1992. "Angela Carter, 1940–92: A Very Good Wizard, a Very Dear Friend." *New York Times Book Review*, March 8.

Sage, L. 1992. "Interview with Angela Carter." In *New Writing*, eds. M. Bradbury and J. Cooke. London: Minerva.

_____. 1994. *Angela Carter.* Plymouth: Northcote House.

_____. 2001. "Angela Carter: The Fairy Tale." In *Angela Carter and the Fairy Tale*, eds. D. Roemer and C. Bacchilega. Detroit, MI: Wayne State University Press.

_____. 2007. "Introduction." In *The Flesh and the Mirror: Essays on the Art of Angela Carter*, ed. L. Sage. London: Virago.

Seifert, L.C. 1996. *Fairy Tales, Sexuality, and Gender in France 1690–1715.* New York: Cambridge University Press.

Shakespeare, W. 2005. *William Shakespeare: The Complete Works.* Oxford: Oxford University Press.

"Shamanism." *Wikipedia.* http://en.wikipedia.org/wiki/Shamanism.

Smith, A. 2007. "Get Carter: An Introduction to the New Edition." In *The Flesh and the Mirror: Essays on the Art of Angela Carter*, ed. L. Sage. London: Virago.

_____. 2010. "Introduction." In *The Infernal Desire Machines of Doctor Hoffman.* London: Penguin.

Smith, P.J. 1994. "All You Need Is 'Love': Angela Carter's Novel of Sixties Sex and Sensibility." *The Review of Contemporary Fiction.* FindArticles.com. 2 September 2010. http://findarticles.com/p/articles/mi_hb3544/is_n3_v14/ai_n28644331/.

Smyth, C. 1992. *Lesbians Talk Queer Notions* London: Scarlet.

Sobshack, T. 1996. "Bakhtin's 'Carnivalesque' in 1950s British Comedy." In *Journal of Popular Film and Television* 23(4).

Stallybrass, P., and A. White. 1986. *The Politics and Poetics of Transgression.* London: Methuen.

Stoddart, H. 2007. *Angela Carter's Nights at the Circus.* London and New York: Routledge.

Stoneham, H. 2010. "Storms and Tempests Be Gone! The Several Perceptions of Angela Carter." *Hannah Stoneham's Book Blog.* http://hannahstoneham.blogspot.com/2010/03/storms-and-tempests-be-gone-several.html.

Suleiman, S.R. 1994. "The Fate of Surrealist Imagination in the Society of the Spectacle." In *Risking Who One Is: Encounters with Contemporary Art and Literature.* Cambridge, MA: Harvard University Press.

Tatar, M. [1987.] 2003. *The Hard Facts of the Grimms' Fairy Tales*, Expanded Edition. Princeton and Oxford: Princeton University Press.

Tester, K. 1994. *The Flâneur.* London: Routledge.

Thackeray, W.M. *Quotes Daddy.* http://www.quotesdaddy.com/tag/Puppet.

Thiher, A. 1987. *Words in Reflection*. London: Chicago University Press.

Todd, J. 1986. *Sensibility: An Introduction*. London: Methuen.

Tolkien, J.R.R. 1965. *Tree and Leaf*. Extract. In "What Is a Fairy Tale?" *SurLaLune*. http://www.surlalunefairytales.com/introduction/ftdefinition.html.

Valéry, P. 1962. "The Position of Baudelaire." *Baudelaire: A Collection of Critical Essays*, ed. H. Peyre. Englewood Cliffs, NJ: Prentice Hall.

Vallorani, N. 1994. "The Body of the City: Angela Carter's *The Passion of the New Eve*." *Science-Fiction Studies* 21, no. 3, November.

VanderMeer, J. 2001. "Angela Carter." *The Scriptorium*. http://www.themodernword.com/scriptorium/carter.html.

van de Wiel, R. 1999. *The Infernal Desire Machines of Deleuze and Guattari — Angela Carter's Picaresque Search for a Feminist Subjectivity*. http://www.raymondvandewiel.org/chapter1.html.

van Gennep, A. 1960. *The Rites of Passage*. Chicago: Chicago University Press.

von Franz, M.-L. 1996. *The Interpretation of Fairy Tales*. Boston: Shambhala.

Vonnegut, K. 1982. *Palm Sunday*. London: Granada.

Warner, M. 1994. "The Uses of Enchantment." In *The Cinema and the Uses of Enchantment*, ed. D. Petrie. London: British Film Institute.

Warner, M. 1995. *From the Beast to the Blonde: On Fairy Tales and Their Tellers*. London: Vintage.

_____. 2000. *No Go the Bogeyman*. London: Vintage.

_____. 2001. "Ballerina: The Belled Girl Sends a Tape to an Impresario." In *Angela Carter and the Fairy Tale*, eds. D. Roemer and C. Bacchilega. Detroit, MI: Wayne State University Press.

Waters, S. 2006. "Introduction." In *Nights at the Circus*. London: Vintage.

Watz, A.F. "Violence as Surrealist Play in Angela Carter's Shadow Dance." In *Forum: University of Edinburgh Postgraduate Journal of Culture and the Arts*. http://www.forumjournal.org/site/sites/default/files/00-play/watz.pdf.

Webb, K. 2010. "Angela Carter at the Movies." *Daily Telegraph*, 3 May. http://katewebb.wordpress.com/.

Weil, S. [1952.] 1977. *Gravity and Grace*. Trans. A. Wills. Lincoln: University of Nebraska Press.

Wilson, E. 1995. "The Invisible *Flâneur*." In *Postmodern Cities and Spaces*, eds. S. Watson and K. Gibson. Oxford: Blackwell.

Winterson, J. 1988. *The Passion*. London: Penguin.

Wisker, G. 1993. "At Home All Was Blood and Feathers: The Werewolf in the Kitchen — Angela Carter and Horror." In *Creepers*, ed. C. Bloom. London: Pluto.

_____. 1994. *It's My Party: Reading Twentieth Century Women's Writing*. London: Pluto.

Zipes, J. 1979. *Breaking the Magic Spell: Radical Theories of Folk and Fairy Tales*. London: Heinemann.

_____. 1991. *Fairy Tales and the Art of Subversion*. New York: Routledge.

_____. 1994a. *Happily Ever After: Fairy Tales, Children and the Culture Industry*. New York: Routledge.

_____. 1994b. *Fairy Tale as Myth. Myth as Fairy Tale*. Lexington: University Press of Kentucky.

_____. 2006. *Why Fairy Tales Stick: The Evolution and Relevance of a Genre*. New York: Routledge.

Žižek, S. 1992. *Enjoy Your Symptom! Jacques Lacan in Hollywood and Out*. London: Routledge.

Index